Race for Citizenship

NATION OF NEWCOMERS
Immigrant History as American History

GENERAL EDITORS: Matthew Jacobson and Werner Sollors

Race for Citizenship

*Black Orientalism and Asian Uplift from
Pre-Emancipation to Neoliberal America*

Helen Heran Jun

NEW YORK UNIVERSITY PRESS
New York and London

NEW YORK UNIVERSITY PRESS
New York and London
www.nyupress.org

References to Internet websites (URLs) were accurate at the time of writing.
Neither the author nor New York University Press is responsible for URLs that
may have expired or changed since the manuscript was prepared.

Library of Congress Cataloging-in-Publication Data
Jun, Helen Heran.
Race for citizenship : Black Orientalism and Asian uplift from
pre-emancipation to neoliberal America / Helen Heran Jun.
p. cm. — (Nation of newcomers)
Includes bibliographical references and index.
ISBN 978-0-8147-4297-6 (cl : alk. paper) — ISBN 978-0-8147-4298-3
(pb : alk. paper) — ISBN 978-0-8147-4332-4 (e-book : alk. paper)
1. Citizenship—United States—History. 2. African Americans—
Social conditions. 3. Asian Americans—Social conditions.
4. Orientalism—United States—History. I. Title.
JK1759.J94   2011
305.896'073—dc22   2010041376

New York University Press books are printed on acid-free paper,
and their binding materials are chosen for strength and durability.
We strive to use environmentally responsible suppliers and materials
to the greatest extent possible in publishing our books.

Manufactured in the United States of America
c   10 9 8 7 6 5 4 3 2 1
p   10 9 8 7 6 5 4 3 2 1

Contents

Acknowledgments

Taking an unreasonably long time to finish a book means that I have an extensive list of people whom I can now thank. The University of Illinois at Chicago is an anomalous place insofar as I am surrounded by colleagues for whom I feel genuine affection. I hear this is a highly unusual state of affairs. I'd like to thank the Institute for the Humanities at UIC for an indispensable one-year fellowship, and its vibrant director, Mary Beth Rose, and the supportive assistant director, Linda Vavra. I was fortunate to have Mark Chiang, Leon Fink, Norma Moruzzi, and Gayatri Reddy as Humanities Institute co-fellows that year. I have received generous and ongoing support administered by the College of LAS at UIC. I presented portions of the book at Cornell University to the Asian American studies department, and Viranjini Munasinghe was an early and much appreciated supporter of my work. Dwight McBride extended a warm and welcoming invitation to share an early chapter with the Chicago Race and Ethnicity study group. I thank African American studies, American studies, and the English department at Northwestern University for various opportunities to present my research, as well as the English department at Loyola University and Asian American studies at the University of Texas, Austin, for their lively engagement.

The faculty in the Department of African American Studies and the Department of English at UIC have always been incredibly encouraging, and I thank each and every one of them for their collegiality, their scholarship, and for just being people whom I truly enjoy seeing and working with. My department heads have been particularly supportive and carefully read drafts of my manuscript at various crucial points: Beth Richie, Paul Zeleza, Nicholas Brown, Walter Benn Michaels, and Mark Canuel. Colleagues in Asian American studies have been steady supporters in the struggle to build the program while keeping our sanity, and their steady presence have made that work possible and rewarding: Mark Chiang,

Anna Guevarra, Kevin Kumashiro, Gayatri Reddy, Rama Mantena, Mary Anne Mohanraj, Karen Su, and Eric Tang.

My writing group consisted of such great people that I looked forward to weekly meetings with unfettered anticipation. Michelle Boyd, with her brilliant and ebullient enthusiasm (tempered by utter impatience for imprecision and nonsense), Cynthia Blair's soothing and steady encouragement, and Badia Ahad's clear-eyed relationship to work and pleasure helped make writing possible over the years. Kerry Ann Rockquemore literally shifted my experience of the time/space continuum with her ingenious faculty mentoring/writing program. There are many people whom I always hope to catch at the next conference, dinner, or performance, and their work and our exchanges have helped shape my work for the better: Kulvinder Arora, Bill Ayres, Paul Cullen, Bernadette Dohrn, Ricardo Bracho, Anna Brown, Kim Dillon, David Eng, Rod Ferguson, Keith Harris, Daniel Kim, An Le, James Lee, Nhi Lieu, David Lloyd, Jinah Kim, Curtis Marez, Chandan Reddy, Dylan Rodriguez, Rosaura Sanchez, Shelley Streeby, and Lisa Yoneyama. I am grateful to Houston Baker and his amazing insights when he generously read portions of the manuscript, and to Charlotte Pierce Baker, with whom I shared memorable evenings out during her year at UIC.

Elaine Kim has inspired and intervened throughout my adult life, and I am deeply honored by her support and grateful for how she has shaped my intellectual and political commitments. George Lipsitz continues to read my drafts, field my last-minute questions, and offer the benefit of his insights and relentless commitment to good work and social change. Sometimes as I go about my day on campus or when I'm in line at the grocery store, I find myself trying to formulate more adequate ways of thanking Lisa Lowe for her mentorship. I know that sounds odd, but that's how much her work and support have meant to me. I am quite certain I am not the only one who does this.

I have an amazing cohort of friends with whom I share an alarming lack of boundaries and who sustain me in innumerable ways. Randall Williams and Stephen Wu took me on as a regular boarder, giving me a place to work, complain, eat, laugh, and languish. Stephen always cheerfully offered brilliant psychiatric expertise (on request) as well as precious apartment space, while Randy's heroic efforts to manage my unwieldy drafts carried me through. The political and intellectual commitment of Randy's worldview and scholarship continually remind me of why the work matters and pushes me to do better. Ben Laya made Chicago into a home for me and continues to cheer me on in ways that dissipate my anxiety with laughter: "You can dew eet." Lisa Cacho and David Coyoca are brilliant colleagues, ideal travel partners, amazing cooks, and general life strategists who consistently help keep me on track and well hydrated. Grace Hong has determinedly picked me up and brushed me off since grad school days, and I've spent many nights talking with her about work and laughing hysterically about less depressing matters. Ever since meeting Victor Bascara in Sau-Ling Wong's Intro to Asian American lit class, his sardonic persona has been a source of great amusement and sharp insight for more than two decades (when did we get this old?). Boone Nguyen, Albert Lowe, and Kevin Pimentel have continued to encourage me to keep on wrrriiittiinng and have empathetically understood and indulged my relationship with Trotsky. Boone has always loved without judgment and with joyful humor. Barry Masuda remembers the beginnings of this project and, fittingly, was also crucial in the last frenetic stages, as he helped revise and copy edit while appeasing my bouts of panic with his varied and delicious preparations of pork. Amie Parry read drafts and made suggestions across time zones so I had someone to engage at 4 A.M. CST. Our all-night conversations and her prescient insights have been the source of much laughter and comfort in whatever country we manage to find each other.

Charlene Barnsdale may know me better than anyone after thirty years, and I thank her for her humor, honesty, and enduring friendship. Gabby and Jackson Baldwin welcomed me into their home and did their best to be encouraging: "That's all you wrote while we were gone ALL day?" An eternal optimist, Jack Baldwin helped sustain me during the most stressful periods of my academic career with his grounded perspective, deep affection, and companionship. Madhu Dubey has been not only a sage and exceptionally committed mentor since my arrival in Chicago but also an endearing friend. I thank her for her amusing (if not perplexing) displays of tough love, the space to write, Chicago insider referrals for all manner of assistance, and a profound capacity for empathy, despite being the most impatient person in the whole world.

My family endured missed holidays, birthdays, cancellations, postponed trips, and deadlines extending into the millennium. My parents, Beyoung and Wha Soon Jun, never made me feel guilty when I couldn't be there and expressed pride in my work, despite its being in a field they had never heard of. Susan Jun and Jeremy Fish have been as encouraging as humanly possible with their sound advice and loving encouragement.

Benjamin Fish graciously and happily accepts birthday and Christmas gifts that arrive six months late. Tommy Jun could always be counted on for matter-of-fact advice after midnight and generous late-night meals in K-town. I thank my late grandmother, Ko Kyoung, who fervently prayed I'd finish, even though I didn't attend church.

Eric Zinner at New York University Press has been extraordinary, and I could not have imagined a more supportive editor. I thank managing editor Despina Papazoglou Gimbel and assistant editor Ciara McLaughlin, for their patience, hard work, and their calming reassurance throughout this very long process. I thank my readers at New York University Press and at *American Quarterly* for invaluable comments and suggestions.

To my friends and family, who helped carry the weight throughout so many years and traveled with me, I owe my deep love and appreciation.

Chapter 1 was first published as "Black Orientalism; Nineteenth Century Narratives of Race and U.S. Citizenship," *American Quarterly* 58, no. 4 (2006): 1047–66. © 2006 American Studies Association. Reprinted with permission of The Johns Hopkins University Press.

Introduction

When vast areas in the city of Los Angeles were set ablaze in the spring of 1992, I was in Northern California approaching the end of my undergraduate education. As a major in ethnic studies and English, I had learned critical histories of Asian Americans, African Americans, Chicanos, and Native Americans. We recognized the distinctiveness of the various cultural groupings, but we also understood that these processes and formations of racialization were related through dominant ideologies of white supremacy. Despite our different histories, we assumed (and not without reason) that racism bound us all together. While our educational training offered us ample opportunity to examine race in a comparative context, the events in late April (from Los Angeles to Las Vegas to Washington, D.C., and beyond) seemed to exceed our analytic frameworks and critical capacities. As the fires diminished and the blue-ribbon commissions were assembled, the social text was revealed as extraordinarily messy and chaotic, challenging us to critically reengage with the significance of race, class, and citizenship in America. This book is not about the uprisings in Los Angeles but has its roots in that maelstrom of theoretical activity in the wake of April 1992, which, as we shall see, stretches far back in time and will no doubt continue well into our "strange future."[1] For our students not old enough to even recall the uprisings, much less the nuances of the discourse that followed, I briefly recount the challenges and constraints of a range of critical responses.

Many liberal voices generally framed the uprisings as yet another divide-and-conquer scenario, signifying a desire to displace the vexing problems of complexity and difference with an unconvincing call to recognize a common and "real" enemy. This insistence that both U.S. Asians and blacks were ultimately being subjugated to white supremacy begged the question of how these groups were being differently racialized by the U.S. state. Another homogenizing account described the uprisings as a modern-day class riot but did not seem to adequately address the racial dimensions of how the black and Latino poor were differently positioned as social actors in the uprising. Nor did the more abstract class analytics seem to consider the possibility that Asian immigrant merchant-class sectors constituted any kind of racially specific petit-bourgeois formation.

Most scholars and public intellectuals from ethnic studies took aim at the cultural essentialist explanations that pervaded the dominant media, by historicizing structural conditions of inequality and stratification. These analyses stressed macro political-economic shifts since the 1970s, such as deindustrialization, urban restructuring, and neoliberal state policies that devastated the black urban poor while facilitating two-tiered immigration (rich and poor) from Asia and Latin America. Although these analyses were the most influential on my own work, it became evident that they did not always engage the discourses being generated by those most affected by these processes. When attention was paid to "micro-level" discourses, the critiques that emerged from Asian American studies and African American studies acknowledged ethnic specificity yet were largely unable to connect the strategic situations of power with the more general states of domination. For instance, many Asian Americanist scholars, myself included, eventually focused on the state's abandonment of Korean immigrant merchants during the rioting as concrete evidence of the enduring disenfranchisement of Asian Americans: proof of second-class citizenship. This politically sound maneuver to critique the state, however, was structured by a logic that essentially demanded that U.S. Asians had as much right as anyone else (i.e., whites) to be protected from "lawless" blacks and Latinos. Therefore, although the Asian Americanist critique of the U.S. state sought to substantiate the denial of citizenship rights without necessarily prescribing "law and order" as remediation, its terms nonetheless capitulated to discourses of black criminality and to the legitimacy of state violence.

In the main, African Americanist scholarship offered analyses of the complex political economy of South Central Los Angeles, situating both the business practices and the racial attitudes of Korean merchants in a genealogy of ironic betrayals that had left a legacy of impoverished black frustration. What seemed difficult to name, however, was that black inner-city resentment of Korean immigrant merchants was not simply animated by the injustice of denigrating forms of antiblack racism (not a new development for inner-city black residents). What seemed to be a driving force in the mobilization of black inner-city communities against merchant exploitation was the perceived audacity of new Asian immigrants who were practicing American racism and were getting away with devaluing black life, just as white Americans had done for centuries. The opposition of black residents to Korean merchant racism expressed an Orientalized indignation that was informed by racialized conceptions that these alien outsiders barely belonged here at all, much less had the right to start thinking and acting like American racists.

It seemed, then, that there was no adequate critical vocabulary for pointing out these contradictions without seemingly undermining the validity of Asian American critiques of the state or of African American critiques of antiblack racism and state violence. Even these important Asian American and African American articulations of injustice emerged as mutually exclusive critiques that unwittingly capitulated to the racialization of the Other. Hence, Asian Americans claiming the right to state protection of their private property reproduced the legitimacy of the state's monopoly on violence and the criminalization of the poor, whereas criticisms of Asian immigrant merchant racism or Korean American demands for state redress challenged these foreigners' excessive sense of entitlement. As a result, it appeared to me that our critical frustration had something to do with how the constraining terms of citizenship, or what I call *race for citizenship*, had come to form the shared basis for a narrow politics and epistemology of justice. In this way, it seemed necessary to begin looking for a history of how struggles for Asian American and African American citizenship have been, at times and variably, intersecting and divergent and to examine how the juridical field of citizenship has consistently and coercively structured struggles and aspirations for national inclusion.

Race for Citizenship is an interdisciplinary study of how Asian Americans and African Americans have been racially defined in relation to each other since the nineteenth century. The tandem character of Asian American and African American racialization has been highly visible since the 1970s when model minority discourse became dominant in defining the relative political, economic, and social location of blacks and Asians. I contend that this is not a novel development but that U.S. blacks and Asians have long been variously situated in interrelation in the economic sphere of labor, the political sphere of citizenship, the social sphere of urban space and the sphere of national culture. I examine three historical conjunctures when crises of Asian American and African American citizenship emerged in particularly salient forms: mid- to late nineteenth-century discourses of the "Negro Problem" and "Yellow Question"; World

War II discourses of race, loyalty, and national identity in the context of internment and Jim Crow segregation; and, finally, post–civil rights discourses of disenfranchisement and national belonging in the context of globalization. As the title of my book implies, this project examines how the institution of citizenship compels racialized subjects to produce developmental narratives of inclusion in the effort to achieve political, economic, and social incorporation. By focusing on how Asian Americans and African Americans have engaged with discourses of U.S. citizenship, it becomes clear that the production of racial meanings is a relational process in which differential inclusions and exclusions are endemic to the institution of citizenship itself.

Race for Citizenship departs from most existing comparative ethnic studies scholarship, which historically has demonstrated a strong teleological investment in multiracial solidarity. Many projects have consequently been oriented toward either documenting exceptional moments of cross-racial consciousness or stressing similar structural conditions by which racial groups share oppression under white supremacy or Western colonialism.[2] Such a focus has illuminated significant linkages that enable us to understand possibilities for social change, which is in no way diminished by inquiry into less ideal, yet pervasive dynamics that are often construed as cross-racial dysfunction. Such a damning diagnosis implicitly positions racialized groups or individuals as somehow inadequately politicized or underdeveloped and consequently fails to analyze the institutional contexts and historical determinations that constrain more radical possibilities. *Race for Citizenship* examines a range of African American and Asian American cultural texts—the nineteenth-century black press, the writing of black feminist Anna Julia Cooper, and Asian American and African American novels and films—and offers an alternative to reading representations of the racial other as signs of either cross-racial identification or dis-identification. My analysis reveals that Asian Americans and African Americans have been unevenly defined in relation to each other and that in their respective struggles for inclusion, they both have had to negotiate the terms by which the other has been racially excluded. Therefore, this book reaches back to the nineteenth century, not to uncover a hidden genealogy of interracial solidarities, but to understand the mutually constitutive formation of Asian American and African American claims to citizenship.

By modifying a comparativist approach, *Race for Citizenship* uses a relational framework to explain how the apparently discrete mechanisms of racialization (specific, particular, nonsystematized) can nevertheless be seen to generate systemic effects. Accordingly, my theorization of Asian American and African American racialization is organized around an analysis of three particular historical periods when the relational nature of the crises of Asian American and African American citizenship was brought into acute relief. Taking a historical long view enables me to track how citizenship is claimed over and against an excluded Other and, more significantly, reveals how residual formations overdetermine contemporary discourses and formations. Therefore, while each chapter stands on its own, I believe we can better understand why discourses of Asian American racial exclusion after 1965 can express contradictory imaginings of blacks as excluded yet enviable cultural insiders of U.S. national culture when read against late nineteenth- and mid-twentieth-century racial formations. In another vein, contemporary notions of black nativism and prejudice in relation to Asian immigrant merchants emerge more clearly as inadequate concepts when read against the contradictory representations of Chinese immigrants in the nineteenth-century black press.

This wide historical range also militates against the tendency to approach African American and Asian American cultural texts as indices of a racial ethic that is subject to being critically assessed as "praiseworthy" or "failed" according to our expectations. The payoff to such an approach is in displacing the ethical presumptions that have come to dominate our understanding of comparative racial formations, as evident in the discourse known as interracial conflict. In other words, in examining cultural institutions such as the press, novels, and films, I suggest an alternative to the commonplace notion that the task of cultural critics is to appraise a text for its hegemonic or counterhegemonic impulses. While cultural production undoubtedly "does" ideological work, it becomes redundant and limited to approach texts in the manner of an insurance adjuster, assessing and measuring critical worth and oppositional potential. Aside from an exceptional and relatively small body of work, most cultural texts inevitably fall under the column declared to be "critically problematic." We can read culture not merely to identify ideological shortcomings (or, conversely, signs of resistance) but to understand that irrespective of intention and impulse, every text can be read for the inevitable contradictions it attempts to manage or reconcile. This more supple methodology can reveal how historically specific contradictions inherent in the institution of citizenship take shape and are negotiated in Asian American and African American cultural production.

Part 1 of *Race for Citizenship* focuses on the tenuous state of black citizenship after Reconstruction, when the anti-Chinese movement was simultaneously reifying the racial boundaries of the national citizenry. I discuss how the mobilization of white labor against Chinese immigrant workers shaped the parameters within which claims to black citizenship could be articulated at that time. My analysis shows how Orientalism ambiguously facilitated the assimilation of U.S. blacks into political modernity and consolidated black national identity following Reconstruction.

The first chapter analyzes the persistence of nineteenth-century black press representations of China, Chinese immigrants, and Chinatown ghettos as embodiments of premodern alien difference. While these representations may not seem significantly different from those of dominant white discourse, I argue that they offered a besieged community a discursive means of negotiating the violence of black disenfranchisement. I refer to this contradictory process as *black Orientalism*, in order to name the paradoxical dilemma endemic to struggles for black citizenship. Nineteenth-century black Orientalism cannot be reductively understood as anti-Asian racism but is instead a concept that situates the contradictions of black citizenship in structural relation to American Orientalism and Chinese immigrant exclusion. My use of the term *black Orientalism* displaces the emphasis on group "intentions" by highlighting how the institution of citizenship compelled narratives of black inclusion that converged with the rhetoric and logic of the anti-Chinese movement.

The second chapter focuses on the work of the nineteenth-century black female intellectual Anna Julia Cooper and examines why discourses of Oriental difference were crucial to her paradigm of black feminism, given her contradictory formation as a Western intellectual. Cooper's well-known advocacy for black women's education and her discourse of modern black womanhood necessarily depart from the struggle for black inclusion as articulated in the black press. The violence waged against black women's bodies in the nineteenth century cannot be adequately redressed through the institution of citizenship, which privatizes black women's economic dependency and sexual vulnerability as lying outside the public domain of politics. Consequently, Cooper has little concern with suffrage or formal rights of citizenship, producing instead a narrative of black female enlightenment that is largely predicated on tropes of the subjugated Oriental woman. Her efforts to distance black women and the space of America from the underdeveloped, despotic Orient nonetheless disclose the barbaric modern history of black female subjugation in the Americas.

Part 2 shifts to the World War II period and provides a context for black urbanization and migration to the West Coast in relation to Japanese American internment, Asian immigration exclusion, and residential segregation. These processes reflected the changing needs of an expanding wartime economy in which black men and women were provisionally incorporated into the industrial labor force and the military during U.S. wars in Asia. On the domestic front, internment and immigration exclusion legally defined Asians as the nation's racial enemy while "foreign" Asian bodies were being violently incorporated through U.S. imperialist wars, ideologies of Western benevolence, and brutal regimes of modernization. This section examines the centrality of discourses of black racial difference in Asian American novels set during World War II, when U.S. national identity was explicitly defined against the Japanese as the racial enemy. I use the term *Asian uplift* to underscore that the formation of Asian Americans as national subjects in this period was necessarily mediated by processes of black racialization. Significantly, these Asian American texts often imagine black subjects as either cultural insiders or indisputably American, even while recognizing their subordination as second-class citizens.

Chapter 3 analyzes how representations of black masculinity and black social spaces inform the production of an Asian American masculine subjectivity in John Okada's *No-No Boy* (1958). This novel is narrated from the space of the multiracial ghetto and negotiates the Orientalist exclusion and national displacement of Asian Americans through gendered discourses of black urban pathology. Blackness is a complex locus of investment in the text, and black social spaces are imagined as being within the cultural boundaries of the U.S. nation even as the novel figures them as racialized sites of deviance to be disavowed. Black male recalcitrance haunts the narrative's failure to produce a cohesive Japanese American masculinity in the context of internment and dis-identification with the U.S. nation. Accordingly, histories of black racial exclusion help disarticulate Asian American masculinity from the white patriarchal authority of a U.S. nationalism that demands the assimilation of Oriental difference.

The fourth chapter builds on the previous argument that gendered representations of black social space and subjects in the 1940s were critical to the narrative production of an Asian American gender identity. This chapter focuses specifically on how blackface in American mass culture was a crucial gendering institution of assimilation through an analysis of Kim Ronyoung's *Clay Walls* (1986). This narrative of Korean American female development cannot thoroughly dissolve Oriental difference into the national citizenry through blackface, nor can it dispel its desire for the "black deviance" that negatively defines bourgeois domesticity. The novel's configuration of black and Asian proximity in segregated residential spaces leads to fractured and contradictory imaginings of a racialized femininity that unexpectedly resignify spaces of black deviance that are formative of U.S. national culture. Discourses of Asian uplift, like black Orientalism, operate in response to the state's racial ideologies that differentially define U.S. blacks and Asians along the axis of citizenship. Besides the internment of Japanese Americans during World War II, Asian immigration restrictions, alien land laws, and wars waged in Asia were all legal means by which the U.S. state repudiated narratives of Asian American citizenship. These two novels bear the marks of a cultural discourse of Asian uplift that attempts to tell stories of Asian American national inclusion in relation to pathologized black formations. The constructions of black resistance in these texts illuminate how the relational history of citizenship produces Asian American fantasies that black racial subjects possess political agency and alternative spaces of belonging in the nation.

Part 3 focuses on the post–1965 period, as a "post–civil rights" era that is defined by global shifts in modes of production and unprecedented immigration from Asia and Latin America. While model minority discourse and reductive culturalist explanations have become the dominant way of understanding how blacks and Asians were situated in interrelation during this period, this section demonstrates that the discourses that we know as "black/Korean interethnic conflict" mark a particular constellation of anxieties around race and national identity in late twentieth-century America. The well-documented processes of deindustrialization, urban restructuring, and mass criminalization in black inner-city communities have generated conditions of spatial isolation and fixity that are in sharp contrast to the mobility that ostensibly characterizes economic globalization in the late twentieth century. In this context, I examine how post-1965 African American discourses of dispossession and displacement were manifested as place-based negotiations with Asian immigrant merchants who became hypervisible in a black national imaginary in the late 1980s and 1990s.

In chapter 5, I begin by looking at two seminal black films: Spike Lee's *Do the Right Thing* (1988) and John Singleton's *Boyz n the Hood* (1991).

I argue that the Korean immigrant merchant became a privileged yet unstable trope for black disenfranchisement throughout the 1980s and 1990s as poor African Americans experienced intensifying conditions of economic and spatial isolation enforced through violent state repression. As opposed to sociological scapegoat or middle-man theories, this chapter does not seek to determine whether black discourses about the Korean immigrant merchant are misplaced or legitimate political grievances. Rather, I frame these discourses as negotiating triumphal narratives of globalization that erase the black poor from a Pacific Century in which Asia figures as the future of capitalist development. I demonstrate that black Orientalism at this historical conjuncture reveals a yearning for national redemption from the very spaces violently ghettoized by the state, a fantasy of black citizenship felt to be displaced by the metanational forces of globalization. As in my discussion of the late nineteenth century, I point to how black Orientalism necessarily produces its own contradictions, evoking a prior moment of ghetto entrapment and the expendability of black life during the U.S. war in Vietnam. In this manner, black Orientalism invokes a repressed national history of U.S. imperialist war in Asia, which the nation and global capital must disavow in the celebratory embrace of global coprosperity, projecting this violent history of U.S. militarization as the regrettable intolerance of the black poor.

Chapter 6 engages discourses of Asian American racial difference in the post–civil rights period, by examining its relationship to the rise of neoliberalism as a hegemonic ideology since the mid-1960s. I argue that Asian American cultural production is uniquely situated to disclose various contradictions of violent neoliberal mandates of self-development and self-enterprise, by analyzing two Asian American films, *Better Luck Tomorrow* (2002) and *a.k.a. Don Bonus* (1995). My reading demonstrates that engaging with the terms of neoliberal discourse is critical to an adequate understanding of race in a post–civil rights era of multicultural inclusion. In this period, Asian uplift entails the production of Asian Americans as idealized subjects of a neoliberal world order, which not only pathologizes the racialized black poor but also reproduces a neoliberal episteme that has devastated the global South since decolonization. While I contend that the vocabulary of global capitalism in the United States has been mediated and constrained by multicultural neoliberalism, both these films can be framed to disclose the pathological violence of an instrumentalizing discourse of privatization. Finally, I conclude my discussion of Asian uplift by linking the narrative of *a.k.a. Don Bonus* with a set of civil rights cases brought against the San Francisco Housing Authority in the 1990s on behalf of Asian immigrant families living in public housing. By looking at the narrative text in relation to these cases, we can see how civil rights can be mobilized to protect impoverished Asian American refugees from black criminality, to the exclusion of the geopolitical violence of imperialist war, refugee displacement, and racialized urban poverty.

The uneven cultural archives from which these chapters draw is indicative of the differential formations of African American and Asian American national subjects that constitute the central concern of this project. An extensive African American literary tradition dating back to the eighteenth century, for example, is an index of how the coercive institution of slavery positioned U.S. blacks to contest their dehumanization by producing an American literature that demonstrated black rationality and humanity according to dominant Enlightenment definitions.[3] Black music and oral folk cultures, or, more precisely, dominant representations of black cultural forms and practices, have long figured as part of U.S. national culture, often in degrading and primitivist contexts. The mere linguistic legibility of this long tradition of black cultural production is distinct from the relative inaccessibility of an Asian American cultural archive, constituted by a range of Asian ethnic groups whose incorporation as exploitable foreign labor did not similarly situate Asian immigrants in relation to "American" cultural institutions. Daniel Kim aptly captures this distinction between Asian American and African American literary traditions: "What Asian American writers seem to face—to rework Gates's phrase—is an onerous burden of *fluency*. To such authors, the African American literary tradition provides a powerful model of emulation but it also throws into relief a certain linguistic lack."[4] Nineteenth-century Asian immigrants, of course, did create their own cultural institutions and practices, but these did not generate a similarly accessible record, nor were they understood as central to U.S. national culture. These distinct historical trajectories persist into the contemporary period, as is apparent in the uneven national visibility of African American and Asian American writers and filmmakers or the frequent conflation of Asian and Asian American cultural production.

Highlighting the uneven relationships of Asian Americans and African Americans to U.S. national culture, this book fights the impulse to produce a false symmetry that would obscure these important distinctions.[5]

Therefore, part 1 does not consider nineteenth-century Chinese immigrant discourses on race and U.S. citizenship, even though this discourse is evident in legal cases and Cantonese newsletters and newspapers, as rigorously researched by historian Charles McClain.[6] The relative scarcity and linguistic difficulty of working with much of this material underscores the very problematic that I seek to examine in part 1: mainly, how do imaginings of Chinese alien difference and their distance from U.S. national culture emerge in nineteenth-century black public discourses that assert claims to citizenship through narratives of black modernity?

Similarly, in the second section, I do not analyze Chester Himes's novels that clearly reference Japanese American internment because it is not my contention that tropes of Asian racial exclusion were central to black literary narratives set between the 1920s and 1940s. Rather, I am arguing that tropes of black racial difference were pivotal to Asian American literary narratives set in that same period, whether in the work of Carlos Bulosan, Younghill Kang, John Okada, Ronyoung Kim, Jade Snow Wong, or Hisaye Yamamoto. Part 2 accounts for why representations of blackness are so salient in Asian American literature and how they variously mediate the manner in which Asian Americans were racialized and gendered by U.S. nationalism in the mid-twentieth century. Close readings of two novels provide an opportunity to trace specific nuances of Asian American subject formation under the U.S. state during World War II in relation to notions of blackness imagined in terms of both longing and disavowal. Because citizenship still was not legally possible for a majority of Asian immigrants during this period, it is instructive to understand how the paradoxical identity of the "Asian American" can be narrativized in the realm of fiction.

In *Race for Citizenship*, the site of public discourse moves from the press to the novel and, finally, to film in the late twentieth century. My readings of black film clarify how complex investments in citizenship are expressed in popular culture when black political equality has been formally secured by civil rights legislation. At this particular historical conjuncture, signifiers of Asian alterity resurface as prominent tropes in black public discourses of the postindustrial urban ghetto. Representations of black racial difference persist in the emergent Asian American popular culture of the 1990s and 2000s, and Asian American film constitutes a powerful medium for registering modes of dislocation that cannot always be categorized as economic and political exclusion. Finally, my focus on black and Asian American film illustrates how broad historical and economic changes are understood and represented through the dramatic oppositions staged in popular culture and that even these fantasies, dreams, and imaginings must negotiate the disciplinary mechanisms of neoliberalism. In a post–civil rights period of ostensible racial equality, coupled with the so-called boundless possibilities of a transnational era, cinematic conventions of narrative resolution fail to contain the revealing contradictions that still animate racialized desires for citizenship and national belonging.

⁓ Part 1 ⁓

Citizenship was an unfolding and highly contested political institution in mid-nineteenth-century America as contentious battles were being waged over the place of blacks, Native Americans, Chinese, and white ethnic immigrants. Although there were relatively few Chinese immigrants in the United States, recent studies have elaborated on the specific dynamic between the Chinese and Negro question in terms of how issues of race, labor, and citizenship revolved around a multivalent racial axis. Historians such as Najia Aairm-Heriot and Moon-Ho Jung have documented the ways in which the specter of Chinese "coolie" labor mediated national debates on free labor and citizenship. According to Jung, "Within the major social crises of the 1860s—battles over the legal, political, and social standing of slaves, masters, blacks, and whites in the United States—coolies represented a vexing anomaly whose contested status would reconstruct American identities after emancipation."[1] Even though there was never any legal definition of what constituted a coolie, the imagining of an influx of unfree Asian labor excited antiblack fears of white workers and the capitalist fantasies of plantation growers. Related to national anxieties about black chattel slavery and emancipation, the racialization of Asian migrants as coolies functioned to reify the immigrant as "white" and the U.S. citizen as non-Asian.[2]

A dimension of the relational nature of black and Asian racialization is evident in the 1870 Naturalization Act, which was ratified to ensure that the alien status of Asian migrants would not be impacted by the Fourteenth Amendment (1868). The Fourteenth Amendment, generally regarded as overturning the infamous Dred Scott decision of 1857, granted former slaves and all their descendants the rights of U.S. citizenship. Securing the legal status of blacks as U.S. citizens was a specific political implication of the Civil War and Radical Reconstruction that was discontinuous from the racialization of Asians as orientalized aliens. Therefore, the 1870 Naturalization Act acknowledged the shifting legal status of U.S.

blacks after the Civil War while seeking to reinstantiate the exclusion of Asians from the national citizenry by specifying that only "white persons and persons of African descent" were eligible for naturalization. Although the Fourteenth Amendment was unable to fully interrupt the negation of citizenship for Asian immigrants, it recognized the citizenship status of "all persons born . . . in the United States" and therefore secured one possible condition for Asian American citizenship: birthright. Severe restrictions on the immigration of Asian women, combined with antimiscegenation laws, were designed to prevent reproduction and to preserve the disenfranchisement of Asian labor, making citizenship by birth a constrained possibility for persons of Asian ancestry.

The first two chapters of this book examine specific dimensions of national discourses of Asian alterity in the nineteenth-century black public sphere. I focus on how distinct yet related discourses of Chinese and black racial difference shaped the emerging parameters of U.S. citizenship and, subsequently, the terms of black political inclusion. In other words, if the specter of coolie labor and the anti-Chinese movement were indeed central to U.S. discourses of freedom and citizenship, how did this affect black claims to citizenship both before and after the Civil War? The black press and the public speeches by Anna Julia Cooper reveal how Western orientalism variously mediated discourses of black political inclusion. Nineteenth-century black citizenship is imagined with different horizons of possibility, and Anna Julia Cooper must reach for a more expansive definition as she constructs a model of modern black womanhood in the United States. As we will see, the gendered meanings of Orientalist discourses had different implications as black disenfranchisement emerged in starkly different terms for black men and women.

1

The Press for Inclusion

Nineteenth-Century Black Citizenship

and the Anti-Chinese Movement

But now observe the practical superiority of slavery over Chinese immigration, as an impelling force for good. Slavery compelled the heathen to give up idolatry, and they did it. The Chinese have no such compulsion and they do not do it. . . . Slavery compelled the adoption of Christian forms of worship, resulting in universal Christianization. The Chinese have no such influence tending to their conversion, and rarely—one or two in a thousand—become Christian. . . . Slavery took the heathens and by force made them Americans in feeling, tastes, habits, language, sympathy, religion and spirit; first fitting them for citizenship, and then giving them the vote. The Chinese feel no such force, but remaining in character and life the same as they were in Old China, unprepared for citizenship and adverse in spirit to our institutions.

—Rev. Blakeslee, Special Report to the
Senate on Chinese Immigration (1878)

In his testimony before the Senate in 1878, a white minister argues for Chinese exclusion, his Orientalist construction of the Chinese alien generating its contrasting Other in the figure of the properly developed, black, Christianized, former slave.[1] What is most disturbing about Rev. S. V. Blakeslee's otherwise predictable discourse of the unassimilable Oriental is his representation of chattel slavery as a necessary civilizing institution that "successfully" transforms African heathens into modern American citizens. Twenty years later, Supreme Court Justice John M. Harlan also constructed a black/Chinese racial tandem in the case of *Plessy v. Ferguson* (1896) when he challenged the Court's majority ruling by constructing the Chinese immigrant as the negative instance of national belonging:

> There is a race so different from our own that we do not permit those belonging to it to become citizens of the United States. . . . But by the statute in question, a Chinaman can ride in the same passenger coach with white citizens of the United States, while citizens of the black race in Louisiana, many of whom perhaps risked their lives for the preservation of the Union, who are entitled by law, to participate in the political control of the state and nation, who are not excluded, by law or by reason of their race, from public stations of any kind, and who have all the legal rights that belong to white citizens, are yet to be declared criminals, liable to imprisonment, if they ride in a public coach occupied by citizens of the white race.[2]

In Harlan's attempt to dramatize the injustice of Jim Crow segregation, he constructs imagined privileges unfairly enjoyed by Chinese aliens to illustrate what was being wrongfully denied to black citizens.[3] That is, Harlan's rhetoric used Orientalist difference to assimilate U.S. blacks into a universalizing American national identity.

Both Blakeslee's and Harlan's statements surprisingly suggest that in the late nineteenth century, the juxtaposition of Chinese immigrants and U.S. blacks could somehow generate a naturalized, commonsensical recognition of the deeply American character of black domestic subjects.[4] This discourse of provisional black inclusion/Chinese exclusion is initially counterintuitive, given how today we often observe that in the nineteenth century, blacks and Chinese were represented as similarly loathsome, or degraded in terms of the "other," that is, the "Negroization of the Chinese" or the "Asianization of blacks." Of course, Harlan's and Blakeslee's public statements on race and citizenship spoke to radically different questions and motivations: one endorsing Chinese exclusion and the other opposing the legality of black/white racial segregation. The differences, however, behind such similar Orientalist figurations in these narratives of black domestication are even more suggestive of the significance of Chinese exclusion and American Orientalism in nineteenth-century discourses of black citizenship.

This chapter examines the nineteenth-century black press's struggles for political inclusion in this dominant discursive context of racialized citizenship, in which the anti-Chinese movement defined the racial, cultural, and political boundaries of the United States. An analysis of black newspapers across the country reveals that Orientalist discourses of Asian cultural difference ambiguously facilitated the assimilation of black Americans to ideologies of political modernity and consolidated black identification as U.S. national subjects. Nineteenth-century discourses of "black Orientalism" can be best understood as a specific formation of racial uplift, generating narratives of black moral, political, and cultural development, which in turn reified the Orientalist logic of the anti-Chinese movement. My argument deemphasizes notions of black intentions, perceptions, or attitudes in order to foreground the narrative demands on U.S. black subjects to constitute their humanity and citizenship through racialized and gendered Enlightenment discourses of morality and rationality. In other words, this chapter looks at how the institution of citizenship produced an imperative for racialized subjects to tell particular stories about themselves and others in the struggle for inclusion. This focus suggests that racist or antiracist principles are not the most relevant terms for interpreting nineteenth-century black press representations of the Chinese; rather, the institution of citizenship is a narrow discursive field in which differentially racialized groups are forced to negotiate their exclusion in relation to others.

Differential Racializations

Although Orientalism has been discussed primarily in the historical context of European colonialism, the discursive production of a foreign, premodern, alien Oriental in opposition to a rational, modern Western subject also has been operative in the United States, albeit in different ways.[5] In the context of mid-nineteenth-century America, Orientalism constitutes an Oriental other through exclusionary U.S. immigration policies and the regulation of Asian labor through the institution of citizenship.[6] Historian John Tchen points out that before the 1850s, there was another Orientalist formation not organized solely around immigration.[7] Instead, during this earlier period, increased trade with China and a growing port culture situated the Chinese as an exotic, curious spectacle for consumption in the emergent industry of urban popular entertainment.[8] Broadly, then, we can understand nineteenth-century American Orientalism as a discursive formation that was determined by and determining of U.S.

economic and political engagements with East Asia and the Pacific and that provided the ideological structure for producing and managing Asian racial difference in the United States. These processes, which involve instances of Asian incorporation (as circus exhibits, as coolie labor, as a U.S. colony) and instances of Asian exclusion (from immigration, citizenship, and U.S. national culture), define an American genealogy of Asian racialization producing the Oriental as alien to the United States.[9]

My objective is not to write an overview of the various forms through which American Orientalism manifests throughout U.S. history but to isolate particular instances of how Orientalism emerges to mediate black racialization. I refer to this contradictory process of negotiation as *black Orientalism* in an effort to capture the critical dilemma that the struggle for black citizenship (or black political modernity) embodies. We can see the contours of this contradiction, for instance, in Blakeslee's observation that slavery "did wonderfully elevate the slave and prepare him for citizenship," with the "one exception" that "it legally denied human rights to the slave."[10] This paradox, in which the systematic dehumanization of racialized populations is the condition for their entry into the "civilized world" to become modern subjects of democratic freedom, is the contradiction endemic to the project of modernity itself.[11] Therefore, in the struggle to challenge their conditions of exploitation and oppression, racialized subjects must negotiate these epistemological contradictions structuring modern institutions and liberal narratives of freedom and liberation. Put another way, racially excluded populations must somehow manage to reconcile their liberatory aspirations promised by enlightenment and civilization, with their brutalization narrated as a historically necessary process of development.[12]

Black Orientalism, as I am using the concept, is in no way an accusatory or reductive condemnation that seeks to chastise black individuals or institutions for being imperialist, racist, or Orientalist. Black Orientalism is a heterogeneous and historically variable discourse in which the contradictions of black citizenship engage with the logic of American Orientalism. Instead of a singular meaning or manifestation, black Orientalism encompasses a range of black imaginings of Asia that are in fact negotiations with the limits, failures, and disappointments of black citizenship.[13] This includes, for example, W. E. B. Du Bois's fascination with China as a utopic site of revolutionary possibility, black admiration for Japanese empire during World War II, and even signifiers of the "Orient" in hip-hop culture.[14] In these instances, one can see that the dichotomous otherness of the "Orient" is precisely what makes it so appealing to dis-identified black subjects attempting to imagine liberatory possibilities, identifications, and historical futures in spaces that have been defined as *not* the United States or defined in opposition to the West.

In the nineteenth century, black Orientalism emerges from the histori-cal conditions of black racialization and the Chinese exclusion movement as a heterogeneous discourse of black citizenship and national identity. To pursue a broader critique of citizenship, this chapter analyzes what might be considered more mainstream, liberal discourses of black national iden-tity rather than often-cited oppositional positions taken by figures such as Frederick Douglass, a well-known and highly vocal opponent of the anti-Chinese movement since the 1850s. As I demonstrate in the follow-ing section, liberal black discourses on citizenship and immigration are in themselves highly complex negotiations that cannot be simplistically regarded as unfortunate and "prejudicial" black attitudes toward the Chi-nese. Comparative race scholarship may miss important opportunities to carefully examine liberal discourses of racialized citizenship owing to a teleological investment in "interracial solidarity," a notion that relies heavily on the premise of identification. The following analysis of the nineteenth-century black press considers black Orientalism as a form of cultural politics that does not illuminate the ideological limits or short-comings of those who engaged in it but reveals the various contradictions of citizenship and modern subjecthood that it ultimately failed to resolve for black national identity.

The Heathen Chinese

Black press representations of Chinese difference engaged with Ameri-can Orientalist ideologies that in the mid-nineteenth century manifested at the national level as the anti-Chinese movement. Anti-Chinese politi-cal agitation emerged in the mid-1850s along the West Coast, fueled by competing white immigrant workers who racially defined free labor in antagonism to blacks and Chinese.[15] Initially a regional and class-based formation, anti-Chinese legislation became part of the national political platform that culminated in the Chinese Exclusion Act of 1882, the first and only time a specific ethnic group was legally barred from immigrat-ing to the United States. White labor, clergymen, and nativists generally constructed Chinese immigrants as an invasive yellow peril that posed a grave moral and economic threat to the survival of the white work-ing man and the American family: "Can we compete with a barbarous race, devoid of energy and careless of the State's weal? Sunk in their own debasement, having no voice in government, how long would it be ere ruin would swamp the capitalist and poor man together?"[16] Anti-Chinese sentiments were not merely racialized expressions of a white working-class ideology, however, but were tied to a larger discourse of American Orientalism that cut across class lines.[17]

In his study of disease and racial classification in San Francisco's Chi-natown, Nayan Shah describes how journalists, politicians, and health officials worked together to produce "a way of knowing" Chinatown as an alien space of filth, disease, and contamination. As Shah argues, "The cartography of Chinatown that was developed in government investiga-tions, newspaper reports, and travelogues, both established 'knowledge' of the Chinese race and aided in the making and remaking of China-town."[18] Hence, white public health officials "scientifically" corroborated the dominant press's sensational descriptions of Chinatown as "ankle-deep in loathsome slush, with ceilings dripping with percolations of other nastiness above, [and] with walls slimy with the clamminess of Asiatic diseases."[19] The overwhelmingly male composition of the Chinese immi-grant community, secured through exclusionary legislation prohibiting the immigration of Chinese women, was central to the discourse of moral panic in areas surrounding Chinatown ghettos. Images of Chinese men as depraved opium addicts and lascivious sexual predators of innocent young white girls dominated an American Orientalist discourse that con-structed Chinatown and its residents as alien contaminants of the white national body.

The black press's representations of Chinatown ghettos and its inhabit-ants also consistently constructed these spaces and persons as embodi-ments of premodern, alien difference.[20] The number and frequency of articles about the Chinese is noteworthy, in that the vast majority of U.S. blacks never directly encountered the Chinese, who began immigrat-ing in significant numbers in the 1850s and were geographically concen-trated in the West.[21] Although much of the coverage in the black press before 1882 concerned legislative/political matters, most were sensational human-interest stories, such as those in the New Orleans Tribune, which described an exotic Chinatown temple where priests "shout, yell, groan, spin around amid the racket of gongs, orums, and fiddlers, and smoke opium until they are quite drunk."[22] The Topeka Tribune reprinted an article describing the immoral depravity of an opium den in Chicago's Chinese quarter, "where some were sprawling on a filthy floor, and others had rolled into dirty bunks, and all were contemplating a glorious orgie [sic]."[23] The *Washington Bee* gave front-page coverage to "The Chinese in New York: Peculiarities of the Orientals Described."[24] In his study of the black press, historian Arnold Shankman observes that "from 1880–1935 almost every time the Chinese were mentioned in the black press, it was in connection with intrigue, prostitution, murder, the sale of opium or children for money . . . superstitious practices, shootings or tong wars."[25]

Stories about Chinese cultural difference even predated the arrival of Chinese immigrants to the United States. As early as 1827, the first issue of *Freedom's Journal* printed an article entitled "Chinese Fashions," which characterized Chinese foot binding as a "well-known" and "ridiculous" custom in China.[26] The description includes a great amount of empirical detail, as in the following:

> The length was only two inches and three-fourths; the breadth of the base of the heel seven-eighths of an inch; the breadth of the broadest part of the foot, one and one-fourth of an inch; and the diameter of the ankle three inches above the heel, one and seven-eighths of an inch.[27]

This highly empiricist, scientific language of ethnographic observation sharply contrasts with the incomprehensible, primitive oriental practice that the article recounts. *Freedom's Journal*, the first black newspaper published in the United States, was a relatively short-lived, but historically significant, paper dedicated to the defense of free blacks and to the abolition of slavery by disseminating "useful knowledge among our brethren, and to their moral and religious improvement . . . and to vindicate our brethren, when oppressed." Other stories in this inaugural issue are more clearly related to the paper's stated commitments. For instance, "Memoirs of Capt. Paul Cuffe," "People of Colour," "Cure for Drunkenness," and "Advantages of Choosing a Wife by Proxy" emphasize male leadership, racial solidarity, temperance, and family, crucial elements in narrating black aptitude for citizenship. Hence, the seemingly random, peripheral article on a backward "Oriental" practice works to underscore a story of black modern development in which "useful knowledge" and "moral and religious improvement" are tied to the paper's commitment to the rights of free blacks and the abolition of slavery.

Producing Black Citizens

As a cultural institution, the black press had a significant role in defining black national identity, and nineteenth-century black newspapers were particularly invested in narratives of racial uplift and development. Benedict Anderson has linked the emergence of print capitalism to the production of nationalist consciousness, arguing that the newspaper produced an experience of simultaneity that enabled imagined "horizontal" identification among strangers across broad geographical areas.[28] Larger, national black newspapers regularly received news from "correspondents" across the country and reprinted articles from black and dominant white media considered relevant to a black national population. This production and consumption of print media not only created an arena for black public discourse but also helped form the very experience of identifying as a subject of a black national community.

The discourses of development, progress, and self-improvement central to *Freedom's Journal* were key to the nineteenth-century black press, which was a particularly effective institution for the production and dissemination of ideologies of racial uplift.[29] Most black newspapers and periodicals aspired to produce narratives of black racial progress while attacking the racist legislation and policies that threatened to impede the development of the race. If we understand the black press as the technical means for "representing" the *kind* of imagined community that defines black racial identity, then the process by which that identity is defined is always a contestation among competing and heterogeneous interests that are homogenized under the unifying rubric of "race." The nineteenth-century black press cannot be understood as a monolithic institution with a cohesive racial or class ideology. But the fact that the majority of editors were educated black men with sufficient financial resources critically informs how black national identity was narrated through print media. As African Americanist historians such as Kevin Gaines and Jane Rhodes note, these editors "promoted the virtues of education, individual progress, and racial uplift as the means for African Americans to transcend the debilitating legacy of slavery and racial oppression."[30] Therefore, while the institutional formation of the nineteenth-century black press was characterized by competing interests and conflicts, ideologies of racial uplift constituted the discursive terrain in which such differences were articulated and debated.[31]

Kevin Gaines discusses how educated blacks engaged in a cultural politics of citizenship that promoted a developmental ideology of racial progress emphasizing black moral and cultural propriety. Negotiating the political, cultural, and social violence of white supremacy, ideologies of racial uplift encouraged the emulation of what Gaines calls middle-class values and ideals, which were the authoritative signifiers of respectability and humanity.[32] Whereas racist discourses constructed blacks as immoral, irrational, and violent savages incapable of self-regulation, the educated black community responded by embracing values of temperance, thrift, chastity, and patriarchal domesticity as a means of proving their worthiness and entitlement to citizenship. Embracing Victorian morality or performing heteronormativity enabled black communities to move as far away from the stereotypes as they could, to give their tormentors no evidence for their charges and to claim a strategic moral superiority.[33]

What is most useful about Gaines's analysis is his theorization of how the violent denial of black political and economic enfranchisement facilitated the formation of a cultural politics that symbolically embodies citizenship. Whereas Gaines's study begins at the end of Radical Reconstruction, his theorization of racial uplift provides insight into black Orientalism as a related form of nineteenth-century cultural politics. Tropes of Chinese underdevelopment enabled the discursive production of black modern subjects capable of being incorporated into a narrative of Western historical progress, despite the brutal material contradictions that countered the very notion of "Western civilization."

The history of white supremacist violence that saturated the political, economic, and social spheres of nineteenth-century America constitutes the "contradictions of black citizenship" to which I continually refer. The abolition of slavery did not resolve these contradictions, nor did the institution of citizenship, which was formally granted to black persons with the passage of the Fourteenth Amendment (1866). Immediately after the ratification of the Fourteenth and Fifteenth Amendments, almost all the former Confederate states quickly instituted black codes that criminalized blacks in ways that effectively negated the abolition of slavery.[34] For example, state laws required that these recently "freed" subjects sign work contracts with plantations (often the same ones on which they worked as slaves) and carry these papers with them at all times. Black persons could be stopped and questioned at any time, and the absence of a work contract was criminalized as "vagrancy," at which point the person was arrested and put to work in the convict lease system. Numerous studies have shown that this systematic economic and political disenfranchisement left many of the "freedmen" as vulnerable to exploitation and violence as they were during slavery.[35]

These postbellum political, economic, and social relations were enforced through campaigns of racial terror that maintained the privilege of whiteness through the violent regulation of black bodies. The well-known work of Ida B. Wells, for instance, demonstrates how the widespread practice of lynching in the South was a crucial means of maintaining the economic, political, and social authority of white supremacist patriarchy.[36] African American feminist critic Hazel Carby notes that in addition to the practice of lynching, the institutionalized rape of black women also was "an instrument of political terror . . . in the South."[37] From the end of the Civil War to the turn of the twentieth century, countless acts of violence were committed against black persons, in addition to the hundreds of documented lynchings enacted as public rituals of torture that used the imagined violations of white women to reconstitute the patriarchal and capitalist authority of white men.[38] It is in this context of racial terrorism that ideologies of racial uplift emerged as strategies of survival against intense dehumanization.

Religious ideologies of Christian morality were central to discourses of racial uplift that sought to contest the historical violence that denied U.S. blacks their humanity and their legal status as citizens. As Reverend Blakeslee's statements implied, Christianity was critically linked to nineteenth-century discourses of black citizenship, in that the Christian conversion of the African heathen was understood as the foundation of moral development and ethical citizenship.[39] Subsequently, ideologies of racial uplift seeking to produce "civilized" black subjects promoted Christian propriety and moral self-improvement to refute the dominant characterizations of blacks as depraved and immoral savages.[40] Racial uplift constituted black Christian subjects, therefore, as part of a larger effort to represent the modern development of blacks under Western civilization.[41] The developmental ideologies of American modernity demanded Christian morality as the precondition for transforming the primitive slave into the modern political subject. This imperative later had profound implications for black understandings of Chinese racial difference.

The heathenism that the Chinese came to signify in nineteenth-century America was a powerful Orientalist trope for black Americans, whose assertions of humanity and claims to citizenship had been largely predicated on discourses of Christian morality. Appeals to Christian ideologies have been crucial to black critiques of white supremacy since the eighteenth century, becoming an important means of refuting their object status in their struggles for recognition as legal subjects of the state. Abolitionist discourse relied predominantly on religious ideology, arguing that slavery violated fundamental principles of Christianity and led to sinful and immoral relations among both slaves and their masters. In addition, the American school of ethnology created damaging, hierarchical classifications of racial groups, which they claimed had emerged from various and unequal origins. Such "scientific" arguments undermined the theological basis of a universal humanity, which had provided U.S. blacks with a fragile, yet important legitimating discourse in their struggle against racialized exploitation. After the formal abolition of U.S. slavery, Christian doctrine and monogenesis posed the greatest theoretical challenge to scientific racism, as various disciplines sought to provide a scientific basis for white supremacy and manifest destiny.[42] Religious discourses, therefore, continued to be relevant to U.S. blacks in their claim to modern institutions, whether citizenship or education.

The following news story shows the fundamental connections between black Christian morality and political aptitude in the nineteenth century, as well as the differential location of racialized groups in relation to religious and cultural institutions of the U.S. nation. This article from the *Pacific Appeal*, a black newspaper in San Francisco, argues explicitly for black rights of testimony and uses an antiracist critique that distances black development from the heathen Chinese and Indian:

> In the same oppressive spirit they deprived the Indian and Mongolian of their right of oath . . . they oppressed them and reduced them to the same social and political level of the Negro. This was inhumane, barbarous, and unjust, but a more plausible excuse might be offered for depriving the Indian and the Chinese of their oaths than the Colored American: they being heathens and not comprehending the nature and obligation of our oath or affirmation. . . . The Negro is a Christian: there is a strong religious sentiment in his nature, a feeling of awe and reverence for the sanctity of an oath which renders his judicial testimony sacred to him . . . perjury is abhorrent to his soul;—he looks upon it as the unforgiven sin.[43]

Indian and Chinese immigrants are represented as atavistic yet wrongfully oppressed subjects of discrimination and are sympathetically characterized as underdeveloped heathens who are nonetheless entitled to recognition by the courts. Even though the article condemns the "inhumane" treatment of "uncomprehending" Native Americans and the Chinese, it consolidates the legitimacy of black male rights to citizenship by describing, in contrast, the proper ethical formation of the black subject who *has* developed the modern capacity to appropriately engage state institutions. This discursive dis-identification must not be interpreted as a hypocritical inconsistency that contradicts the article's critique of racist exclusion. Instead, emphasizing the Christian formation of the black national subject is an ideological imperative in narrating black fitness for citizenship, which, by consequence, Orientalizes, or discursively disciplines, Chinese and Indians as inadequate subjects of political modernity.

Recalling Gaines's analysis, black Orientalism functions as a cultural politics of citizenship even in the absence of an explicitly "political" discourse, such as the case of *Freedom's Journal* and its seemingly apolitical article about Chinese foot-binding. This next article, from *Frederick Douglass' Paper*, was submitted by a San Francisco correspondent and chronicles the "progress made by the colored people in this city," describing the three black churches, school, and literary association that have "given tone and character to Society."[44] The emphasis on black religious, educational, and cultural institutions in this article reflects their ideological significance to the ethical formation of proper subjectivities that the article tries to bring into representation. The narrator shifts abruptly from the black community's "large number of respectable ladies and their influence" to conclude the report with an ethnographic description of Chinese immigrants:

> San Francisco presents many features that no city in the Union presents. Its population is composed of almost every nation under heaven. Here is to be seen at a single glance every nation in minature [*sic*].— The Chinese form about one-eighth of the population. They exhibit a most grotesque appearance. Their "unmentionables" are either exceedingly roomy or very close fitting. The heads of the males are shaved, with the exception of the top, the hair from which is formed into a plaited tail, resembling "pig tail tobacco." Their habits are filthy, and their features totally devoid of expression. The whites are greatly alarmed at their rapid increase. They are very badly treated here. Every boy considers them lawful prey for his boyish pranks. They have no friends, unless it is the colored people, who treat everybody well, even their enemies. But I must close this already too long letter.[45]

The representation of the Chinese immigrant's "grotesque" and "filthy" appearance, undergarments, and habits are in sharp juxtaposition with the proper formation of the black community's "intelligent audiences," "handsome" churches, "respectable ladies," and "eminently qualified . . . gentlemen" who speak with "eloquence" and "chaste and elegant" language. Once again, these polarized representations cannot be reductively interpreted as an instance of racism or anti-Chinese sentiments, which the article strongly criticizes and disavows, even asserting that the Chinese are befriended by only "the colored people."[46] As in the *Pacific Appeal*, this article clearly expresses empathy towards the "persecuted" Chinese, even as it simultaneously objectifies Chinese immigrants through an anthropological gaze that methodically recounts their foreign signs of bodily and cultural difference.[47] This Orientalist account is neither a "negative or positive" representation but narrates the alien formation of the Chinese immigrant to negotiate black exclusion, which the article briefly acknowledges in an otherwise celebratory testimonial:

> We suffer many deprivations, however. We have no oath against any white man or Chinaman. We are debarred from the polls. The Legislature refused to accept our petition for the right to testify in courts of justice against the whites; but not withstanding all these drawbacks, we are steadily progressing in all that pertains to our welfare.[48]

In response to the degradation of black disenfranchisement, the article's Orientalist gaze constitutes a modern black subject of the West, just as the refined churches, schools, and literary association are the markers of black development and civilization.

While papers such as the *Pacific Appeal* and *Frederick Douglass' Paper* had expressed earlier sympathetic positions regarding the Chinese, by 1873 the black press in California emphasized the derogatory impact of Chinese immigrants on the black community and the nation as a whole. These papers consistently discussed the cultural and moral underdevelopment of the Chinese in an effort to distance blacks from the dangerous implications of anti-Chinese legislation that occupied California's political discourse.[49] One telling article published in 1867 denied any link between the black and Chinese situations, arguing that "there is no analogy between the cases," since "the negro is a native American, loyal to the Government . . . American in all his ideas . . . and a believer of the truths of Christianity" who "ask[s] for the rights of citizenship as [his] just due."[50] Discourses of the Chinese as a racial problem were not confined to California, as evidenced by the *New Orleans Lousianian*, which stated that "the Negro question was being replaced by that of the Chinese."[51] As the anti-Chinese movement gained political momentum throughout the nation, it became increasingly necessary and commonplace that black claims to citizenship articulate Orientalist dis-identification with Chinese immigrants.[52] The formulaic narration of black military service, Christian morality, and nationalist identification to represent blacks as unambiguously *American* subjects became a repetitive and frequent refrain with respect to discourses of Chinese exclusion.

Black Orientalist discourses of dis-identification were not merely nativist ideologies, since they were also deployed to demonstrate the assimilability of black immigrants. One article rhetorically dismissed the notion of Chinese immigration as a "problem" while discussing the modification of naturalization laws that would allow immigrants of African descent to become naturalized citizens. Arguing that such legislative changes had little relevance to the Chinese, the article characterized West Indian immigrants as "already Americans; their habits, customs, and associations are identical with ours. . . . They have practically renounced their allegiance to their original government and are truly Americanized . . . the same advantages should be extended to the colored alien as are enjoyed by white foreigners."[53] The article contrasts the alien Chinese with black immigrants from the West Indies whose formation under European colonialism has made their "habits, customs, and associations . . . identical with ours" and therefore easily assimilable into the U.S. national body. It is particularly striking that the allegiance of West Indian black immigrants "to their *original* government" is linked to a colonial state whose importation of African slave labor produced a "Western" black colonial subject "known for . . . adherence to our customs and institutions." The suppressed ambiguity surrounding the black immigrant's national identification is an index of how the history of the African slave trade and Euro-American colonialism positioned blacks in the Americas in a radically different relationship to the institution of citizenship from the Chinese, who were not similarly incorporated as cultural or political subjects of the West during the nineteenth century.

Although black Orientalism was a means of narrating the development of black subjects into American modernity, the passage of the Chinese Exclusion Act in 1882 did not consolidate black national identity but exposed the tenuous status of black citizenship itself. Hence, when the anti-Chinese movement gained national support for federal legislation to prohibit Chinese immigration, the black press voiced almost unanimous opposition to this unprecedented form of race-based immigration policy.[54] As the *Christian Observer* stated, "One of the most hopeful signs of the times is the unanimity of the press, especially the religious, in opposition to the Chinese bill."[55] While the *San Francisco Elevator* was one of the few exceptions and was criticized in the black press for having "failed to stand up for equal rights," other black presses on the West Coast condemned Chinese exclusion.[56]

Historians studying black press representations of Chinese immigrants have found this pervasive opposition either surprisingly anomalous or a commendable sign of the black community's alliance with another racially oppressed group.[57] If we understand the ideological relationship of black Orientalism to discourses of black modernity and citizenship, the black press's opposition to the Chinese Exclusion Act is neither a "curious" aberration nor transparent evidence of the black community's "dedication to the image of America as a composite nation of diverse peoples."[58] The discursive limits of black Orientalism as a means of narrating the modern development of the black American subject were exceeded when the Chinese Exclusion Act unequivocally signified the racial reification of U.S. citizenship that undermined aspirations for black national incorporation. In other words, whereas an Orientalist discourse on Chinese alien difference was a form of cultural politics that could underscore the Americanness of black subjects, the Chinese Exclusion Act was itself a clear threat to the circumscribed legal rights already undermining black citizenship. Hence, black Americans rightly felt threatened by the notion that federal legislation employing racially exclusionary language with respect to Chinese immigration could next be aimed at them.

Frederick Douglass waged the most prominent and vocal critiques of the anti-Chinese movement, recognizing the dangerous consequences of race-based exclusion for liberal principles of American democracy.[59] Douglass's *New Era* criticized both Republican and Democratic politicians for supporting the anti-Chinese movement in an effort to secure the trade unions' political support.[60] Douglass was hardly alone, however, and the religious and secular black press alike strongly condemned the Chinese Exclusion Act and recognized its racist implications for blacks, whose recent political gains had been violently contested by white ethnics:

Only a few years ago the cry was, not "The Chinese must go," but "The niggers must go"; and it comes from the same strata of society. There is not a man to-day who rails out against the yellow man from

China but would equally rail out against the black man if opportunity only afforded. Nor have they given up all hope of that opportunity coming in the near future.[61]

The "same strata of society" is a clear reference to the white working class and its political institutions, which not only exercised considerable power in the Democratic Party but also practiced racist union policies that culminated in violent hate-strikes and riots that targeted black laborers.[62] Black Americans were particularly antagonized by Irish immigrants, whose political, economic, and cultural incorporation often came at the expense of black displacement.[63] Therefore, the proponents of Chinese exclusion—the white ethnic working class—were largely regarded as enemies of black workers throughout the country. Black critiques of the Chinese Exclusion Act did not necessarily oppose the general idea of immigration restrictions, which the black press often advocated, but criticized the political power of white labor to mobilize federal legislation that was racially exclusive. Hence, several papers urged creative solutions to slowing Chinese immigration, such as prohibiting the common practice of sending the deceased back to China, which would not require federal legislation that employed exclusionary race-based language and yet might achieve the same desired results.[64]

It would be imprecise, therefore, to understand black press opposition to the Chinese Exclusion Act as evidence of black subjective identification with the Chinese, whose alien and immigrant formations were in cultural, linguistic, and religious contradiction to black national identity. Many articles opposing Chinese exclusion were careful to simultaneously mark black Orientalist dis-identification: "We honestly confess that we have no sympathy for the Chinese. Their habits, customs, modes of living, manner of worship . . . [are] an abhorrence to us."[65] Despite the overwhelming evidence of black opposition to Chinese exclusionary legislation, the black press's fascination with Chinese immigrants and Chinatown ghettos as grotesque sites of immorality, filth, and alien difference was a discourse that consistently shaped black "ways of knowing" Chinese racial difference from the 1850s well into the twentieth century. The Chinese Exclusion Act's interruption of black Orientalism suggests that while the possibilities for black and Asian identification are often highly constrained (or even formed in mutual exclusion), owing to specific historical processes of racialization, such identification was not necessary to generate black opposition to the Chinese Exclusion Act. Race emerged as the contradiction to the promise of universal equality, revealing the vulnerability of the status of black Americans as nonwhite citizens of the state.

It should be neither surprising nor disappointing that after the ratification of the Chinese Exclusion Act in 1882, black press Orientalism persisted and even intensified, with a particularly strong emphasis on Chinatowns as depraved sites of criminality and sexual vice.[66] While nineteenth-century black Orientalism might have been an effective means of provisionally emphasizing the deeply "American" character of blacks in the United States, this discourse of inclusion had stark limitations. The black press's concerns that the Chinese Exclusion Act would be followed by more race-based legislation were dramatically substantiated less than a decade later by the Supreme Court's decision that racial segregation was an entitlement of white citizenship. If the Chinese Exclusion Act defined the U.S. citizen in opposition to the Oriental alien, the constitutionality of *Plessy v. Ferguson* suggested that although U.S. blacks were not Orientalized immigrants, the reification of black racial difference would remain at the very core of American national identity.

"When and Where I Enter . . ."

Orientalism in Anna Julia Cooper's

Narratives of Modern Black Womanhood

> *In Oriental countries woman has been uniformly devoted*
> *to a life of ignorance, infamy, and complete stagnation.*
> *The Chinese shoe of to-day does not more entirely dwarf,*
> *cramp, and destroy her physical powers, than have the*
> *customs, laws, and social instincts, which from remotest*
> *ages have governed our Sister of the East, enervated and*
> *blighted her mental and moral life.*
>
> —Anna Julia Cooper, *The Voice of Anna Julia Cooper*

Anna Julia Cooper's essay "Womanhood: A Vital Element in the Regeneration and Progress of a Race" was originally delivered as a speech in 1886 to a congregation of black ministers in Washington, D.C.[1] Cooper is perhaps best known for the black feminist formulation that has become central to paradigms in ethnic studies and women's studies: "Only the BLACK WOMAN can say, 'when and where I enter . . . then and there the whole Negro race enters with me.'"[2] In the late nineteenth century, Cooper's arguments and critical discourse positioned black women's education and development as fundamental to the possibilities of black historical progress. More than a century later, her work is widely read and circulated, and Cooper has been recognized as one of the earliest black feminist intellectuals who linked the "race and woman" question.

Significantly, Cooper's renowned essay opens with an Orientalist narrative of China and Turkey as immobile sites of women's degradation and backward social development. The Western world's fascination with the "barbaric" patriarchal practice of Chinese foot-binding has been one of the most enduring and powerful legacies of Orientalist discourse and has survived well into the present. These narratives of the subjugated Oriental woman, however, bear a complex ideological relation to Cooper's struggles to address the horrific conditions of black women's subordination in late nineteenth-century America.

Anna Julia Cooper's writings negotiate black women's multiple displacements from the racial and gendered terrain of citizenship. *A Voice from the South* (1892), a collection of Cooper's polemical essays, explicitly challenges the ideologies of both the patriarchal discourses of black citizenship and the racism of the white women's movement.[3] Like many other black female intellectuals of the nineteenth century, Cooper turned primarily to Christian ideologies to reconstitute black women as ethical subjects and to reconcile the "underdevelopment" of black women with discourses of modern progress. The assimilation of black women into American modernity demands a narrative of development that Cooper provides by advocating for the education of black women in her attempt to construct a disembodied and "enlightened" black female subjectivity. Cooper's text creates an ideologically complex paradigm of modern black womanhood, often deploying Orientalism in an attempt to negotiate particular racial and gender ideologies of modern progress. Orientalism is a particularly useful discourse for Cooper, as she seeks to centralize black women's conditions while negotiating the racial imperative to offer black men "unconditional support in pursuit of [their] manhood rights."[4] Hence, black Orientalism discursively attempts to assimilate black female difference into the institutions and temporality of American modernity yet also generates new contradictions that undermine Orientalism as a discourse of Western civilization.

After citizenship had been formally granted to African American men in 1870, only to be systematically denied following the demise of Radical Reconstruction, the dominant discourse of nineteenth-century black politics sought to reconstitute black men's political authority as full citizens. Prominent black male intellectuals such as Martin Delany, Booker T. Washington, and W. E. B. Du Bois struggled to produce various paradigms of black citizenship that could reconcile the brutal history of black racialization with ideologies of emancipation and progress. These black nationalist discourses were also deeply imbricated with gendered ideologies of racial uplift. According to Kevin Gaines, ideologies of domesticity were constitutive of nineteenth-century discourses of racial uplift: "Oppression kept African Americans from fulfilling the majority society's normative gender conventions, and racist discourses portrayed society's denial of the authoritative moral status of the patriarchal family as a racial stigma, a lack of morality. . . . For educated blacks, the family and patriarchal gender relations became crucial signifiers of respectability."[5] Under the daily horrors of "living Jim Crow," which attempted to subvert the social, economic, and political advancement of the black community, the black family became one of the few viable arenas in which to exercise patriarchal authority and to assert not just black humanity but also a cultural form of black citizenship.[6] The resulting dominant narratives of nineteenth-century black politics thus formed a masculine citizen-subject whose modern development reified the privatized social, political, and economic subjugation of black women. This gendering of racialized citizenship often placed "black women writers at odds with a nationalist, masculinist ideology of uplift that demanded female deference in the cause of elevating black men."[7]

Black female intellectuals during this period were negotiating specific aspects of Euro-American definitions of modernity, which were particularly salient to the racialization of black women in the United States. Because racial uplift ideology espoused domestic patriarchal authority, middle-class black women were increasingly subjected to strict gender conventions, and black women across class lines were vulnerable to the gendered and sexual horrors of "living Jim Crow." Cooper's concerns that black men seemed to have particularly strong investments in traditional gendered conventions are underscored in the following passage regarding black women's education:

> While our men seem thoroughly abreast of the times on almost every other subject, when they strike the woman question they drop back into sixteenth century logic . . . women may stand on pedestals or live in doll houses, (if they happen to have them) but they must not furrow their brows with thought or attempt to help men tug at the great questions of the world. I fear the majority of colored men do not yet think it worthwhile that women aspire to higher education.[8]

Even though white men are positioned as the primary agents of black women's subordination in Cooper's work, she also identifies the patriarchal response of black men to white supremacy as one of the main obstacles to black women's emancipation. By describing black men's patriarchal investments as following "sixteenth century logic," Cooper challenges masculinist narratives of black progress by characterizing black men's response to "the woman question" as outmoded and premodern. The intensification of the black woman's confinement to the home, founded in the domestic ideologies and traditions of the white bourgeoisie, is clearly recognized by Cooper as a stultifying tradition that black women had never shared with white women and that would not offer emancipation through "inclusion." Narrating the black female's modern development, Cooper necessarily had to interrogate the ways in which narratives of black progress normalized black women's subordination through separating the private sphere ("women may . . . live in doll houses") from the public ("colored men do not think yet think it worth while that women aspire to higher education").

As African American feminist historians and critics have observed, black women's experiences during and after slavery confound the public/private separation of family from market relations, state intervention, and formal political equality.[9] However, the ways in which black women understood the links between public and private lives did not mirror the critiques employed by white women during the suffragist movement of the late nineteenth century. Suffragists demanded white women's political participation at the expense of eroding even the limited gains of African American men while multiply displacing black women from the terrain of citizenship, which reified a bourgeois construction of public and private spheres. As feminist scholar Nancy Fraser notes, white feminist scholarship has often used the term *public sphere* to refer to anything outside the domestic sphere and the site of the family, which therefore "conflates at least three analytically distinct things: the state, the official economy of paid employment, and arenas of public discourse."[10]

Black feminist scholarship has demonstrated that this imprecise notion of the public can generate reductive critiques of (white) women's oppressive "confinement" to the domestic sphere that also fail to account for black women's historical "exclusion" from domestic ideologies and institutions and their terrifying "inclusion" as slaves and exploited low-wage workers in the U.S. labor market. Fraser's emphasis on a nuanced understanding of the organization of public and private spheres of activity resonates with black feminist critiques that underscore the political significance of domestic ideologies and institutions to nineteenth-century black women's writing.[11]

For instance, African American cultural critic Ann duCille criticizes dominant feminist studies of nineteenth-century women's political fiction for recognizing only a rights-based discourse as a legitimate articulation of feminist concerns. DuCille contends that "the right to speak, the right to vote, the right of married women to own property—needs to be expanded to encompass broader public and private concerns."[12] Her critical insights weaken liberal narratives of political emancipation restricted to a narrow politics of inclusion, which situates nineteenth-century black women's political concerns with marriage, family, and black female morality outside the parameters of the political domain.[13] Black women were both women and dehumanized reproductive slave property. They physically labored both inside and outside the home; they were legally denied the marriage contract, motherhood, and their families. And they were also exploited as sexual concubines and domestic laborers, often functioning as "mammies" for the families of others. That is, black women in the United States occupied material and discursive sites that contradicted the gendered spatial logic of the public and private sphere.

This context is relevant to analyzing Cooper's construction of the domestic sphere as inherently political. By construing the domestic sphere as an expansive institution that determines the formation of the citizen and the nation's historical destiny, Cooper politicizes the home, regarding domestic life as crucial to a nation's modern development. Rhetorically, she draws on Orientalist imaginings of the East as her evidence for the relationship between home and nation, enabling her to strategically navigate the gendered ideologies underlying both racial uplift and claims to black citizenship.

The oriental woman's life of "ignorance, infamy, and complete stagnation" embodies a traditional, premodern existence of sexual degradation that Cooper links to the deterioration and historical regression of Asian civilizations. A depraved domestic life, she argues, is destined to destroy the nation as a whole, which is exemplified in an Orientalist text that she quotes to sustain her claims:

Says a certain writer: "The private life of the Turk is vilest of the vile, unprogressive, unambitious, and inconceivably low." And yet Turkey is not without her great men. . . . But these minds were not the normal outgrowth of a healthy trunk. . . . There is a worm at the core! The homelife is impure!

Cooper cites the "brilliant minds" and intellectual accomplishments of Turkish men that were nonetheless undercut by the depravity of their domestic life, which ultimately contaminated the national body.[14]

Cooper immediately follows this conventional Orientalist narrative of impurity and stagnation by constructing Western civilization in masculinized, developmental terms of modern progress and democratic possibility:

> It is pleasing to turn from this effete and immobile civilization to a society still fresh and vigorous, whose seed is in itself, and whose very name is synonymous with all that is progressive, elevating and inspiring, viz., the European bud and American flower of modern civilization. And here let me say parenthetically that our satisfaction in American institutions rests not on the fruition we now enjoy, but springs rather from the possibilities and promise that are inherent in the system, though as yet, perhaps, far from the future.[15]

By capitalizing on the discursive logic of Orientalism, Cooper attempts to produce black masculine dis-identification from the patriarchal practices of a society characterized as "effete and immobile," as well as masculine identification with the "American flower of modern civilization" that "rests not on the fruition we now enjoy, but rather springs from the possibilities and promise that are inherent in the system." Cooper uses this narrative of Oriental domestic depravity for an audience of black male ministers struggling to identify as subjects of Western civilization, from which they also are excluded as degraded racial Others. Given the commitment of racial uplift to embody black gentility, refinement, and civilization (see chapter 1), Cooper's Orientalist depiction of the despotic and barbaric subjugation of Oriental women is a potentially effective means of persuading black leadership that embracing restrictive "traditions" of domesticity undermined black historical progress. "Unprogressive" and "unambitious"—terms used to describe the Turk's home life—were particularly degrading and loaded terms in ideologies of racial uplift. Narratives of black progress and development were deployed to counter racist discourses of black regression into savagery,[16] and therefore black association with primitive, backward, or undeveloped behavior was systematically repudiated.

Cooper, therefore, negotiates patriarchal ideologies of black citizenship by using Orientalist tropes of premodern stagnation to revise discourses of black domesticity. But even these revisions spoken through and represented by black Orientalism cannot completely displace and, in many ways, disclose the violences underlying black women's modern formation in the United States. The construction of the enslaved, subordinated Oriental woman often functions in dominant colonial discourses as a sign of the "uncivilized practices of the oriental rather than as a critique of social and cultural institutions that subordinate women."[17] Such representations often reify the West as the site of civilization and construct the Western woman as a sign of civilized culture. In the logic of black Orientalism, the domestically confined and undeveloped woman is an emblem of barbarism rather than of civilization, which serves to position the modern black woman in Western civilization while also constructing patriarchal gender roles as signifiers of underdevelopment:

> Mahomet did not know woman. There was no hereafter, no paradise for her. The heaven of the Mussulman is peopled and made gladsome not by the departed wife, or sister, or mother, but by houri-a figment of Mahomet's brain, partaking of the ethereal qualities of angels, yet imbued with all the vices and inanity of Oriental women. The harem here, and—"dust to dust" hereafter, this was the hope, the inspiration, the summon bonum of the Eastern woman's life! With what result on the life of the nation, the "Unspeakable Turk," the "sick man" of modern Europe can to-day exemplify.[18]

In this instance, Orientalist discourse (for which the subjugated woman is a privileged trope) is the embodiment of the traditional domestic degradation that Cooper attempts to relegate to the historical past of Western civilization. Deploying the discursive logic of Orientalism is not only a means of legitimating modern gender ideologies that enable black women's development but also a way of narrating this progress as an uncontested formation in the current conditions of a nonstagnant West.

The Chinese woman's bound feet as well as the harem—in which the oriental woman is confined to a despotic form of sexual slavery—both imagine and locate the degraded, racialized female body in the premodern Far East, but the figure of the oppressed Oriental woman cannot entirely displace Cooper's modern formation under U.S. slavery, in which both she and her mother embodied her father's right to property protected by the state. Cooper's recurrent invocation of the bound foot and the harem as signs of the oriental women's bondage and sexual subjugation are not strikingly dissimilar from the signs of black women's subjugation during and after U.S. slavery. In a separate essay regarding the need for black women's education, Cooper asserts that the "old, subjective, stagnant, indolent, and wretched life for woman has gone. . . . The question is not now with the woman, 'how shall I so cramp, stunt, simplify and nullify myself as to make me eligible to the honor of being swallowed up by some little man?'"[19] Her rhetorical construction of traditional, restrictive gender ideologies employs the same language that she uses to describe the present conditions of Oriental women, who are "uniformly devoted to a life of ignorance, infamy, and complete stagnation" and whose shoes, customs, and laws "entirely dwarf, cramp, and destroy her physical powers."[20]

Of course, these resonating images of female subordination emerge from highly differentiated historical contexts. But these tropes of bondage and sexual slavery are also precisely the dominant signifiers for the exploitative conditions suffered by black women. The dehistoricizing tropes of the Oriental woman's bondage and her function as a sexual concubine recall the history of black women's exploitation in the United States even as they attempt to distance these histories across time and space. If the bound foot and the sexual slave are the signs of barbarism that measure "a nation's rank in the scale of civilization,"[21] the consolidation of America as the site of modernity and civilization is undone by the material history of black women, which destabilizes any binaristic relation between modern America and a despotic Orient. In other words, Cooper's use of black Orientalist discourse as a means of linking women's subjugation with underdeveloped, backward societies works to recall and reveal the contradictions that black women's history poses to ideologies of American modernity.

The sexual violence and exploitation of black women in the United States forms a material history that contradicts the "American flower of modern civilization." Nonetheless, Cooper must privilege the modern American West as a utopic site of "promises and possibilities" for black women. Having entered into American modernity through the institution of slavery, Cooper wrestles with the contradictory political imperative for black women to assert their personhood and womanhood by claiming dominant, domestic gender ideologies. But as African American literary critic Hazel Carby points out, black women were historically excluded from domestic ideologies of true womanhood, and "black female sexuality was nevertheless used to define what those boundaries were."[22] Racial uplift thus demanded black women's acquiescence to a racialized ideology of idealized womanhood that was defined over and against black women's sexuality. For Cooper, the "promises and possibilities" of American institutions were not to be found in marriage and motherhood; rather, she advocates a modern transformation of black women's gender roles, which find their telos in higher education.

In Cooper's essays, black women's sexual vulnerability to rape, abuse, and seduction is the fundamental horror that necessitates black women's development through higher education. Gaines notes that "amidst the self-congratulatory optimism of the spate of commemorative volumes testifying to Black progress,"[23] work like Cooper's, which addressed the rape of black women, was rare and uncommon. Yet he also contends that her appeals for black women's protection were located outside the context of political power and the legal system, reducing the matter to "self-help and moral conduct" and indicative of the "political disadvantage faced by southern blacks."[24] The state's political or legal institutions, however, could not adequately address Cooper's concerns, since she understood the sexual exploitation and commodification of black women as a consequence of a normalized patriarchal structure of socioeconomic relations that characterized the rhetoric of racial uplift.

It is therefore important to recognize that when Cooper addresses the rape of black women as a primary facet of their subjugation, she is extending her critique to the normative social and economic options of pseudovoluntary relationships that exploited black female sexuality. Cooper's description of that "fatally beautiful class" of young black women who were "full of promise and possibilities" and yet "before the fury of tempestuous elements . . . so sure of destruction . . . in the midst of pitfalls and snares, waylaid by the lower classes of white men, with no shelter, no protection nearer than the great blue vault above"[25] is not only an indictment of coerced sexual violence. She also links the subordination of black women to the racialized economy of heteronormative gender relations that made black women's survival contingent on their sexual commodification through marriage or less socially legitimate arrangements with white (or black) men.[26] While Cooper clearly looks to the black middle class as an agent of uplift that can save the "unprotected, untrained colored girl of the South,"[27] she also interrogates the highly uneven system of heterosexual courtship and coupling in the black community that leaves poor black women vulnerable to what she regarded as seduction and sexual manipulation with few economically viable options. Her critique points to the limits of modern political institutions, which cannot adequately address black women's oppression insofar as the heteronormative institution of marriage constitutes the naturalized private sphere that is "protected" from state intervention.

Cooper argues that industrial and liberal education could resolve the economic dependence and sexual commodification endemic to black women's sexuality that impeded their development. Education could provide black girls and women with institutional support and skills for the labor market that would render them less vulnerable to sexual exploitation. Even more important to Cooper was the notion that education could develop a black female subject who could transcend the degradation of sexual embodiment through the development of her mind:

> I grant you that intellectual development, with the self-reliance and capacity for earning a livelihood which it gives, renders women less dependent on the marriage relation for support (which by the way, does not always accompany it). Neither is she compelled to look to sexual love as the one sensation capable of giving her tone and relish, movement and vim to the life she leads. . . . Here, at last, can be communion without suspicion; friendship without misunderstanding; love without dependency and sexual jealousy.[28]

Refiguring marriage from sexual coupling to friendship was a component of the late nineteenth-century Victorian ideology of "passionlessness," which was particularly critical to the elevation of black womanhood and cleared a discursive space for black women's intellectual development and enlightenment.[29] Hence, according to Cooper, a proper educational formation granted black women moral integrity by desexualizing their social relations and subjectivity, which was crucial to narrating black female transcendence. Cooper describes the importance of allowing black women educational access and opportunity so that "she can commune with Socrates . . . she can revel in the majesty of Dante, the sweetness of Virgil, the simplicity of Homer, and strength of Milton."[30] While such a liberal education would hardly be accessible to poor black girls and women in industrial schools, it is an imaginary means of incorporating black women into the transcendent universality of Western civilization.

Cooper's struggles to realize an enlightened, moral, and disembodied black female subjectivity through higher education reveal the paradox endemic to the project of modernity itself. The particularity of American modernity emerges from its racialized national formation. America's

Declaration of Independence from British rule and the U.S. Constitution were articulations of the racialized liberal political ideologies of Enlightenment philosophy, whose emphasis on the individual, property rights, and representative forms of government provided the key terms in the formation of a liberal democratic state. America's self-defined break from European feudalism and aristocracy was critical to the formation of U.S. nationalism, which declared itself the embodiment of modern ideals that promised novel and unprecedented democratic institutions designed to secure the rights and freedom of its citizens.

The institution of slavery was constitutive of American liberal ideologies of freedom and emancipation. As historian Orlando Patterson observes,

> Slavery is associated not only with the development of advanced economies, but also with the emergence of several of the most profoundly cherished ideals and beliefs in the Western tradition. The idea of freedom and the concept of property were both intimately bound up with the rise of slavery, their very anti-thesis.[31]

For U.S. blacks, placing themselves into an Enlightenment narrative of development and modern progress produced a critical contradiction. Cooper's imagining of black women's assimilation into the universality of Western liberal humanism can hardly be a seamless process when the violent particularity of black female difference continually emerges in contradiction to ideologies of Western civilization.

In the mid-nineteenth century, ethnological discourses posited that blacks were irrational and driven primarily by their emotions and therefore incapable of progressive development and self-government. Scientific racism directly negated black narratives of modern development by "fixing" black intelligence and ability, claiming that blacks and other nonwhite races were inherently incapable of advancement. Yet romantic racialism, emerging in relation to the abolitionist movement in the United States, characterized the black subject as the purest embodiment of Christian virtue: meek, naïve, emotional, innocent, and childlike.[32] Romanticist and religious discourses gave precedent to "feelings over intellect" and framed black racial difference as virtuous with respect to the cold rationalism of Anglo-Saxons.[33] Blacks were, therefore, morally superior to white Anglo-Saxons, who were driven by rationality, intellect, aggression, and a non-Christian desire for dominance. Both scientific racism and Christian romantic racialism imagined black Americans as primitive and underdeveloped, although religious discourses allowed for the possibility of redemption and transcendence. The innocent and childlike construction of black Americans in romantic racialism also ascribed to blacks a moral authority that social Darwinism did not.

Hazel Carby observes that black women in the nineteenth century transformed dominant ideologies of domesticity that espoused Victorian morality and Christian doctrine by redeploying these discourses to reconstitute the moral authority of black women, condemn the immorality of slavery, and indict the institutionalized rape of black women after emancipation.[34] Cooper's recourse to Christian ideology as a means of contesting the teleology of scientific racism is fundamental to how she challenges ethnological studies, which legitimated and naturalized racialized processes of domination. These ideological negotiations are borne out in Cooper's response to colonization schemes that were still being discussed in the 1890s as a possible solution to America's "race problem."

Having only been recently emancipated from slavery, Cooper explains the capacity of black Americans for development by characterizing them as children of civilization:

> The race is young and full of the elasticity and hopefulness of youth. All its achievements are before it. It does not look on the masterly triumphs of the nineteenth century civilization with that blasé world-weary look which characterized the old washed out and worn races which have already, so to speak, seen their best days. . . . Everything to this race is new and strange and inspiring.[35]

Constructing the black population as eager young children, Cooper produces a naturalized narrative of developmental growth that tries to displace racial scientific discourses that construed black persons as inherently primitive and backward.[36] Black men and women would develop into civilized "adulthood" to embody the historical agency ascribed to a modern subject that shapes the course of progress. Romantic racialism was a patronizing ideology that feminized and infantilized African Americans so they could assume a Christ-like innocence that was being unfairly exploited by Anglo-Saxon masculinity.

Condemning the "barbarian brawn, greed and brutality" that have governed the formation of the civilized world, Cooper critiques its evolution into a self-righteous ideology of manifest destiny. She quotes Percival Lowell at length, whose work she disdainfully characterizes as "Barbarian brag":

As for Far Orientals, they are not of those who will survive. Artistic attractive people that they are, their civilization is like their own tree flowers, beautiful blossoms destined to never bear fruit. If these people continue in their old course, their earthly career is closed. Just as surely as morning passes into afternoon, so surely are these races of the Far East, if unchanged, destined to disappear before the advancing nations of the West. Vanish, they will, off the face of the earth, and leave our planet the eventual possession of the dwellers where the day declines.[37]

Cooper's critical discussion of Lowell's description of Western progress emerges from her challenge to racialized discourses of social Darwinism, which pervaded America by the turn of the century. Cooper's response to Lowell's imperialist vision of manifest destiny firmly embraces a nonsecular Christian ideology that she articulates through discourses of romantic racialism, inverting the racial logic of moral authority:

Whence the scorn of so-called weak or unwar-like races and individuals, and the very comfortable assurance that it is their manifest destiny to be wiped out as vermin before this advancing civilization? As if the possession of the Christian graces of meekness, nonresistance and forgiveness, were incompatible with a civilization based on Christianity.[38]

Cooper's unequivocal critique of Lowell may seem striking in comparison with her own frequent Orientalist articulations, but it is not contradictory in the context of how she reconciles discourses of development with ideologies of romantic racialism. Cooper's sarcastic disparagement of Lowell does not interrogate the construction of an effeminate, premodern, and aestheticized Orient, which is consistent with her own Orientalist imaginings. What produces Cooper's strong indignation is Lowell's complacent presumption regarding the "annihilation" of a feminized civilization, which implies the erasure of blacks and other "nonmodern" populations from the historical future.[39]

Romantic racialism enables Cooper to critique the masculinized ideology of imperialist dominance over a feminized Orient, and it underlies her condemnation of anti-Chinese racism in the United States. The work of Lisa Lowe and sociologist Yen Espiritu demonstrates how immigration restrictions produced Chinese immigrant bachelor communities that were "concentrated in feminized forms of work—such as laundry, restaurants, and other service sector jobs," which effectively "feminized" Chinese immigrant men "in relation to white male citizens."[40] To this degree, the ideology of romantic racialism, which analogized race with gender, converged with the discursive racialization of Chinese immigrants. Cooper recounts a white woman's unsympathetic reaction to the harassment of a Chinese immigrant in San Francisco:

> The incorrigible animal known as the American small boy, had pounced upon a simple, unoffending Chinaman, who was taking home his work, and had emptied the beautifully laundered contents of his basket into the ditch. "And," said she, "when that great man stood there and blubbered before that crowd of lawless urchins, to any one of whom he might have taught a lesson with his two fists, I didn't much care." This is said like a man! It grates harshly. It smacks of the worship of the beast. It is contempt for weakness.[41]

Cooper's empathetic, feminizing narration of the Chinese male immigrant presents the emotionalism and docility of the crying "Chinaman" as virtues in contradistinction to the violent aggression and racist contempt typified by the "American small boy" and the white woman recounting this story. Although black men are similarly and consistently figured as docile and childlike throughout Cooper's text, this does not necessarily produce equivalence or identification between blacks and Chinese immigrants as subordinated racial minorities.[42] Cooper's sympathetic characterization of the feminized Chinese immigrant is displaced when the black American is situated in relation to an immigrant labor force supplanting black workers. Cooper writes,

> America needs the Negro for ballast if nothing else. His tropical warmth and spontaneous emotionalism may form no unseemly counterpart to the cold and calculating Anglo-Saxon. And then his instinct for law and order, his inborn respect for authority, his inaptitude for rioting and anarchy, his gentleness and cheerfulness as a laborer, and his deep-rooted faith in God will prove indispensable and invaluable elements in a nation menaced as America is by anarchy, socialism, communism, and skepticism poured in with all the jailbirds from the continents of Europe and Asia.[43]

Cooper nuances romantic racialist discourse by emphasizing the loyalty and docility of black laborers during a period when the racially exclusive organizing efforts of white immigrant workers were causing considerable social upheaval. The black American is strongly differentiated from an immigrant population whose Catholicism, heathenism, and political ideologies are markers of foreign identifications threatening the moral and political integrity of the U.S. national body. In this context, Cooper's sympathetic feminizing narration of the docile and sensitive "Chinaman," who is unfairly subjected to Anglo-Saxon aggression, is displaced by another Orientalism that forms black national identity over and against alien immigrants from "the continents of Asia." Although Orientalism is central to Cooper's arguments and rhetorical strategies, negotiating discourses of underdevelopment through the Christian ideology of romantic racialism enables her also to critique Orientalist writers and imperialist ideologies. Using the ideology of romantic racialism enables her to counter the "underdevelopment" of black and nonwhite populations by reconstituting their Christian moral authority and by imagining for them a redemptive space in the historical future.

Cooper herself occupies the contradictory position of being assimilated into the very discourses that defined and dominated nonwhite populations as the backward and underdeveloped Others of the West. Her own elite formation as a black female intellectual generated numerous contradictions to that body of Western knowledge through which she was incorporated. Throughout her arguments, for instance, Cooper continually cites and refers to more than twenty Euro-American intellectuals, almost all of whom can be categorically described as Orientalists, such as Thomas Macaulay, François Guzoit, Percival Lowell, George Eliot, Lord Byron, Matthew Arnold, and Hippolyte Taine. Furthermore, Cooper's doctorate from the Université de Sorbonne was completed under her adviser, Celestin Bouglé, another prominent Orientalist scholar in French sociology.[44] Throughout the nineteenth century, both American and western European higher educational institutions produced a subject formed through Orientalism.

Cooper's paradoxical formation as a Western intellectual was highly conflicted, and she found herself challenging her own eminent adviser, Professor Bouglé, who argued that "backward" nonwhite populations lacked the capacity to modernize into democratic institutions. During her dissertation defense, Cooper responded to Bouglé, an atheist, that God's presence in all human beings, or "the singing something,"[45] was the origin of the principles of equality, justice, and democratic freedom.[46] Although Cooper's intellectual formation was shaped by an Orientalist education

and her writings clearly indicate her own acquiescence to Western imaginings of the Orient and Oriental people, her specific material history as
a black woman in the United States necessarily challenged Orientalism
as an epistemology. Orientalism scripted all nonwhite populations out of
the historical future because it justified the colonization, eradication, and
exploitation of nonwhites as inherently underdeveloped people. Cooper's
invocation of "the singing something," reflective of God's presence in all
human beings, challenges the epistemological foundations of Orientalism by seeing all people as equally able to become modern subjects and
therefore also equally deserving of the promises in this telos of modern
development: "equality, justice, and democratic freedom."

Black Orientalism as manifested in the writings of Anna Julia Cooper gives us little indication of a singular position or perspective on Chinese immigrants. At some points, Chinese immigrants are constructed
similarly to black Americans as feminized and virtuous racial minorities
subjected to discriminatory practices and white racial violence. At other
moments, the Chinese are figures of foreign difference that threaten U.S.
national culture and are differentiated from the domestic loyalty of black
Americans. Similarly, Cooper represents the "Orient" as a monolithic premodern site of stagnation and despotism, particularly through the trope
of the subjugated Oriental woman, yet she also imagines the Far East as
a feminized site to be defended and protected from the dominance of
Anglo-Saxon aggression. Black Orientalism clearly cannot be understood
as a racial "attitude" but, rather, as a set of discursive negotiations seeking to reconcile particular racial and gendered contradictions that emerge
in the production of a developmental narrative regarding black women's
incorporation into American modernity. The ideological maneuvers that
Cooper must perform in order to advocate for the humanity and entitlement of black women and men produce numerous contradictions, which
are neither an index of Cooper's inconsistencies nor her presumed ideological "shortcomings"[47] but indicate the discursive constraints in which
black female emancipation could be narrated.

%% Part 2 %%

Previous chapters examined the ways in which discourses of black citizenship from the mid- to late nineteenth century deployed American Orientalism to negotiate the vulnerable political status of black Americans. Part 2 inverts this analytical trajectory to examine how processes of black racialization are variously represented in Asian American novels that produce narratives of national belonging during the World War II period. This shift to fiction enables us to examine how Asian American national identity could be imagined or narrativized when the notion of the Asian as an American citizen was both paradoxical and legally negated. We can understand World War II as a period when black racial exclusion became a political contradiction for the U.S. state, whereas the expulsion of Japanese Americans from the national citizenry did not pose a similar crisis of legitimation. For instance, A. Philip Randolph's threat of a black "march on Washington" succeeded in pressuring President Franklin D. Roosevelt to sign Executive Order 8802, ordering the desegregation of industrial labor in all plants with federal contracts. The political expedience of expanding black civil rights at this historical conjuncture was discontinuous with the wartime internment of Japanese Americans, whose claims to U.S. citizenship did not similarly resonate when racially defined as a national threat. This relationship between the expansion of civil rights and U.S. war in Asia was sustained throughout the twentieth century as racial liberalism became critical to U.S. geopolitical legitimacy in the fight against fascism and the cold war. The increasing political legitimacy of black claims to full inclusion during the mid-twentieth century registers in Asian American cultural production through imaginings that agency, racial recalcitrance, and even national belonging are in the domain of blackness.

The relationship between mass culture and U.S. national identity was also a critical dimension of discourses of citizenship in this period. The ascendance of radio and film after the 1920s constituted new technologies in the making of U.S. national consciousness and identity, and the immediacy of President Roosevelt's radio "fireside chats" produced a new subjective experience in the making of the citizen-subject. Commercial entertainment programs were even more important to the national culture, and blackface was at the center of these emergent cultural institutions. From *Amos 'n Andy*, to D. W. Griffith's *Birth of a Nation*, to the wildly popular Al Jolson films, American national identity incorporated white ethnic difference and was consolidated through mass cultural consumption of performative disavowals of black racial difference.

The following chapters examine how two Asian American novels variously represent black subjects and black social space in an effort to redress the exclusion of Asian Americans from the national citizenry during the World War II period. Gendered discourses of black urban pathology are a central feature of *No-No Boy* and *Clay Walls*, functioning as an ambivalent form of Asian American cultural politics that negotiates the state demand for assimilation. John Okada, a *nisei* (second-generation Japanese American) who served in the U.S. Army during World War II, sets his novel *No-No Boy* in the Central district of downtown Seattle where he was born and raised in the multiracial ghetto before and after his family's internment. Ronyoung Kim's novel, *Clay Walls*, could be characterized as autobiographical fiction, recounting the experiences of her Korean American family in Los Angeles between the 1920s and 1940s. Kim, who was born and raised in South Central Los Angeles, writes in a manner that is similarly characterized by a textured familiarity with the nonwhite urban neighborhood that is the setting of the novel. The novels' publication dates are not determining factors in the following chapters, as my analysis is not predicated on a periodization of Asian American literary production. Rather, I focus on how Asian American authors narrate their national formations in the particular racialized sociopolitical context of ghettoized urban space in the World War II period. These novels negotiate Asian American racialization and respond to the violent mandate of assimilation by constructing ambivalent relationships of both disavowal of and longing for black urban space and black working-class culture.

3

Blackness, Manhood, and the Aftermath of Internment in John Okada's *No-No Boy* (1957)

> *"Jap!"*
>
> *His pace quickened automatically, but curiosity or fear and indignation or whatever it was made him glance back at the white teeth framed in a leering dark brown which was almost black.*
>
> *"Go back to Tokyo, boy." Persecution in the drawl of the persecuted. The white teeth and brown-black leers picked up the cue and jigged to the rhythmical chanting of "Jap-boy, To-ki-yo, Jap-boy To-ki-yo."*
>
> —John Okada, *No-No Boy*

John Okada's novel, *No-No Boy* (1957), is a postwar maladjustment story of a young Japanese American's struggle to reincorporate into the national citizenry in the aftermath of his internment and incarceration as an alien racial enemy.[1] In the novel's opening, the *nisei*[2] protagonist, Ichiro, is walking home after spending two years in federal prison and two years in an internment camp when he has a hostile encounter with a group of young black men, who derisively call him out as a "Jap." More than just a commentary on the "sad irony" of interracial hostility, the preceding passage comments on the ways in which these differently racialized characters negotiate their exclusion from the national body through discourses of Orientalism and antiblack Americanism. The narrative's reference to the black men as "the persecuted" draws an implicit connection between the "no-no boys"[3] and the black male community that also had struggled during World War II with the dilemma of whether to fight abroad for the freedoms denied them at home. However, this passage clearly shows that the Japanese American and black male characters do *not* share an equivalent dilemma of racialized citizenship, indicating instead that they are mutually constituted as "American" through the racialization of the other. These young black men, spilling out of a poolroom bar, are represented as unruly and underdeveloped working-class subjects, and hence the novel situates them as the fringe of an already marginal black community. But by depicting African American participation in the anti-Japanese discourse that defined U.S. national identity during World War II, the novel imagines a modality of black national belonging that is nonetheless available through Asian American displacement.

While the black men's racial remarks reproduce the Orientalist logic that locates the Asian American outside the national body, the narrative's description of the black men is what most clearly contradicts the notion that the Asian American is an alien national subject. The passage's fixation on black bodies, which are reduced to dismembered parts of "white teeth" and "brown-black" leers that "jigged . . . to rhythmical chanting," invoke some of the most enduring American signifiers of black racial difference. The narrative's caricatures of blackness draw from a national cultural repository that dates from the antebellum period to the U.S. minstrel stage and thus inadvertently demonstrates a strikingly "American" formation. Ichiro counters the black men's emasculating anti-Japanese remarks with an assertion of antiblack Americanism ("friggin niggers") in an attempt to undermine the nationalist authority that these black men are figured to possess. It is significant that this brief, but loaded, exchange takes place in the opening of a Japanese American novel that struggles to claim the paradoxical promises of inclusion and universality in the face of racialized exclusion and differentiation. In this World War II narrative of Japanese American masculine formation, the displacement and alienation of Asian American subjectivity are expressed through various imaginings of black national belonging and black alterity. These imaginings are posited in specific social spaces and suggest that a historical and literary analysis of social space is critical to understanding the significance of black racial difference in the production of an Asian American national identity.

The previous chapters examined the ways in which discourses of black citizenship during the post-Reconstruction period deployed American

Orientalism to negotiate the vulnerable political status of black Americans in the mid- to late nineteenth century. This chapter inverts this analytical trajectory to examine how processes of black racialization are variously represented in a Japanese American novel that struggles with the contradictions of Asian American citizenship during the World War II period. *No-No Boy* is told from the space of the multiracial ghetto and negotiates Orientalist exclusion and national displacement through gendered discourses of black urban pathology. Blackness is a complex and ambivalent signifier in this narrative of Asian American formation, and black social spaces are imagined as being in the cultural boundaries of the U.S. nation even as the novel them as racialized sites of deviance disavows. Black social space disrupts narratives of Asian American identification with either "Oriental tradition" or "American modernity," thereby forming a "third space"[4] that is an alternative to the space of national culture and the political space of the state. Against the symbolic resolution of social contradictions that identification with national spaces would compel, the figuring of black social space enables this Japanese American novel to explore and manage the contradictions of Asian American national identity.

The novel's figuration of racialized social space invokes a genealogy of social and spatial practices that differentially racialized black and Asian Americans from the mid-nineteenth century through World War II. The material processes and the discursive representation of Asian and black im/migration, urbanization, and ghettoization demonstrate that the racialization of Asians as noncitizens is a spatial process in which black urban culture emerges as a racially deviant yet American formation that mediates Asian American political and cultural disenfranchisement.

Since the mid-nineteenth century, Asian American citizenship had been a conceptual contradiction or paradox, since American Orientalism legally and ideologically racialized the Asian as permanently alien to the U.S. nation. From 1882 to 1954, a series of exclusion acts effectively barred immigrants from China, Japan, Korea, India, and the Philippines, and Asian immigrants were the only group to be racialized as "aliens ineligible for citizenship."[5] Asians could become U.S. citizens only if they were born in the United States, an impossibility for most groups due to antimiscegenation laws and rigid restrictions preventing the immigration of Asian women.[6] Japanese immigrants were an exception, however,[7] and were able to form family units in significant numbers in the United States and the U.S. colony of Hawai'i. Accordingly, two-thirds of the Japanese American internees during World War II were U.S. citizens. This formal status, however, obviously provided little protection from the anti-Japanese nationalism that resulted in the relocation and incarceration of Japanese Americans, despite their U.S. citizenship. The internment of Japanese Americans during World War II, therefore, is a dramatic yet unremarkable instance in the history of American Orientalism that located U.S. Asians outside the boundaries of the national citizenry.

While Asian immigrants were thereby defined against the American citizenry, a related set of processes defined them in relation to U.S. blacks. Asian immigrant labor functioned as a permanently disenfranchised and tractable labor force, more often than not contained in racial ghettos that were highly regulated as alien spaces that threatened to disease and contaminate the nation. Throughout the West, the Orientalist racialization of Asian Americans as foreign racial elements was also an expression of white workers' racialized anxieties about a free and enfranchised black labor force. Despite attempts to criminalize black mobility after the abolition of slavery through vagrancy laws that sought to confine black labor to the southern agricultural economy, black migration and urbanization began in the late nineteenth century, culminating in the "Great Migrations" during World Wars I and II. These processes of migration and urbanization generated black urban ghettos and working-class cultures that were pathologized by the black middle class, white intellectuals, and progressive reformers. However, since the mid-nineteenth century, the appropriation of black culture had been definitive of U.S. popular culture, and America desperately needed its "Negroes," not just as an exploited labor force, but also as the foundation of its collective, yet racially exclusive, culture and identity. For U.S. Asians who have been legally, politically, and culturally defined as racialized aliens of the nation, this constitutive relationship between black culture and U.S. national identity emerges as a crucial axis in negotiating the contradictory formation of Asian American citizenship.

The exploitation of Asian immigrant labor in the development of the West and Pacific began in the mid-nineteenth century, precisely when regional conflicts over the South's dependency on black slave labor were escalating. The newly annexed western territories were claimed as non-slave or "free-labor" states, which were maintained not by the abolitionist movement but by the white working class, which regarded slavery and free black labor as grave economic threats. Even before the formal abolition of slavery, white workers across the West mobilized in a series of campaigns to prohibit black migration to these "free-soil" states in order to protect white workers' wages. As historian Alexander Saxton argues, these intense anxieties concerning black labor were intimately linked to the anti-Chinese movement on the West Coast: "One of the earliest efforts to exclude the Chinese from California by state law was passed in the Assembly as a companion piece to a measure barring entry of Negroes."[8] It seems clear that "white" migrants in mid-nineteenth-century California imagined Chinese immigrants and black workers in relation to each other as degrading nonwhite labor forces that needed to be contained and excluded. Saxton's insights into the relationships between white labor and the racialization of black and Chinese immigrant workers resonate with Du Bois's understanding of how the defeat of "abolition Democracy" and the rise of Chinese exclusion not only were events that happened in succession but also made each other possible and desirable.

Before World War II, low-wage black labor was never employed in significant numbers in the capitalist development of the West and Pacific. Although most western states had contained small black communities since the mid-nineteenth century, the black population was not sufficiently large enough to constitute a racial threat, since anti-Asian sentiment defined the racial axis in the West. Therefore, pre–World War II black communities in the West were not subjected to highly rigid forms of residential segregation, and early black migrants experienced relative freedoms compared with those of the rest of the country.[9] Although many black residents lived close to other black households and black businesses, rigid forms of residential segregation emerged in West Coast cities only after the massive migration of black workers during the industrial boom produced by the war.

Asian immigrants, however, as the largest and most economically threatening nonwhite population since the mid-1800s, were strictly contained in racial ghettos throughout the nineteenth to mid- twentieth century. Chinatown ghettoization constituted not only an attempt to regulate the economic threat of Chinese labor, but, as Saxton suggests, also was the expression of intense national anxieties around the containment of an impending free black labor population of four million.[10] The discourses surrounding Chinatowns and other Asian immigrant ghettos persistently constructed these spaces as alien sites of contamination, disease, vice, and immorality. For example, in response to the threat of bubonic plague contagion in San Francisco's Chinatown, local officials imposed strict quarantines and other regulatory measures passed in the interest of public health, literally constructing a policed boundary around the Chinese ghetto.[11] This "medical" discourse of disease and contamination became the primary rationale for Chinese racial segregation, as well as subjecting Chinese immigrants to a variety of dubious medical examinations as a condition of their entry into the United States.[12]

The waves of Japanese and Filipino immigrant workers (to the U.S. mainland) that followed the Chinese exclusion were also confined to Asian ghettos, often directly adjacent to or near the older existing Chinatowns. Along the West Coast, housing discrimination and restrictive covenants against the Japanese and Filipinos were pervasive throughout the early to mid-twentieth century, with real estate agents citing losses in property values and claiming that "no one wants to live near them."[13] Filipino immigrants were composed almost exclusively of young men and were also regulated as a sexual threat to white women, owing to their participation in urban commercialized leisure, such as taxi dance halls.[14] Door signs posted in West Coast restaurants and other establishments in the 1920s and 1930s reading "No Dogs or Filipinos Allowed" are indicative of the persistence of ethnically differential yellow peril discourses that debased Asian immigrants through their association with filth and contamination. While the pathologization of Chinatown ghettos that began in the 1850s and persisted as the dominant signifier of the Asian urban ghetto expresses anxieties extending to the containment of black racial difference, it also indicates the racialized specificity by which Asian urban ghettos were constructed as foreign and contaminating spaces that needed to be expunged from the nation.

The Asian American cultural practices that emerged from these ghetto spaces were indelibly marked as foreign, whether as curiously "exotic," sensationally repulsive, or dangerously subversive. After the bombing of Pearl Harbor, Japantown's religious leaders, language teachers, and the heads of other community institutions were immediately arrested by the FBI, and the internment literally emptied these ghetto spaces of their communities and culture. Many families hurriedly burned photos, letters, books, and any other cultural "signs" that the U.S. state would interpret as subversive and anti-American.[15] Similar to the nineteenth-century razing of numerous Chinatowns, either killing or displacing its residents, the destruction of Japanese American culture during World War II was understood as a matter of national security. The meanings ascribed to Asian urban ghettos reveal that Asian American culture became the negation of U.S. national culture, in contrast to the appropriation and commodification of black culture that have defined U.S. national identity since the nineteenth century.

From the late nineteenth century through the 1940s, processes of black migration and urbanization were central to the racialization of the social space of the city. After the dismantling of Radical Reconstruction, black migration to urban centers (in the South and North) increased at a slow rate until 1917, when hundreds of thousands of black southerners headed to northern cities. Black southern migrants organized both formal and informal networks to abandon the South's racial social order and an agricultural economy in which they were increasingly expendable in order to seek new lives and labor opportunities in northern cities, which had experienced labor shortages during the war. This "Great Migration" was followed by a continuing pattern of black northern settlement, and by 1930, an estimated 700,000 African Americans had left the South.[16] The rapid influx of black migrants into Chicago, New York, Philadelphia, and Detroit was met with labor hostility, race riots, and rigid residential segregation, which functioned to contain and ghettoize black racial difference as well as provide the conditions for a thriving working-class and middle-class black urban culture.[17]

Northern urbanization failed to meet most of the expectations of black migrants. In addition, the poverty, poor housing conditions, and cultural practices in the black ghetto were treated as a social crisis or "problem" by academics, black middle-class reformers, and white progressive reformists.[18] Since the turn of the twentieth century, black working-class urban culture has been pathologized by constructing crime, vice, and sexual immorality as the causes of poverty and poor living conditions in black urban ghettos. In the 1920s and 1930s, white sociologists "urbanized" existing theories of black pathology, focusing on black family structure and the negative impact of black female "independence," which was linked to "rising rates" of sexual immorality, vice, and criminality in the city.[19] Black community leaders expressed anxieties about black urbanization, concerned that "the rush of our young people to large Northern cities . . . [makes them] easy prey to the vices of the slums and alleys."[20] The emphasis on black sexuality and vice as constituting black working-class urban culture is the ideological thread running throughout these various articulations. Therefore, black urbanity itself was not a problem, and the enthusiastic patronage and reception of black artists and writers during the Harlem Renaissance indicate that in fact, black urban "high culture" was not just tolerated but highly celebrated and consumed by a cosmopolitan and multiracial bourgeoisie.

The Harlem Renaissance, which included a multitude of black urban writers and artists who worked with various forms and themes, captures one dimension of the commodification of black urban culture after the Great Migration. As in every other period of American history, national culture in the 1920s was largely defined through white fascination with "blackness," including working-class black urban culture. Both avant-garde and middle-class whites in the 1920s regularly inhabited black social spaces for leisure purposes, otherwise known as "slumming," which was considered the practice in which white urbanites or "social superiors [engaged in] temporarily exploiting people and institutions on the margins, usually for pleasure, leisure, or sexual adventure."[21] But white leisure activity was not confined to edgy yet elegant evenings at New York's Cotton Club, which featured black performers but prohibited the entry of black patrons. The pathologization of black urban working-class culture as sexually licentious, underdeveloped, and animalistic also produced white desires for black transgression, resulting in the "black and tans" and "speakeasies," which were spaces in which interracial dancing, socializing, and other "deviant" sexual relations were practiced. Kevin Mumford refers to these sexually nonnormative urban spaces as *interzones* that both defined and destabilized modern discourses of race and sexuality. Because these interzones were also sites that produced alternative subjectivities, they were intensely policed, categorized, and regulated.[22]

Specific "reform" policies and policing strategies confined vice districts to black neighborhoods during the 1920s and 1930s and reified discourses of black urban pathology, identifying unregulated black sexuality as the cause of poverty, crime, high infant mortality, unemployment, and deplorable housing conditions. As in many Asian ghettos throughout the early twentieth century, vice districts were largely situated in black urban neighborhoods, but it was the Great Migration that enabled progressive reformers and selective policing practices to relocate vice zones to black neighborhoods.[23]

The black middle class, which could not move out of vice zones because of residential segregation, was consequently compelled to regulate and discipline the black working class as a means of asserting black respectability. The spectacle of black urban culture as "transgression" was also central to the emergence of early twentieth-century notions of modern womanhood and sexuality, which were largely predicated on the further degradation of black working-class women as the negative limit of acceptable womanhood. As Hazel Carby observes, young and single black women were particularly targeted by white and black intellectuals, reformers, and institutions as the locus of a multitude of anxieties incited by migration, displacement, and urbanization. As one black female reformer stated, unregulated black female sexuality in the urban North was a direct threat to the "headway which the Negro had made toward the state of good citizenship."[24] While the gendered pathologization of black urban space led to a strong middle-class imperative to perform heteronormativity, that same urban space gave rise to a thriving black working-class women's blues culture and community.[25]

Gendered discourses of black urban pathology are central to Okada's *No-No Boy*. In this novel, representations of black urban deviance function as a form of cultural politics that addresses the contradictory demands for Asian American assimilation during World War II. This process by which contradictions of Asian American citizenship are negotiated in relation to black racialization is termed *Asian uplift*. Like black Orientalism, what I call Asian uplift is not reducible to antiblack racism, nor does it signify the "successful" resolution of Asian American assimilation. Instead, Asian uplift is an analytical paradigm that sees Asian American racialization as a relational process to which black racial formation is integral.[26] Asian American novels show that the pathologization of black working-class subjects and black urban space is constitutive of U.S. national culture and a critical means by which liminal subjects become "American." This mode of national incorporation is predicated on the reproduction of dominant discourses of black racial difference as well as the production of distance from black urban place. Throughout the West, practices of residential segregation in the 1940s confined most Asians, African Americans, Chicanos, and some Jews to "unrestricted" housing districts. Okada's novel explores processes of Asian American racialization and responds to the discursive pressure of assimilation by constructing ambivalent but crucial relationships to black urban space and black working-class culture. The novel is haunted by histories of black racial exclusion that uneasily contradict the developmental narrative of assimilation that thematically and formally structures the Asian American novel.

For Asian Americans, who are racialized as perpetual and immutable aliens of the U.S. nation, the developmental ideology of assimilation is the central discursive means by which their national identity is disciplined and narrated. This narrative of assimilation, a long-standing feature and demand of U.S. nationalism,[27] emplots the formation of Asian American identity as the movement from Oriental tradition to American modernity. U.S. Orientalism constitutes this development of national identification as either impossible or perpetually deferred and hence demands that the Asian American subject "choose" a national identification, which is always already outside the domain of choice. This contradictory imperative that Asian Americans "develop" into a national formation that has already been denied is exposed and negotiated in the realm of Asian American culture.

In the twentieth century, national culture became the site in which subjects are constructed as American by being incorporated into a corpus of stories, images, rituals, and icons that define and represent the nation's values and identity. As compulsory public education became the primary means of Americanization in the early twentieth century, the American bildungsroman, or novel of formation, emerged as a significant cultural institution that constitutes the U.S. national subject through identification with a protagonist who ultimately reconciles with the social order.[28] These narratives of development, which form the national canon, are defined as quintessentially "American" stories that embody universal struggles, dilemmas, and resolutions that are representative of American identity, life, and society, thereby demanding an erasure or subordination of difference and particularity through the logic of representation.

The Asian American novel must always negotiate the demand to produce a narrative of national formation. Usually this story requires that the foreign Asian immigrant assimilate into the American citizen, or it demands a resolution of an orientalized struggle between "Asian tradition" and "American culture." This largely accounts for the prominence of the family in so many Asian American narratives in which "intergenerational conflict" is the crisis to be resolved through assimilation or vacuous multicultural mantras as in "the best of both worlds."

Lisa Lowe argues that while such narratives may attempt to "produce cultural integration" and dutifully narrate "the absorption of cultural difference into the universality of the national political sphere," the material history of racialization that locates the Asian American outside the racial boundaries of the nation reemerges in opposition to such a resolution. These irreconcilable instances and memories of racialization (not limited to Asian exclusion) interrupt the developmental temporality of assimilation and its mythic telos of universality, locating Asian American culture as an alternative formation "that produces cultural expressions materially and aesthetically at odds with the resolution of the citizen in the nation."[29] The cultural text analyzed in this chapter demonstrates that the relentless demand of assimilation is itself an expression of Asian Americans' racialization, which in turn is often negotiated by imagining or invoking black racial exclusion in a variety of ways.

The internment of Japanese Americans is a dramatic instance of the state's violently contradictory demand for national identification, in which Japanese Americans were incarcerated as racial enemies of the nation and dispossessed of property rights as a condition of their formation as loyal citizen-subjects. In *No-No Boy*, although the protagonist refuses to pledge his allegiance to the United States during his internment, the narrative is hardly a systematic critique of the U.S. state. Instead, it is riddled with guilt, self-loathing, and a desperate longing for the American dream. In this manner, the novel is shaped by the discursive violence of assimilation, which is constitutive of Asian American racialization. In other words, the novel has no purpose or intention to critique assimilationist ideology but is rather produced out of its internalization. The violent recruitment of national subjects is also always a gendered process, and in *No-No Boy*, the Japanese American protagonist is constructed as a multiply deviant subject of the nation.

The importance of notions of racial, class, and gender deviance can be discerned in the way that *No-No Boy* posits the contradictions of Japanese American subjectivity through representations of key social spaces. The internment camp, the prison, the racial ghetto, the Japanese American home, the white employer's office, and the point of industrial production are all social spaces in which the narrative situates Ichiro's formation as an emasculated and racialized subject. *No-No Boy*'s spatial representations map a nexus of relationships among race, gender, class, and citizenship that configure the novel's negotiation of narratives of development. An analysis of these racialized spaces and nationalist narratives reveals how the novel posits Japanese American subjectivity in and against the multiple meanings ascribed to black masculinity.

No-No Boy begins with Ichiro's bitter homecoming in the fall of 1945 and quietly underscores the temporal and spatial displacement produced by the state's violent regulation of Japanese American national identity:

Two weeks after his twenty-fifth birthday, Ichiro got off a bus at Second and Main in Seattle. He had been gone four years, two in camp and two in prison. Walking down the street that autumn morning with a small, black suitcase, he felt like an intruder in a world to which he had no claim. It was just enough that he should feel this way, for, of his own free will, he had stood before the judge and said that he would not go in the army. At the time there was no other choice for him. (*No-No Boy*, 1)

Ichiro's detention in the internment camps and his subsequent imprisonment for draft evasion are simply described as a period of four years. This passage of time is never described in detail and reveals little of the history of Ichiro's incarceration, but it is registered through the physical and psychic sense of spatial dislocation that characterizes the entire novel: "He felt like an intruder in a world to which he had no claim. . . . What the hell have I done? What the hell am I doing back here? Best thing I can do would be to kill some son of a bitch and head back to prison" (*No-No Boy*, 1). This dislocation from the space of the nation manifests his sense of racial and gender deviance from the citizenry. Ichiro's refusal to be inducted into the U.S. military provokes a crisis of national identity as well as racialized masculinity, since the discursive terrain of citizenship makes the soldier the classical embodiment of manhood and national representative. The narrative's relentless anxieties regarding citizenship and masculinity determine its representations of the Japanese immigrant family and home, the urban racial ghetto, and the universal space of the nation.

The internment itself can be understood as a dominant spatial practice that racializes and genders the Japanese American community and subject. The state's evacuation of families from their homes, the practice of removing male heads of household before other family members, and the dispossession of property structurally displace the patriarchal authority of the Japanese American family and thus feminize the community in its subordination to the paternalistic authority of the U.S. state. Ichiro's racialized crisis of masculinity is not merely a result of having missed "an opportunity" to secure American identity and citizenship as a U.S. soldier but is also critically linked to the racialized feminization of the Japanese American community at large.

Lisa Lowe contends that oedipalization is constitutive of the masculine subject in colonial (as well as nationalist) narratives, insofar that the subject becomes a citizen at the point when he identifies with the paternal state and subordinates a "prior" identification with a precolonial motherland.[30] Lowe suggests that U.S. nationalism recruits subjects through this oedipalization narrative, in which the male subject must disavow identification with the feminized site of racial "origin" in order to identify with the patriarchal authority of the U.S. state.[31] Understanding the discursive mechanisms by which nationalism interpellates citizen-subjects provides an analytical framework for *No-No Boy* that reveals the gendering racial logic of citizenship and identity and suggests how and why black masculinity emerges as an unstable trope in the novel.

Throughout the text, it is difficult to separate the alienation, self-disgust, and shame that disciplines Ichiro as a Japanese American male subject from the racialized spaces he occupies in the Central district of downtown Seattle, a working-class, racial ghetto formed around the main thoroughfare of Jackson Street. As Ichiro walks through the neighborhood after his release from prison, his descriptions of the urban ghetto invoke multiple histories of racialization:

> For Ichiro, Jackson St. signified that section of the city immediately beyond the railroad tracks and between 5th and 12th Avenues. That was the section which used to be pretty much Japanese town. It was adjacent to Chinatown and most of the gambling and prostitution and drinking seemed to favor the area. Like the dirty clock tower of the depot, the filth of Jackson St. had increased. (*No-No Boy*, 4–5)

From the nineteenth century onward, racially exclusive housing practices placed virtually all of Seattle's Chinese, Japanese, and Filipino populations into a four-mile-square quadrant south of downtown, which was known as the Southside or lower Jackson Street.[32] By the late 1870s, a Chinatown formed around the streets of Third and Washington as Chinese immigrants came to Seattle mainly to work as contract laborers in logging and the canneries and eventually as builders of the railroad. Immigration restrictions and the stratified labor market racialized and gendered the Chinese male community, which was feminized by the absence of heteronormative family units and the performance of domestic labor as cooks, laundrymen, and servants: work traditionally performed by women, who were largely absent from this frontier community.[33] The virulence of anti-Chinese sentiment that was typical of West Coast cities was manifested in the formation of the Puget Sound Anti-Chinese Congress, and in 1886, white mobs forced the Chinese from their homes and "in one week virtually the entire Chinese population of Seattle was deported and the city's original Chinatown was history."[34] Despite immigration exclusions, Chinatown did in fact reemerge at Second and Main as a result of in-migration from other states,[35] but the Japanese in the 1890s and Filipinos in the 1920s soon surpassed the small community.[36]

The Chinese Exclusion Act of 1882 was followed by the immigration of Japanese laborers,[37] and a Japantown formed directly adjacent to the small second Chinatown on the Southside. In Seattle between 1900 and 1930, Japanese immigrants were the largest racial minority.[38] Then in 1942, the entire Japanese American community was relocated to internment camps, and Japantown "disappeared" until 1945. Jackson Street represents a spatialization of this history of anti-Asian legislation and displacement that defines Asian racial difference.

In the novel, Jackson Street figures as a racialized space of deterioration, deviance, and marginalization and thus mirrors the internment camp and prison from which Ichiro ostensibly had been freed. The intense dislocation that Ichiro experiences as a racialized national subject is linked to the very formation of the Central district's Southside. "Coming home" after his release from state detention cannot be figured through tropes of freedom, since the dominant spatial practices that ghettoize Jackson Street through the containment and regulation of Asian populations are directly related to the dominant spatializing practices of internment and incarceration. The racial ghetto, however, has also been radically transformed in Ichiro's absence, and these demographic changes exacerbate his sense of dislocated alienation in an already marginalized space. Ichiro's rage, regret, and confusion over his decision to refuse the U.S. state's demand for identification result not only in his displacement from the discursive nation but also from the racialized ghetto where he finds himself further situated as a foreigner.

The marginality and deviance that Jackson Street symbolizes to Ichiro is clearly related in the novel to the dramatically increased presence of black men in the neighborhood.[39] Owing to acute wartime labor shortages, mechanization in southern agriculture, increased ease of transport, and black density in northern urban cities, black southerners moved to the West, where they entered the industrial labor force in unprecedented numbers.[40] The relatively low visibility of the black community in Seattle before this "Second Great Migration" had initially circumvented the strict patterns of residential segregation that had bound the city's Asian immigrants.[41] But by World War I, new housing developments were already governed by restrictive covenants to keep black residents out.[42] As this massive influx of black people transformed the racial composition of the factory floor, social segregation forced almost all wartime black migrants into the small Southside district, which offered some housing and business opportunities after the evacuation of Japanese Americans. The spatial practice of confining tens of thousands of new black migrants to the Asian ghetto was not a "neutral" logistical matter of urban policy.[43] This pattern of World War II black settlement was repeated throughout the West Coast, where the containment of blackness in a space of alien unincorporability was an anxious response to the threat of black incorporation into the workplace. The novel represents these historical processes as the further displacement and disciplining of Japanese American masculinity.

Ichiro's description of how these processes had transformed "his" neighborhood during the war speak to the many anxieties regarding space and displacement:

> The war had wrought violent changes upon the people, and the people, in turn, working hard and living hard and earning a lot of money and spending it on whatever was available, had distorted the profile of Jackson Street. The street had about it the air of a carnival without quite succeeding at becoming one. A shooting gallery stood where once had been a clothing store; fish and chips had replaced a jewelry shop; and a bunch of Negroes were horsing around raucously in front of a pool parlor. Everything looked older, dirtier and shabbier. He walked past the pool parlor, picking his way gingerly among the Negroes, of whom there had been only a few at one time and of whom there seemed to be nothing but now. They were smoking and shouting and cussing and carousing and the sidewalk was slimy with their spittle. (*No-No Boy*, 5)

The novel represents the spatial transformation of Jackson Street during the racialized industrial wartime expansion as a chaotic process of structural and moral deterioration. In this scenario, high production demands and high wages drive a male-oriented leisure market that caters to unproductive and escapist black working-class forms of recreation that in turn contributes to the neighborhood's degeneration. The narrative's preoccupation with signs of the neighborhood's filth, decay, and general disorder is clearly racialized, identifying working-class black male bodies as the underdeveloped and contaminating elements that discipline and displace Ichiro in the already marginal space of the urban ghetto.

Although this narrative of Jackson Street's transformation conforms to a dominant bourgeois pathologization of black urban culture, it is also an expression of an ambivalent longing to inhabit black social space, born of Ichiro's formation through specific modes of racial and gender discipline.

The portrayal of the neighborhood as having "the air of a carnival" and as "dirtier and shabbier" does not merely signify a bourgeois revulsion with dirt, disorder, or chaos. The socially exhilarating experience of carnival as an uninhibited celebration and communal play must be read in relation to the isolation, rigidity, and disruption of community produced by the internment camp and prison. Jackson Street has been transformed by its black residents into a space of recreation, leisure, and play that enables a "reclaiming" of the body from the disciplinary demands of wartime production.[44] The black men described as "horsing around raucously in front of a pool parlor . . . smoking and shouting and cussing and carousing and the sidewalk slimy with their spittle" are not simply signs of vulgarity and deviance in the narrative but also signify freedom from multiple regimes of bodily discipline. The pathologization of black working-class urban space as an underdeveloped site of immorality, indulgence, and criminality is constitutive of a specific racialized masculinity that Ichiro and other Asian American male characters cannot embody. Although the novel is structured by the assimilationist imperative to disavow racialized and racializing spaces in order for Ichiro to develop into a universal bourgeois citizen-subject, the particularity of his racialized emasculation produces contradictory desires to inhabit the pathologized spaces in which black masculinity and community are produced. Since Ichiro is situated as a foreigner who can move only "gingerly" through this black male space, the narrative's central concern with reconstituting Ichiro's racialized masculinity involves negotiating with white patriarchal authority as well as black masculinity.

In the novel, social spaces outside the ghetto, such as the industrial workplace, occasion encounters with white patriarchal authority that reconfigure how relations between black and Japanese American men can be represented. During World War II, when white women and black men worked together on the factory floor, the industrial workplace became a locus for anxieties about miscegenation as a means of preserving white privilege in the industrial working class. Given this context, the novel's depiction of racial antagonisms between white male workers, on the one hand, and Japanese and black male workers, on the other, in the workplace departs from the novel's earlier imaginings of black working-class men in the racial ghetto. Instead, the narrative constructs the relationship between Birdie, a black male worker, and Gary, a passive "no-no boy," as a close alliance or gendered "partnership" in a hostile workforce that targets and punishes Gary as a traitorous coward. Birdie, "who used to spar with Joe Louis," continually protects Gary from the hostile workforce, which is defined as mainly inhabited by white men:

> Birdie pretty near got in a couple of fights over me, but only because it seemed to bother him for some reason. I kept telling him not to go to bat for me, that I didn't mind not being spoken to or being called names, but he couldn't see how that could be. . . . He was suffering for me, really suffering. There's plenty of good people around you know. (*No-No Boy*, 226)

The narrative thus situates Gary in a hyperfeminized relationship with Birdie, whose principled defense of the Japanese American against the racism of white workers takes on almost biblical proportions: "He was suffering for me, really suffering." While spaces outside the ghetto enable these imaginings of black and Japanese American partnership, the novel's representations of the hypermasculinity of black men cannot help but situate Gary in a feminized relation to Birdie, even in the context of this imagined coalition. Birdie, the novel's best-developed black character (which is nonetheless still wanting), seems to function as a fantasy savior figure born from Japanese American desires for an alliance with black men against the authority of white nationalist masculinity.[45] These desires indicate how gendered processes of Asian American racialization are negotiated in a triangulated relation to white citizenship and liberal democratic promises of universality as well as to the gendered processes of black racialization and the contradictions constitutive of black citizenship. The novel's fantasy of an alliance between black and Japanese American men emerges as a response to the authority of white national patriarchy, which disciplines the Japanese American home and family as a foreign and feminized site that must be disavowed.

The Japanese immigrant working-class "home" in the Jackson Street ghetto is represented as an alien space where the lack of hierarchical division between social spaces produces deviant gendered familial relations. Ichiro's response to arriving home where his parents have resettled after leaving the internment camp is one of intense disavowal:

> Then he was home. It was a hole in the wall with groceries crammed in orderly confusion on not enough shelving, into not enough space. . . . The short round man who came through the curtains at the back of the store uttered the name preciously as might an old

woman. "Ya Ichiro, you have come home. How good that you have come home!" The gently spoken Japanese which he had not heard for so long sounded strange. He would hear a great deal of it now that he was home, for his parents, like most of the old Japanese, spoke virtually no English. On the other hand, the children, like Ichiro, spoke almost no Japanese. . . . The father bounced silently over the wood flooring in slippered feet towards his son. Fondly, delicately, he placed a pudgy hand on Ichiro's elbow and looked up at his son who was Japanese but who had been big enough for football and tall enough for basketball in high school. He pushed the elbow and Ichiro led the way into the back, where there was a kitchen, a bathroom, and one bedroom. He looked around the bedroom and felt like puking. It was neat and clean and scrubbed. His mother would have seen to that. It was just the idea of everyone sleeping in one room. (*No-No Boy*, 6–7)

The gendered construction of public and private spheres is represented as highly distorted in the working-class Japanese immigrant home.[46] As both a small commercial store and house, the domestic sphere cannot be separated from the space of paid production and economic enterprise. His father occupies no position in the male public domain, effectively consigned to an effeminate role as some kind of ineffectual househusband. The narrative presents this home as the feminizing space of Asian alien difference from which Ichiro must be differentiated in order to achieve an American masculine subjectivity. This process of dis-identification is facilitated through a number of disavowals, including his father's "strange" foreign language, in contrast to Ichiro, who "spoke almost no Japanese," and in juxtaposing the father's effeminate gestures with Ichiro's embodiment of American male physicality, which was "big enough for football and tall enough for basketball" (*No-No Boy*, 6–7). The family's single-bedroom house fails to individuate social space. The Japanese immigrant working-class home is the dystopic countersite to normative middle-class domestic space in which the gendered separation of work and private life enables proper subject formations. Ichiro's revulsion of his working-class home, which is constructed simultaneously as a foreign and feminized space, is explicitly linked to his immigrant mother.

The most deviant gender and racial identity that emerges from Ichiro's foreign, working-class family is clearly his mother, Mrs. Yamada, a domineering, fanatical, and insane Japanese nationalist. Several critics have pointed out that Ichiro's formation seems "grounded in the apparent rejection of negative Japanese traits projected onto the Asian immigrant mother."[47] Lisa Lowe's paradigm of oedipalization clarifies that in this Asian American novel of male formation, U.S. nationalism demands a narrative in which the feminized and racialized home is a site that must be repudiated in order for Ichiro to develop into identification with the state.[48] The novel is saturated with this dynamic, and the protagonist obsessively blames his demonized mother for his decision to not fight in the U.S. army while being disgusted and ashamed of his feminized and infantilized father. Patricia Chu states that the mother's insanity and her eventual suicide enables Okada to "symbolically purge the Japanese American psyche of these unwanted traits so that Ichiro and others in his community can psychically and politically reconstruct their Japanese American subjectivities free of this disturbing, unassimilable element."[49] The novel is ultimately unable to produce this narrative of assimilationist development insofar as Ichiro repeatedly retracts and qualifies the blame he places on his family or mother: "Sometimes I think my mother is to blame. Sometimes I think it's bigger than her" (No-No Boy, 152).[50] The larger context that he vaguely gestures toward in this quotation is the social context of white supremacy, which the novel cannot clearly identify as being responsible for Ichiro's internment and his inability to feel American. Since anti-Asian racism is so difficult to identify or name, owing to the deep internalization of assimilationist ideologies, antiblack racism and black exclusion furnish a discursive space in the text in which race and inequality can be explicitly articulated.

The novel acknowledges that black exclusion and black spatial distance has been a primary means by which white ethnic immigrants and racial minorities gain entry into the national social formation. In one scenario imagined through an omniscient third-person narrator, the text denounces this process of antiblack "Americanization" with respect to eastern and southern European immigrants:

The woman with the dark hair and large nose who has barely learned to speak English makes a big show of vacating her bus seat when a Negro occupies the other half. She stamps indignantly down the aisle, hastening away from the contamination which is only in her contaminated mind. The Negro stares silently out of the window, a proud calmness on his face, which hides the boiling fury that is capable of murder. (No-No Boy, 135)

This passage racializes the white ethnic immigrant woman, as her "dark hair and large nose" and her inability to speak English mark her as a foreign and undesirable element of the nation, yet she is able to secure her liminal position through antiblack Americanism. The narrative imparts both strength and dignity to the black character, in contrast to her "contaminated" and unprincipled lack of integrity, because it is he who represents the legitimate national subject, as a historical and cultural "native" of the United States.

This character's "boiling fury that is capable of murder" is a sign of his dignity and manhood, insofar as such rage is indicative of his refusal to accept the ubiquitous forms of racism to which he is subjected. Yet it also consolidates and ennobles black masculinity through recourse to dominant discourses of black male violence and criminality, irrespective of how the narrative rationalizes his potentially violent outrage as a legitimate response. In criticizing the processes by which white ethnic immigrants become "white" through black exclusión, the narrative produces an admirable and dignified black male subject through terms of racialized manhood and masculinity.

The novel also rejects Japanese American incorporation at the expense of black displacement, and this principled position is clearly produced from the narrative's negotiations with Asian American masculinity. Gary's story about Birdie's inspiring interventions triggers Ichiro's own memories of his acceptance into a white church while working on a sugar beet farm during his internment. Ichiro is elated by the church's compassion and Christian acceptance until he witnesses their "civil" and unspoken exclusion of an elderly black man, who is left standing throughout the service. Neither approached nor acknowledged, the old man leaves alone. The white church, as the archetypal space of morality and universal acceptance, is revealed to be a thoroughly corrupted site, and Ichiro refuses to return. Afterwards, Ichiro expresses his disgust with another internee, castigating the Japanese American's willingness to participate in black racial exclusion as cowardly and effeminate:

And then Tommy had revealed himself for the poor, frightened, mistreated Japanese that he was. "Holy cow!" He had exclaimed in a frantic cry, "they like us. They treat us fine. We're in no position to stick out our own necks when we've got enough troubles of our own" . . . When he [Ichiro] left . . . he thought he heard a whimper. (*No-No Boy*, 232)

Ichiro returns to spending his Sundays gambling, drinking, and carousing with other men in the internment camp, and the novel shores up his masculinity through this refusal to be included in a space of white morality predicated on spatial distance from African Americans. The text's explicit critique of Japanese American inclusion through black displacement imagines such a process to preclude the possibility of idealized manhood and masculinity, insofar as it entails Japanese American submission to corrupted white patriarchal authority. It is important to note that the narrative's rejection of this form of Asian uplift emerges from the intersectional relations of white, black, and Japanese American masculinity.

The implications of this masculine disavowal of Japanese American incorporation at the expense of black displacement become clearer in the context of the oedipal imperative that the Asian American subject repudiate feminized sites of foreign Asian difference in order to identify with the patriarchal authority of the U.S. state. Owing to black migration and residential segregation, the former Asian ghetto has become a multiracial, predominantly black social space, and hence Americanization for the Asian American subjects demands distance from black social spaces and communities. However, black racialization emerges in *No-No Boy* to mediate rather than merely to converge with U.S. nationalism and its oedipalization of the Asian American male subject. In other words, this World War II Japanese American narrative of national identity is haunted by not just Asian American racialization but also a history of black racial exclusion, offering a model of racialized masculinity that is imagined in a nonfeminized and defiant relation to white male supremacy. While Japanese American and African American male subjects are not constructed through terms of identification, black male recalcitrance and black social space clearly affect how narratives of Asian American incorporation and citizenship interpellate masculine identifications with the U.S. state.

For instance, the novel's characterization of Mr. Carrick, who embodies white male paternalism and approval, is a dramatic expression of the narrative's subordination to the discipline of white patriarchal authority. Carrick appears only briefly in the text and offers Ichiro a national apology, a good job in Portland, and even forgiveness for his sins, stating that "the government made a big mistake when they shoved you people around. . . . I don't feel as proud as I used to. . . . We can still be the best damn nation in the world. I'm sorry things worked out the way they did. . . . When do you want to start?" (*No-No Boy*, 150–51). Ichiro cannot allow himself to accept the job, and the novel's utopic imagining of white

male benevolence is poignant as it reveals the depth of Ichiro's formation as an undeserving and pathological subject, who is unworthy of the
kind opportunities that Carrick has the power to offer. It would seem that
the state's disciplining of Ichiro as a deviant racial subject who cannot be
incorporated into the nation has produced an irreconcilable contradiction: Ichiro's intense desire for inclusion and acceptance cannot subsume
the racialized differentiation that he has come to embody.

> Then, as he thought of Mr. Carrick and their conversation time and
> time again, its meaning for him evolved into a singularly comfort-
> ing thought. There was someone who cared. Surely there were others
> too who understood the suffering of the small and the weak, and yes,
> even the seemingly treasonous, and offered a way back into the great
> compassionate stream of life that is America . . . when he thought
> of Mr. Carrick . . . and of what he had said, and still more, what he
> had offered to do, he glimpsed the real nature of the country against
> which he had almost fully turned his back, and saw that its mistake
> was no less forgivable than his own. (*No-No Boy*, 153–54)

Here, the narrative seems to be at a crucial moment of resolution, but Ichiro turns down the job and returns to the Southside ghetto and his family, stating, "They were not to be ignored, to be cast out of mind and life
and rendered eternally nothing" (*No-No Boy*, 154). While the novel casts
white masculine authority in utopic and obfuscating terms, it is ultimately
unable to narrate Ichiro's identification with Carrick. Ichiro cannot leave
the ghetto neighborhood that he seems to detest so thoroughly, instead
turning down a good job in a new city and returning to Jackson Street,
where he wanders through the same dirty streets and dark alleys until the
novel's conclusion. This unresolved return is largely predicated on the novel's ambivalent relationship to gendered discourses of black racial difference and the centrality of black masculinity as an alternative embodiment
that mediates the patriarchal authority of white nationalist supremacy.

The novel's spatial mappings, therefore, interrupt the developmental
temporality of assimilation that would emplot Ichiro's progress from the
localized confines of the racial ghetto to white middle-class spaces that
parade as "universality." The narrative is so saturated with the discursive
violence of assimilation that the racialization of black men functions
as a means by which the text disarticulates the disciplining demands of
assimilation. Resistance to white patriarchal authority, or recalcitrance, is

largely how black masculinity signifies in the novel, in contrast to the narrative's positioning of Ichiro and other Asian American men's desperate desires of national inclusion. The black men in this novel are extremely minor characters, appearing in brief and fleeting instances and passages, such as the black shoe shiner and hustler, whose dialogue with Ichiro is restricted to "Good boy. If they had come for me I would have told them where to shove their stinking uniform too" (*No-No Boy*, 238). These peripheral black characters collectively play an important function in the text as alternative models of racialized masculinity to those embodied in the Japanese American community.

Black men are variously represented as critical subjects who do not seek or depend on white male approval and acceptance, thereby enabling them to inhabit racialized masculine identities that are imagined as unavailable to Japanese American characters who have internalized racial shame and have no sense of national entitlement. Ichiro's decision to remain in the Southside ghetto suggests that this marginalized racial space emerges as an alternative to the paradoxical demand that he identify either with the U.S. nation that repudiates his American identity or with Japan, which he has never known yet which is racially ascribed as his motherland. If identities are always produced in relation to social spaces, then the seedy bars, prostitution quarters, gambling houses, and differentially racialized communities of the Southside ghetto indicate that such "deviant" particularities will not readily dissolve into the universality of the nation. The opening confrontation in *No-No Boy* that began this chapter reminds us that the multiracial ghetto of the 1940s and the differential histories of racialization that are spatialized by and in Jackson Street cannot be figured as an alternative site of identification between blacks and Asians. Instead, this space represents what is in excess of identity itself and discloses how histories of black racial exclusion mediate the denial of Asian American citizenship in ways that destabilize assimilationist narratives of Asian American national identity.

4

Becoming Korean American

Blackface and Gendered Racialization

in Ronyoung Kim's Clay Walls *(1987)*

> *Harold and John knew how to talk jive; they learned*
> *because they did not want to get picked on by the boys*
> *in the neighborhood. But Momma would not allow them*
> *to speak it in the house. Once, when Harold and John*
> *bantered in jive talk, Momma said, "Stop that! You sound*
> *like Amos and Andy." I had laughed when the boys took*
> *it as a cue to shuffle out of the house, swaggering like*
> *Lucerne Luke and his friends. Even Momma had laughed.*
> —Kim Ronyoung, *Clay Walls*

Kim Ronyoung's semiautobiographical novel *Clay Walls* (1986) reconstructs the experiences of a Korean immigrant family living in the
multiracial ghettos of Central Los Angeles between 1920 and 1945. This
particular scene of Korean American teenagers performing "blackness"
situates Asian Americans in a complex and contradictory relation to
American culture. The mother's reference to the popular *Amos 'n Andy*
show foregrounds the centrality of blackface in U.S. popular culture,
avidly consumed since the nineteenth century by white ethnic immigrants as part of the process of becoming American subjects. In this
regard, the Korean immigrant family seems similarly located in relation
to a national culture founded on the performative disavowal of blackness:
the boys' speech and bodily manipulation as well as the scene's comic
resolution underscore that they are *not* black. But the narrative assimila-

tion of the family as consumers of blackface mass culture is mediated by their racialization as "Orientals" who are restricted from white areas and living in a black neighborhood with a thriving urban youth culture. The boys' adoption of black social practices, therefore, is also indicative of a more "local" process of Americanization by virtue of sharing residential and social space with black Americans.

Narrated from the perspective of their younger Korean American sister, signifying is represented as a primarily masculine practice, although Faye tries "talking jive" herself after being teased outside: "'Whatchu mean, man?' I repeated to myself, trying to sound like Lucerne Luke. I tried several times under my breath, but it didn't sound right" (*Clay Walls*, 198). Faye's failure to reproduce a local black vernacular locates her outside black social space, which is crucial to her narrative development into proper femininity and womanhood. Nonetheless, Faye's attempts to "sound like Lucerne Luke" and his friends on the corner reveal desires to occupy the racialized and gendered public space from which she is excluded, as well as a longing for social relations and spatial imaginings that are not predicated on privatized bourgeois domesticity. In this manner, black and Asian proximity due to residential segregation produces fractured and contradictory imaginings of a racialized femininity, which unexpectedly destabilize the discursive apparatus of blackface as well as ideologies of black deviance.

Written by a Korean American woman, *Clay Walls* can be read as somewhat analogous to Okada's *No-No Boy* insofar as representations of black social space are also critical to Ronyoung's gendered production of an Asian American subject. However, in this immigrant narrative of female development, the racial and gender "deviance" of ghettoized social space is presented in complex relation to the racialized ideologies of proper femininity disseminated by American mass culture. *Clay Walls* demonstrates that a gendered Asian American cultural formation emerges from the intersection of the dominant culture predicated on blackface and the working-class black urban culture into which the characters are simultaneously incorporated. The female Korean American characters are strictly confined to the boundaries of racially segregated and domestic spaces, yet they "freely" enter the arena of national culture as avid consumers of Hollywood film, popular music, and radio programs.

The narrative's imperative to develop Faye into a bourgeois feminine subject is linked to the discursive racialization of black men and women. Although *Clay Walls* constructs the domestic space of the Korean immigrant home through terms of both constraint and safety, it clearly demonstrates that Faye's achievement of proper womanhood is predicated on her distance from the alleged deviance and sexual immorality of black social space. Bertha, a black neighbor and playmate, for example, urges Faye to come out and play after dinner by suggestively stating that "[a] lot can happen between seven and nine," but when Faye asks her mother, her request is vehemently denied:

> "Absolutely not! You cannot go out after dark, not in this neighborhood." "What about the boys?" I asked.
> "They're boys and have to learn how to take care of themselves." . . .
> She motioned me to a chair. "Come and listen to the radio. You don't understand now, but one day you'll thank me." (*Clay Walls*, 201)

In this early passage, Faye's confinement to the domestic sphere emphasizes that her femininity is constituted through a discourse of protection from the racialized working-class neighborhood in which they live. Faye's mother, Haesu, who works ceaselessly at home as a piece-rate seamstress, encourages Faye to join her isolation as a privatized consumer of mass culture, offering the radio as a substitute for participating in a predominantly black working-class community that is defined over and against normative domesticity.

The conventional leitmotif of mass culture as a primary institution of cultural assimilation and gender formation takes on particular significance owing to the historical setting of *Clay Walls*.[1] The novel persistently locates the production of American femininity and domesticity in the Hollywood studio industry, which displaces education as the nation's primary institution of Americanization. Haesu drops out of her adult English-language courses and starts going to the movies:

> She made a delightful discovery. She was able to follow the story by reading the captions, able to make connections between what a person said and what he did. Settling back into her seat, she found the movies were an entertaining way to learn about life in America, much more satisfying than from the rides on streetcars, and much less embarrassing than reciting in front of a class. (*Clay Walls*, 33)

Haesu's retreat into the movie theater is a fictional register of the sociohistorical processes that historian Michael Rogin ascribes to the ascending "1920s motion picture palace, with its narrativized features . . . and mass audiences, [which] silenced and incorporated the participant, immigrant crowds."[2] As Haesu is "settling back into her seat" in the dark theater, she undoubtedly figures as one of those silent participants in Rogin's "immigrant crowds" who finds immense relief from her inadequate performance in English-language classes. In *Clay Walls*, mass culture is prominently figured as a primary institution of assimilation, as Hollywood films and icons produce racialized models of gender normativity while also naturalizing the ideology of romance and bourgeois domesticity as the telos of female development. Hence, even the staunch Korean nationalist immigrant mother buys dresses that remind her of Greta Garbo (*Clay Walls*, 86), curls her daughter's hair like Shirley Temple (62), and arranges the furniture in her home as "she had seen in a Buster Keaton movie" (38).

According to Rogin, the modern Hollywood studio industry underwent enormous development and expansion, and by the 1920s, motion pictures had been transformed from "sites of class and ethnic division to arenas of modern, mass entertainment, from threats to agents of Americanization."[3] As with other forms of U.S. popular culture, this consolidation of a national identity was largely enabled through the disavowal of black bodies. African American studies has long demonstrated that U.S. national culture has appropriated black dance, music, dress, and language in the forms of blackface caricature. Numerous scholars have produced different interpretations of the discursive logic of blackface, from a white cultural politics of black disavowal, to notions of blackface as both love and theft. But it is clear that by the end of the nineteenth century, blackface had provided a "'distinctive national identity' during slavery and had unified a heterogeneous [white] ethnic population through the repudiation of Blackness."[4]

Blackface minstrelsy was the first form of American popular culture, beginning as early as the 1820s when white men literally blackened their faces to perform as absurd black caricatures for working-class, white ethnic immigrant audiences. James Snead's notion of "exclusionary emulation" aptly describes the relationship of white performers and audiences to blackness and black culture. According to Snead, minstrelsy imitated the "power and trappings of black culture" while the "black originators are segregated and kept at a distance."[5] This seemingly contradictory dynamic of black imitation and repudiation points to the complexity of U.S. racial formations in which American identity and culture are founded not only on "racial aversion" but also, as Rogin argues, on "destructive racial desire."[6] What had been disparaged as "low-brow" working-class entertainment had become a "commercial, scripted and mass spectacle" for audiences that by the 1840s included middle-class participants released from "civilized restraint."[7] Rogin argues that U.S. nationalism was organized through the unifying principle of racial division and that blackface minstrelsy enabled white ethnic subjects to remake themselves into Americans by "fixing the identities of African Americans."[8] Blackface, therefore, must not be narrowly understood as merely another "racist" cultural form of American entertainment but as a significant discursive mechanism or cultural technology that produces U.S. national culture and identity through the reification of the black body as Other.[9]

Clay Walls is saturated with signs of American popular culture between the 1920s and 1940s; such references index the place of blackface in the formation of Asian American national identity.[10] During the golden age of the Hollywood studio system, blackface films and musicals were among the most beloved and critically acclaimed talking pictures, beginning with the immense popularity of the first talking picture, The Jazz Singer (1927), starring Al Jolson (see Clay Walls, 92). Unlike previous motion pictures that conventionally used actors in blackface, most of these musicals thematized blackface or, in Rogin's words, made "blackface . . . [a] conscious film subject."[11] Shirley Temple musicals frequently paired her singing and dancing routines with Bojangles Robinson, and blacking up little Shirley was a "charming" theatrical gesture that enhanced the pleasurable and innocent spectacle of blackface performances.[12]

The genre of the blackface musical, Rogin notes, is defined by both "the ideology of its content—organic nationalism—and the ideology of the form—self-making, performance, artifice."[13] Sentimentality and nostalgia, therefore, pervaded blackface musicals during the Depression and war, which imagined the nation's "home" in the old South and claimed Mammy as a nurturing force in the remaking of an infantilized (white) self.[14] Songs such as "My Mammy" "set the precedent for talking pictures in Hollywood." Amos 'n Andy was the most popular radio show in the country when Jolson was enjoying the height of his film career.[15] Blackface and minstrelsy in the golden age of Hollywood produced racialized national icons like Stepin Fetchit, Aunt Jemima, and Hattie McDaniel's award-winning performance as Mammy in Gone with the Wind.

The racialization of Asian Americans in the first half of the twentieth century made it impossible for blackface to fully dissolve oriental difference into the national citizenry, in the same way as it had transformed white ethnic immigrants into Americans. In *Clay Walls*, unstable racial fractures of national belonging are visible in the representation of a Japanese American family whose participation in U.S. national culture ultimately fails to constitute them as Americans. The Naganos seem to be a model of normative Asian American bourgeois domesticity, living in a large, well-furnished, and spotless home where family snapshots are "turned just-so on the mantelpiece." The father is a proud patriarch who "always wears a suit" as he leisurely reads a paper after work while the pleasant mother brings tea and snacks from the kitchen (*Clay Walls*, 213). Signs of the family's racial difference are marked by a Buddhist shrine and pictures of Mount Fuji and the emperor of Japan. Such signifiers of foreign domestic culture, which hang "perfectly straight on the wall," are seemingly reconcilable with the wholesome American domicile where the Japanese American children perform skits every Friday evening.

In one scene, the young girl announces, "Ladies and gentlemen. My first number will be 'Home Sweet Home,'" which she sings as her sister's arms and hands gesture dramatically to the lyrics, finally ending with "There's no place like home" (*Clay Walls*, 215–16). The structural details of their performance are central to understanding the form of the blackface musical, a genre that rejected Hollywood's shift toward a realist aesthetic driven by technological innovations. The blackface musical retained the formal elements of artifice, trickery, and other theatrical qualities, promoting an ideology of self-transformation that celebrated the possibilities of remaking the self.[16] While the sisters do not literally blacken their faces, they perform a blackface nostalgia piece that involves elements of bodily illusion. The ideological context of "Home, Sweet Home" is paradigmatic of the blackface musical that evinced a nostalgic longing for an imaginary and idealized home (the antebellum South), producing an "organic nationalism" in response to (im)migrant displacement.[17] As Rogin observes, this particular narrative of blackface nostalgia, which claims the plantation South and the mammy as having mythic national origins, consolidated national identity during the Depression and war by obliterating the historical violence against black bodies through slavery, lynching, rape, and exploitation for a white ethnic population.[18]

The Nagano family's participation in blackface, however, does not negate Japanese racial difference during World War II, as they are later interned as enemy aliens. Nick Browne argues that World War II was a "particularly crucial moment of displacement" when cinematic representations posited Asians as the more historically appropriate Other for an emergent U.S. global hegemon.[19] Browne's analysis suggests that World War II was a liminal moment for Asian and African Americans who were positioned as possibly unstable participants as well as constitutive Others of U.S. nationalism. Despite the Naganos' refined performances of heteronormative domesticity and U.S. national culture, six years later the family stands in the back of a crowded truck with other Japanese Americans who are being forcibly removed to internment camps. Like the pictures of Mount Fuji and the emperor of Japan hanging on the wall of the Nagano home, Japanese American culture emerges as an Orientalist sign for what threatens the nation, indicating that for Japanese Americans, "home, sweet home" cannot claim a mythic U.S. origin.

In stark contrast to the bourgeois domesticity embodied by the Nagano family, Faye's father is permanently absent, having left in search of migrant labor, while her mother Haesu is fixed to the kitchen table as a piece-rate seamstress supporting three children. Haesu experiences a rapid decline in economic and social mobility when she settles in the racially segregated neighborhoods of Los Angeles. As a working-class "colonial" subject, Faye is intimidated by the Naganos' middle-class domesticity, which governs her own nonnormative family through discourses of colonialism: "I recognized the word 'Chosen-jin' and knew it was about me. I felt ill at ease. Was it about my ignorance of Walt Whitman? . . . or about the way I laughed? Was it about me being Korean?" (*Clay Walls*, 216). Even though Faye is initially delighted by the skit, she unwittingly associates blackface performance with Japanese colonialism in Korea, thereby implicitly illuminating the violence at the center of assimilation and national identity.[20]

In the novel, Faye literally flees the Nagano home, although this cannot be interpreted as a rejection of blackface, since even as Faye escapes the classed and ethnic disciplining she experiences, she abruptly imagines Lucerne Luke as the potentially threatening black male: "I walked rapidly. Someone could be hiding behind the stumps of the palm trees, someone like Lucerne Luke. What did Mrs. Nagano say? It was driving me crazy not to know" (*Clay Walls*, 217). Feeling multiply disciplined as she recounts her recent experience at the Nagano household, Faye conflates her anxieties about her improper formation with the imagined sexualized threat of black masculinity. Her inability to recognize and name Walt Whitman's poem leads her to feeling that she has failed to represent herself as proficient in the classics of American culture, exacerbating the anxieties caused by her class and colonial underdevelopment.

The novel constructs this moment as one in which this space—a middle-class bourgeois Japanese American home governed by conventional gendered roles—disciplines her as an underdeveloped subject. Faye feels that she is not American enough, too "colonial" and ethnic, not bourgeois enough, and lacking a modern formation of proper femininity. What finally negotiates these self-conscious anxieties is Lucerne Luke, the black male imagined as lurking behind the bushes. Although Faye's enjoyment of the sisters' performance could not override her ethnic and class differentiation from the proper bourgeois home of the Americanized Naganos, blackness as masculine sexual threat is one way in which the novel reintegrates her into bourgeois femininity. Black male characters are consistently constructed as blackface caricatures, and Lucerne's absent presence helps her imagine that she inhabits the proper formation that the Naganos' domestic space revealed that she did not have.

Dominant signs of black masculinity as a sexualized threat saturate the novel's representations of black social space. The novel introduces the character Lucerne Luke in an early scene depicting a rare instance when Faye must walk alone through the neighborhood to help her mother with a large bundle of fabric. As she nears the bus stop where her mother is waiting, she assiduously tries to avoid a group of young black men by pretending "to look at something on the other side of the street" but nonetheless feels forced to engage:

> "Hey China girl! Ain't you a little young to be pushing a baby carriage? Come on give us a look-see at this miracle of nature."
> I knew his name. It was Lucerne Luke; he lived on our street. He was dark, muscular, and intimidating. I always knew when he was around but I would try to avoid him. (*Clay Walls*, 197)

The mythology of the black male rapist clearly determines the narrative's construction of Lucerne Luke, who is described in explicitly racialized sexual terms when he states, "We can help China girl fill the buggy with a bronze bundle of joy" (*Clay Walls*, 198). The suggestive remark is a gratuitous elaboration, since the signification of Lucerne Luke already emerges from a century-old discourse of the imagined sexual dangers posed by black masculinity. The constructed threat of black male sexuality has historically defined white womanhood while erasing the sexual exploitation of black women.[21] In the context of twentieth-century urbanization and suburbanization, the myth of the black rapist continues to reproduce capitalist relations of production and is constitutive of proper femininity.

The ideological construction of the American home as a site of protection and safety has been historically defined over and against a racialized public that threatens to violate or degrade proper femininity. At ten years old, Faye's first-person narrative voice makes it clear that her dreaded encounter with Lucerne and his friends generates anxieties mediated by the racialized threat of rape:

> I saw my chance and ran. No one was chasing me but I wanted to get as far away from their gibes as I could. . . . Lucerne Luke had resumed his place among his friends. They continued to watch the scene on Western Avenue, as if waiting for something to happen that would amuse them. They were through with me. (*Clay Walls*, 198)

Faye's intimidating encounter with these boys is coded in terms of rape and violation. She deliberates an escape ("I saw my chance and ran") and comments afterward that "they were through with me." But the boys are clearly not rapists, nor do they ever pose any kind of physical threat to Faye. Instead, the passage's implication of intimidation and differentiation is part of a gendered performance of heteronormative femininity defined through the construction of black male sexuality as a threat.

Black masculinity is consistently figured as both a criminal and a sexual threat to the integrity of the family and home. Faye's brother John is arrested for selling stolen items that he receives from Lucerne Luke. After John appears in court, Faye has a nightmare in which the terrifying specter of black masculinity combines the blackface minstrel and the black(face) rapist of D. W. Griffith's *Birth of a Nation*: "That night, I dreamt about Lucerne Luke. His eyes were bulging out of their sockets. He had huge wings and was hovering overhead as I ran to find a hiding place. I kept looking up at him to see how close he was until I stumbled into a deep hole" (*Clay Walls*, 207). While Faye ostensibly fears the possible reprisal that her brother will suffer after Lucerne is released from juvenile hall, the demonic and haunting construction of black masculinity displaces the mounting material constraints that have long undermined this family. After the mother discovers that the police are searching for John, she attempts to send him to his father, "safely away from the neighborhood" (*Clay Walls*, 205). But when she writes to the farm where the father was last seen, the letter is returned because he has already moved again in search of work. Faye's father sends minimal amounts of money that can hardly cover the growing heap of unopened bills that pile up in the house, filling a large box. In Faye's childhood blackface nightmares, the threat of black masculinity is imagined as the agent of deterioration of the normative family household that they never were.

Yet the myth of the black male rapist is reproduced in the novel in the context of another discursive register that belies these dominant representations of black masculinity. In Los Angeles during the 1940s, a "pluralistic and diverse street culture emerged to challenge the dominant cultural narratives of public and private life."[22] Although the multiracial neighborhoods in *Clay Walls* cannot "reflect" the sociohistorical processes of segregation in the West during World War II, these communities are mediated representations that express both dominant and oppositional racialized gender ideologies. Faye's narrative is filled with frustration over differential gender codes, prompting her to angrily ask her mother, "Are you glad you're a woman?"(*Clay Walls*, 202). When read alongside her attempt to "talk jive" (198), this shows that Faye strongly wants to participate in a set of black cultural practices that are related to a thriving community, an alternative racialized femininity, and unregulated access to public space.

The novel's racialized imaginings of neighborhood and community as black social space are mediated representations of Los Angeles's racially segregated history from the 1920s through the 1940s. Place is important to situating the narrative in a historical context because the spatialization of race in Los Angeles differs from the historical production of most urban ghettos on the West Coast. As noted in chapter 1, although the presence of blacks in the West was numerically unremarkable until World War II, the city of Los Angeles was a noteworthy exception.[23] Los Angeles's black population increased sevenfold between 1900 and 1920.[24] As a consequence, patterns of black ghettoization could be found earlier in Los Angeles than in other western states where black urban populations faced relatively little opposition in residential housing until the second Great Migration. From 1910 to 1920, the spatial concentration of black residents of Los Angeles increased dramatically, and black dispersal throughout the city shifted into "a few restricted areas which amounted to a spatial ghetto and which had some of the social, economic, and psychological characteristics of a ghetto in the broader sense of the term."[25]

By 1920, the majority of the black urban population lived in several tracts that included thirty blocks of Central Avenue and a few eight- to nine-block areas of "unrestricted housing," which included West Jefferson, Temple, Holmes, and the larger area of Watts. From 1920 to 1945, Los Angeles's ghettos were not exclusively black, as they also included Asians, a large number of Mexicans/Chicanos, and some Eastern European ethnic immigrants, all of whom lived in racially defined areas but also among one another in areas designated as "unrestricted." These "islands" of unrestricted housing, which were generally within a mile of Central Avenue (with the exception of Watts, which is more than ten miles to the south) were surrounded by residential blocks of white resistance, invested in protecting their boundaries through a more systemic use of restrictive covenants and block association restrictions. By the summer of 1942, the massive influx of tens of thousands of black migrants joined the great numbers of white migrants to Los Angeles, which greatly exacerbated the citywide housing shortage and reified already existing patterns of residential segregation that had begun in the 1920s.[26]

Dominant spatial practices were designed to isolate and ghettoize black and other nonwhite subjects, but in turn, these racially segregated populations transformed South Central into a vibrant space of urban culture and social life, which was described by the well-traveled pianist Fletcher Smith as "one of the swingingest streets in the world, man."[27] Black musicians found work performing musical scores for Hollywood's growing talking pictures industry while playing gigs on Central Avenue with artists such as Count Basie, Lester Young, Les Hite, Buddy Collette, Louis Armstrong, Jelly Roll Morton, T-Bone Walker, and a young Charles Mingus. Jack Kelson, a musician born and raised in the Central district, recalls that Central Avenue offered opportunities to exercise a form of black cultural politics for those who participated in the vibrant jazz/blues scene of Los Angeles:

> Everybody was just immaculately, you might say, splendiferous in their appearance, and they took great pride with everything about their appearance. The way they walked, you know: proud. And they could tell stories, and the body language, and all this. And the economy of language, sometimes there would be just maybe one verbal sound or a word or a syllable . . . more eloquent than a paragraph. . . . I have come to realize, later, in life, that the appearance of the clothing was very, very important, but also their posture.[28]

Kelson's astute insights resonate with Robin Kelley's analyses of black working-class culture, which emphasize black dress as well as verbal and bodily performances as important forms of black urban cultural politics that contested the denigrating discourses of black urban pathology and the bodily regimes of workplace discipline.[29] Kelson's vivid memories of Central Avenue as exhibiting "more glamour [than] anywhere in the world" and as a place where "there's not enough tape in the world to record all that glory" offer powerful counternarratives to the pathological construction of black urban space as underdeveloped, depraved, and immoral.[30]

As documented in the oral history project *Central Avenue Sounds* (1998) and Horace Tapscott's autobiography *Songs of the Unsung* (2001), it was the everyday actions of locally respected musicians and residents that played a crucial role in building generative and interrelated social spaces of collectivity. Music was a cultural practice that transformed the space and relations of Central Avenue, or in the words of Horace Tapscott, music "was part of the social fabric of the community."[31] Tapscott's recollections of the 1940s effortlessly link "all these blues cats" looking to date his sister to women's church choirs where that "blues became the spiritual" to elementary school music teachers whose young students lived on the same block and still performed together at local venues more than fifty years later. Tapscott and many of the musicians, activists, and/or teachers included in *Central Avenue Sounds* give remarkable testimonials that reveal how music and cultural praxis were the means of linking what had been discrete social spaces in the remaking of the Central Avenue district during the 1930s and 1940s.[32]

Like the representations of black social space in *Clay Walls*, these oral histories of African American musicians who lived in the Central district of Los Angeles are always also discursive mediations of the "real." But to understand the various discourses being orchestrated in this Korean American novel's representations of black social space, it is useful to note how this place is remembered by African Americans who are engaged in their own narrative reconstructions of the neighborhood. In other words, these various accounts help provide a sense of the related yet differential historical circumstances and social stakes in reimagining South Central Los Angeles of the World War II period.

In an analysis of the possibilities engendered by new spatial relations in wartime Los Angeles, historian George Lipsitz observes, "Physical proximity embodies culture in a way that can undermine even the most deeply held prejudices and ideologies."[33] Lipsitz's insights into the potentially radical cultural formations that emerged from the spatial organization of Los Angeles during the World War II era are elucidated in *Clay Walls*'s narration of the development of Korean American and other racialized femininities. Faye's isolation in the privatized space of the home is starkly contrasted with representations of the vibrant "public space" of the black working-class neighborhood:

> As soon as I made the turn, the sounds of people working, walking, shopping, and driving cars became louder. Colored people were yelling to friends on the street. Most of the owners of shops lived upstairs or in the backs of businesses. Cooking smells hovered over their cash registers. I looked past the gaudy window displays as I pushed the carriage, passing by the handmade signs that said, "Come In." As I neared the poultry I held my nose, careful to avoid running the carriage into the rabbi. . . . Count Basie's music filtered into the street. . . . Some boys were hanging out around the record shop. We shared the neighborhood with blacks but when they grouped together, it became their territory. I pretended to look at something on the other side of the street and walked rapidly by them. (*Clay Walls*, 197)

The de-rationalized organization of black social space generates cultural practices and subjectivities that threaten to contaminate or degrade Faye's development into bourgeois femininity. Social, commercial, and domestic spaces are inextricably fused in this description, and the ideology of separate spheres breaks down, as economic and commercial space are simultaneously "domestic" sites of reproductive labor as well as social and cultural practice and exchange. The passage is both disciplined by and disciplinary of black urban space, which is represented as a chaotic, disorderly, and vulgar place, assaulting all the refined senses of the bourgeois subject with the noises, smells, and "gaudy window displays." The sights, sounds, and smells of black urban space travel across and invade the imagined necessary distance that separates the privatized bourgeois individual from a collective urban public.[34]

However, the isolation of the privatized domestic sphere that engenders proper femininity also produces a longing for social participation in the black urban space that is available precisely because of its nonnormative formation. Faye's family hardly embodies normative bourgeois domesticity or its privileges, despite the mother's compensatory efforts to claim an elite Korean past to displace the material conditions and racialization that they endure as Asian immigrants. Faye's commitment as a young girl "to not upset" her mother, who is physically and emotionally struggling with the strains of poverty and a failed marriage, threatens to bind Faye to her mother's legacy of isolation and domestic confinement. Faye's sense of fear and intimidation as she moves through the black urban neighborhood is central to the novel's construction of a proper bourgeois feminine subject. Yet as a working-class Korean American girl in the 1930s, she is radically dislocated from the national citizenry and can never represent or embody proper womanhood and domesticity. The figurative and literal signs of social exchange and public life in black social space ("Come In"), although represented as "gaudy" or vulgar, are also compelling invitations to an Orientalized subject, who feels confined to domestic isolation in the working-class Asian immigrant home, which is constructed as the only possible site of safety or belonging.

However, throughout the narrative, the family is displaced and evicted from numerous houses because they cannot pay their rent, and the working-class immigrant home is hardly a stable privatized space of domestic bliss. After losing his job, the father leaves indefinitely in search of migrant labor work, and eventually the family is forced out of the small home that they had purchased through a white business partner. When Faye fears that their continual relocations will prevent her father from ever finding them, the mother scoffs, "'How far can we go? We can't move beyond Vermont or Western Avenues or Jefferson and Exposition Boulevards.' She made it sound like we lived on a board in a game of Monopoly" (*Clay Walls*, 189). Their multiple evictions not only undermine the ideology of the domestic sphere as a protected space separate from the "external" pressures of economic commerce, but in addition to alien land laws, residential segregation further underscores how the Korean immigrant home cannot be separated from the political sphere.

The text ultimately represents Faye's incorporation as a consumer and a peripheral participant of the black urban culture that emerges from the multiracial spaces of South Central Los Angeles. Much to her mother's dismay, Faye begins to practice the jitterbug, a form of swing dance associated with black urban culture, and which her mother describes as "savage."[35] The jazz and blues scene of Central Avenue is figured as similarly shaping Faye's and her brothers' tastes in music, as exemplified by her record collection, which includes Count Basie's (rather than Benny Goodman's) "One O'Clock Jump."[36] Thus the novel's mapping of the production of social space, which represents multiracial "unrestricted" neighborhoods as generative of a nonwhite working-class urban culture, becomes central to challenging the gendered ideological production of separate spheres. For Faye, the urban culture and social space of Los Angeles offer an alternative formation of racialized femininity.

While black racialized femininity is consistently represented as deviant, it simultaneously provides an alternative to the protected, domestic bourgeois womanhood that Faye's mother offers her by consuming American popular culture safely inside their home. The black character, Bertha, plays a recurring role in the text, and she is consistently represented as occupying the neighborhood corners and public streets from which Faye is restricted by her mother. The text never locates Bertha in a domestic space, as she appears in the novel only on street corners, sidewalks, and outside storefronts as an embodiment of the transgressive black female. Bertha engages in premarital sex, is sexually promiscuous, has an abortion, and has a "street" knowledge that is antithetical to the text's construction of Faye as a naïve girl, confined and regulated to the space of her home. Bertha's deviant femininity, though disciplined in the novel, is simultaneously idealized and admired for embodying a critical agency that Faye and other racialized young women are represented as lacking.

Bertha's capacity to critique racism unequivocally in a variety of contexts mirrors Okada's construction of black men as contestatory and critical subjects. Conversely, whereas racial recalcitrance constitutes a romanticized black masculinity in *No-No Boy*, Bertha's vocal critiques in *Clay Walls* situate her outside the domain of proper femininity, which is defined precisely against black female deviance. Consequently, black female recalcitrance is figured as ennobling and admirable but, at the same time, comes at the cost of being disciplined by bourgeois femininity as a sexually immoral and deviant formation. The novel always represents Bertha's critical articulations in the context of her various sexual transgressions of female propriety. In one instance, Faye bumps into Bertha when they are both teenagers. Their discussion of Bertha's pregnancy serves to frame Bertha's construction as an autonomous female subject who is incapable of accepting racial subordination:

> I noticed then that she was pregnant. 'When did you get married?' I asked.
>
> Her mouth dropped open. 'Girl, you haven't changed nohow. I'm not married." . . .
>
> "What's wrong with Texas?" I asked as she pulled me down to sit next to her.

"Take everything that's wrong with L.A. and double it. Hotter than blazes, can't not only live where you want, can't sit where you want. Have to look like a nigger, dress like a nigger, and act like a nigger. I wasn't ready for that. I came back." . . . "My folks stayed in Texas. 'They said, "It's our home, baby.'" "Some home! A place where white folks think they're 'good people' if they're civil to us. I wanted none of it." . . . "I'm paying my own way." . . .

Bertha was back and I was glad to see her. (*Clay Walls*, 246)

In this instance, the novel situates Bertha in the context of her family only to narrate her displacement from the social space of the family and home. The passage figures female autonomy and racial resistance in contradiction to domesticity and familial cohesion. Bertha's already "illegitimate" pregnancy is further disarticulated from discourses of motherhood when she states, "I'll probably put it up for adoption or something. It's not easy to find a guy looking for a ready-made family" (*Clay Walls*, 246). The novel represents Bertha's predicament as an unmarried, pregnant teenager living without her family as a condition of her integrity and strength that enables her to challenge racism and other social constraints.

Bertha ends up having an illegal abortion, another violation of the sacred reproductive function ascribed to true womanhood. Once again, sexualized transgression serves to frame Bertha's antiracist position when she voices her opinions about the internment:

Bertha was the first to make me realize what it meant. I was surprised to see her at our door. "I came to say good-bye and to let you know that I think the whole thing stinks. . . . It's so dumb. Hauling off everyone to a camp because they can't tell who's spying." . . .

"Not us. The Japanese," I explained.

"That's not you?"

"No we're not the same." As soon as I noticed it, I blurted out, "You've had your baby!"

She ran her hand over her stomach. "Do you mean you don't have to go?" I nodded. "When did you have it?"

She hugged me. "I'm glad. I know you ain't done nothing."

"Was it a boy or a girl," I asked.

"I don't know. . . . I had an abortion." . . . She wrinkled her brows. "I had to. I couldn't take care of it myself. . . . I'm sure glad you don't have to go to no concentration camp. Ain't that some confession of stupidity? They can't find the spies so they lock everyone up."

"Yeah," I said. (*Clay Walls*, 263–65)

Faye's inarticulate "Yeah" concludes the chapter, further emphasizing her characteristically vague and reticent response to Bertha's unambiguous and sustained critique of the "stupidity" of internment, which she calls a "concentration camp." At various points in their dialogue, the two young women are almost having two different conversations, so that the discussion of Bertha's pregnancy and abortion becomes literally inseparable from her vocal attack against the state's anti-Japanese racism. The novel is unable to bring Bertha's critical and resistant subject formation into representation without simultaneously constructing her through discourses of black female pathology that characterize her racialized sexual body as "fallen" from the elevated ideals of bourgeois femininity.

But it is precisely Bertha's displacement from normative femininity through discourses of black female deviance that enables the novel to represent her as an alternative model to racialized womanhood. After the novel's relentless construction of Bertha through sexualized discourses of transgression, Faye states near the conclusion that "Bertha was the only girl I knew who took hold of her life and made things happen. 'Girl, don't you know anything?' she always said to me. Remembering made me smile" (*Clay Walls*, 284). Faye's admiration for Bertha is an ambivalent expression of the constraints of the bourgeois femininity that the narrative attempts to develop. The institutions of marriage, heterosexual coupling, and motherhood are narrated as the telos, which requires a woman's reconciliation with the social order. Bertha is the novel's device for undermining ideologies of romance, love, and marriage without directly implicating the Korean American female protagonist as a deviant subject. Bertha clearly articulates what the novel cannot otherwise represent, which is a critical voice that sees through the transparent mythologies of love and romance that exist only on Hollywood's movie screens.

Although the novel differentiates Bertha's deviant formation from Faye's attempts to follow a proper one, the novel also draws vague and unstated relationships connecting the two young women. Their relationship to each other is not presented through terms of either identification or dis-identification, as when Bertha initiates the idea of finding work:

"Maybe I can get a job in a war plant. They can't be fussy, they'll be needing people like me."

"A job? Will they need people like me?"

"If they take me, they'll take you." . . .

I took her hand. "Let me know about the job. I'm serious," I said. "My mom can't refuse to let me work if it means I'm helping to win the war." (*Clay Walls*, 265)

The ambiguity of social distinction and identity in the phrase "people like me" suggests the refusal of any logic of correspondence in defining marginal social identities. This exchange does not collapse the many differences between Faye and Bertha, yet it also points to a provisional, shared location that they occupy as young nonwhite women with respect to the specific space of the factory workplace, or as Bertha states, "If they take me, they'll take you too." The relationship between the subjects of "me" and "you" is forged out of intersectional axes of race, gender, and class that retain a space of contingency for the shifting conditions that underlie their differential incorporation into wartime industrial labor at a specific historical conjuncture.

The multiracial neighborhoods in *Clay Walls* cannot be read as reflections of the sociohistorical processes of segregation in the West during the World War II period but are mediated representations that express racialized gender ideologies specific to the moment of the novel's production. Kim's "fictional autobiography" was published in 1986 when the welfare state had been thoroughly dismantled as the Reagan administration waged its "antistatist" campaign of fiscal austerity through discourses of black male criminality and black female dependency. The novel's representations of black social space and culture are aesthetic expressions of these gendered ideologies of black urban pathology and dependency, which saturated public discourse and legitimized corporate subsidization and the systematic deprivation and disciplining of inner-city communities during the 1980s. Okada's *No-No Boy* (1958) may also be "retrospective" in its representation of a previous decade; however, Okada was writing during the early civil rights struggles for desegregation as white suburbanization exploded in the expanding cold-war economy and before the tremendous demographic changes of post-1965 immigration. *Clay Walls* reconstructs the pre–World War II urban landscape of Los Angeles twenty years *after* the passage of civil rights legislation, nationwide black inner-city insurgencies, the devastation of urban renewal and development policies, the emergence and containment of radical social movements, and the mass immigration of both unskilled and middle-class Asian and Latino workers. Kim's novel, in other words, was produced in the context of a radically transformed, de-industrialized global economy that fueled a backlash discourse of "reverse discrimination," as neoconservative ideologies of individualism, merit, and personal responsibility legitimized brutal assaults on the racialized poor in the name of a "color-blind" society.[37] By the 1980s, the ideological construction of Asian Americans as a model minority, defined solely in relation to their cultural, educational, ethical, and even residential distance from "underdeveloped" African Americans living in "cultural poverty," was crucial to this neoconservative campaign. While *Clay Walls* tells a story of Korean Americans' and African Americans' shared social space and history before World War II, the novel defines Asian and African Americans through an uneven and disciplinary relationship. In the novel, dominant ideologies of black urban pathology constitute the Korean American female national subject whose narrative resolution is bound to a historical future in which black urban womanhood is severely debased and pathologized. However, from the intense divisions of race and class that organize the segregated, de-industrialized space of late twentieth-century Los Angeles, the novel's representations of multiracial ghettos and of black urban culture in the 1930s and 1940s project contradictory imaginings that directly counter contemporaneous discourses of black female dependency, suggesting utopian desires for an alternative present.

%% Part 3 %%

In part 2, questions of Asian American national identity and the expansion of black civil rights were posed in the context of an expanding wartime economy in the first half of the twentieth century. The last two chapters of this project describe the contours of Asian American and African American discourses of national belonging under the transformed political economic landscape of U.S. deindustrialization and globalization in a post–civil rights era. In this political context of full "equal rights," the inclusion of racial difference has become an important dimension of U.S. neoliberalism, and therefore racialized dispossession cannot be adequately captured by the same discourse of exclusion that was operative before 1965.

The concepts of black Orientalism and Asian uplift introduced in previous sections are brought together to examine how enduring conditions of inequality and exclusion after the passage of civil rights are represented and narrativized in contemporary black and Asian American film. These films engage and negotiate the black/Asian racial tandem that currently manifests as model minority discourse: virtuous Asian American mobility as evidence of the pathological failure of the black poor. This disciplinary relationship is negotiated in disparate ways in African American and Asian American cultural production, and the following analyses provide an alternative to the moralistic logic that structures discourses of "black/Asian conflict" that have become dominant since the 1980s.

The formation of a black/Asian racial tandem after 1965 was central to the reproduction of a U.S. neoliberal episteme that has radically transformed conceptions of both citizenship and the state. Under neoliberalism and economic globalization, the notion of the U.S. citizen has shifted from a post–World War II Keynesian subject of "rights" and "entitlements" to state resources, to a subject of "self-enterprise" whose civic duty is largely defined as being free of state dependence. This transformation was ideologically secured in the United States by racializing and pathologizing both poverty and welfare assistance as black dependency. In accordance with neoliberal principles, the U.S. state was no longer imagined as it was after the New Deal as an institution functioning in service to its (white) national citizenry but, rather, as an entity facilitating the flow of global capital for "general" prosperity.

Within this shifting context, dispossession and disenfranchisement do not operate through racial categories as they did before the passage of civil rights when nonwhites had racially restricted access to housing, employment, voting, cross-racial marriage, education, and social space. While segments of nonwhite populations in the post–civil rights era now experience political, economic, and social incorporation, the scope of inequality has massively increased with unprecedented concentrations of wealth and poverty that are characteristic of a neoliberal world order. There is a persistent racial dimension to U.S. inequality, although appeals to racial exclusion are readily countered with a moralistic discourse that capitalizes on notions of individual agency.

U.S. neoliberal ideologies have quite successfully reduced massive systemic inequities to a matter of personal defect and individual moral failure. Discourses of the Asian American as model minority have long been recognized as performing this type of ideological work—as undermining the legitimacy of the political grievances of those "not making it." While there has been much critical attention to countering ideologies that construct surplus populations as the product of their own deviant cultural values, I contend that there has been an unwitting reproduction of the moralistic implications of these dominant discourses.

This becomes evident in how the behaviors and worldviews of structurally vulnerable nonwhite communities are evaluated in relation to cross-racial dynamics and formations. Therefore, the depiction of Asian immigrant merchants in black public discourse constitutes a troubling problematic that would best be "absolved" from racial prejudice. The violent crimes of impoverished black residents against Southeast Asian refugees are regrettably racist, as are the antiblack racist narratives expressed by Asian refugees and immigrants. Such statements belie a strikingly pious yet sympathetic position that mistakenly believes that such moralistic assessments are relevant terms of social justice, even while the larger geopolitical formation is governed by the brutal indifference of inequality under global capitalism.

The last two chapters contexualize this misplaced ethical burden, which characterizes discussions of contemporary Asian American and

African American discourse and cultural production. By refusing disingenuous mandates of multicultural neoliberalism, we can better recognize how discourses of African American and Asian American national belonging evidence complex negotiations with broader global processes. Such an alternative interpretive framework is neither celebratory nor apologist in examining the inevitable contradictions that are disclosed in these constrained discourses that nonetheless persistently strive to imagine forms of community and freedom.

Black Surplus in
the Pacific Century

Ownership and Dispossession
in the Hood Film

The Mobile and the Immobile

The accelerated mobility of capital, goods, and bodies has become a defining feature of contemporary discourses of globalization. In the United States, formal racial equality, global shifts in modes of production, and unprecedented levels of immigration from Asia and Latin America distinguish the post-1965 experience of race. In contrast to the nineteenth century, in this age of heightened capital mobility Asia now figures as the site of capitalism's future.[1] At the same time, however, the much-vaunted mobilities of the post–civil rights era are contemporaneous with the intensification of mass displacement (deindustrialization, gentrification, incarceration, etc.), which is particularly acute given the relative immobility of impoverished urban populations. The inordinate impact of the new urban enclosures on working-class black communities, in particular, has only exacerbated the conditions of spatial isolation and fixity, which stand in stark contrast to the hypermobilities of capitalist globalization. In the dominant imaginary, these countervailing movements have come to provide the contrasting poles through which contemporary ideologies of development are racialized. Out of this complex matrix of mobilities and some twenty years after the passage of civil rights legislation, it is the black urban poor who have become "Orientalized" in contemporary discourses of development. In the modified terrain of symbolic pasts and futures, the black urban poor now occupy the place of the atavistic, underdeveloped Others of global progress: incapable of being incorporated into the national citizenry, let alone into a world economy.[2] In this chapter I examine the figure of the Asian immigrant merchant in post–civil rights discourses of black dispossession and disenfranchisement as one critical sign of how this new, global racial imaginary has recast the race for citizenship.

In my analysis, the concepts of black Orientalism and Asian uplift provide an alternative means through which to interrogate the assumptions of "racial prejudice" and "racial conflict," which tend to short-circuit our analyses of U.S. black and Asian racial formations. As described in preceding chapters, the discursive registers of black Orientalism and Asian uplift should not be regarded as unfortunate psychological complexes of "racial prejudice" but, rather, as a form of cultural politics integral to negotiating the contradictions endemic to Asian and African American citizenship. Echoing the previous analysis of nineteenth-century discourses of black citizenship, my point is not to identify whether black Orientalism is racist or problematic. Instead, in the post-1965 period, black Orientalism names how the persistent failures of black citizenship—the inadequacy of legal equality, intensified residential segregation of the black poor, disenfranchisement through mass incarceration—are negotiated in relation to global restructuring, mass immigration, and a dominant cold-war American Orientalism that is wary of a future shaped by Asian economic domination.

Current discourses of black Orientalism are distinct from dominant forms of American Orientalism, insofar as these discourses serve as a strategic means to engage with the abandonment and disenfranchisement of the black urban poor. Contemporary black Orientalisms, like their antecedent historic forms, cannot simply be reduced to Asian scapegoating, since black disenfranchisement is structurally related to new Asian immigration and the rise of the so-called Pacific Rim economy. In this way, rather than dispute the existence of anti-Korean or anti-Asian sentiments during, say, the Los Angeles uprisings or merchant boycotts, black Orientalism directs our analytical focus to the complexity of black national formation in contemporary transnationalism, in which Asian labor, markets, and capital constitute both America's dream of future prosperity and the likely realization of its worst yellow peril nightmare. In particular, I show here that an understanding of the contradictions endemic to the institution of U.S. citizenship help leverage the "ethical frame" in which contemporary black/Asian antagonisms are contained through the dominant liberal episteme. In other words, the reductive imposition of situational ethics through which black collective resistance is persistently figured, individualized, and neutralized (as in "do the right thing") requires a different kind of critical reckoning with the past in the present, a reckoning that Marx so eloquently depicted in his 1852 account of French history in the making:

> Men make history, but they do not make it just as they please; they do not make it under circumstances chosen by themselves but under circumstances directly encountered, given and transmitted from the past. The tradition of all the dead generations weighs like a nightmare on the brain of the living. And just when they seem engaged in revolutionizing themselves and things, in creating something that has never yet existed, precisely in such periods of revolutionary crisis they anxiously conjure up the spirits of the past to their service and borrow from them names, battle cries and costumes in order to present the new scene of world history in this time-honoured disguise and this borrowed language. . . . In like manner a beginner who has learnt a new language always translates it back into his mother tongue, but he has assimilated the spirit of the new language and can freely express himself in it only when he finds his way in it without recalling the old and forgets his native tongue in the use of the new.[3]

The sociological analyses and film scripts, the boycotts and the riots, that I take up in this chapter bear the traces of "this time-honoured disguise and this borrowed language," but they are not merely repetitions of the old. What is new in these critical vernaculars can be discerned by attending to how the "tradition of all the dead generations" continues to operate in and on the present.

Black Surplus and the Pacific Rim

By the late 1970s, the economic ascendance of East Asian countries had given rise to an American discourse of the "Pacific Rim," in which the United States, Japan, the East Asian Newly Industrializing Countries (NICs), and a second tier of developing Pacific nations were imagined as a regional space for the expansive flows of capital and coprosperity.[4] The United States invested large sums of money in postwar Japan to ensure its emergence as a regional capitalist bulwark. By the 1960s, however, Japan's export manufacturing–based economy was growing annually at three times the rate of the U.S. economy, and a decade later, "over a third of America's trade deficit came from Japan alone."[5] By 1985, Japan's rapid economic expansion propelled Japanese banks to displace "the Americans as the largest holders of international assets," with Tokyo "topping New York for the first time in 1987" as the world's most important financial center.[6] Countries such as South Korea and Taiwan also rapidly industrialized with U.S. military, political, and economic intervention, and by the 1980s, Asia's "economic miracles" were themselves looking offshore in pursuit of cheaper labor as well as profitable opportunities, many in the United States, for foreign investment.

As Chris Connery explains, the Pacific Rim was an invented spatial imaginary in which

> Japan and the NICs represent capital's transformative promise— their recent history is capital's teleology. China is the certain future. The discourse of equality and connectedness reflects, in part, a reaction to East Asian "success": when Japan is number one, the only way to not be number two is to transcend the nation.[7]

As the 1973 global recession and capitalist crisis destroyed utopic hopes of America's infinite postwar expansion, the "Pacific Rim" became a means of figuring a new extranational space in which economic growth could be a shared global enterprise, an invention by globalizing forces and institutions that had the most to gain from these linked international circuits.

Nowhere has the presence of Pacific Rim discourse been more in evidence than in Los Angeles, "the jewel of the Pacific Rim," as city boosters tout their geographic advantage as the port of call for Eastern capital. Since the 1970s, Los Angeles has been an extremely profitable site for Japanese, South Korean, and Taiwanese capital, which could house their financial headquarters in a downtown area that was relatively "undeveloped" and devalued compared with other major U.S. metropolitan centers such as New York, San Francisco, and Chicago. Unlike most other de-industrializing U.S. urban centers, Los Angeles benefited significantly from capital restructuring in Asia by functioning as the literal gateway to the Pacific and as "the second largest customs district in the nation."[8] Financial and banking institutions became increasingly concentrated in the LA area, serving as the headquarters of numerous Asian financial institutions.[9] Such expansion in the increasingly international sector of banking and finance led to a major office-building boom in the undeveloped downtown area, which generated substantial real estate speculation, yet another important site of Asian capital investment in Los Angeles throughout the 1980s until Japan's economic crash in the early 1990s.

The increased visibility of Asian capital and Asian professional labor throughout California's urban centers can operate as a sign of the selective "Pacific Rim" prosperity that this influx has generated for all professionals working in well-paid positions in finance, banking, insurance, and real estate. But dystopic Orientalist imaginings (the classic *Blade Runner* scenario) of a future of Japanese or Asian economic domination are always the anxious underside of official celebrations of the "Pacific Century."

According to Rob Wilson, although the "Pacific Rim" (which shifted to the rubric of the "Asia-Pacific" by the mid-1990s) is constructed in the United States as a more "porous, user-friendly space of post–cold war, post-binary, 'post-Orientalist' interaction" for the global flow of capital, these celebratory regional constructs cannot completely transcend "the 'cold war demonology' and historical trauma of war and immigration which continue to haunt 'the U.S. political imaginary.'"[10] Indeed, as Wilson argues, "Orientalism refuses to be posted or deconstructed inside the US national imaginary even during this hyper-interactive moment of transnational/transcultural flow," and he points to the "lurid . . . racially phobic and politically regressive" characterizations so recently ascribed to the Asia-Pacific.[11] In order to keep the past at bay, the U.S. construction of "the Pacific Rim" as a vast space of future coprosperity strives to produce what Bruce Cumings calls "a forgetting, a hoped-for amnesia" of how the region was "fashioned in warfare" from 1941 to 1975.[12]

By the late 1980s, the more or less successful erasure of the imperialist past had made it possible for the Pacific Rim to become the sign of the future itself. Rhetorically shorn of any vestiges of the turbulent, deadly past, the Pacific was now to be embraced as the means to take hold of the new millennium, with all the shiny, techno-utopic promise of limitless growth and prosperity. It was this vision of the Rim that the megadevelopers, corporate barons, and civic leaders of Los Angeles seized as their ticket to win the race to become the American city of the twenty-first century:

Just as New York, London, Paris stood as symbols of past centuries, L.A. will be THE city of the 21st century. The potential for Los Angeles as a prosperous international center for communications, trade, investment and culture is immense. It will be a leading hub of world trade, especially as the U.S. gateway to the Pacific Rim nations, where

the combined economies are expanding at the rate of $3 billion
a week toward a projected 27% share of the world's gross product
before the end of the century.[13]

Despite the ebullient rhetoric of official LA boosters ("$3 billion a week"),
the embrace of the Pacific Rim by the West has been an anxious enterprise on at least two important fronts. On the one hand, the historic specter of imperialist wars in Asia continues to haunt the dreams of a har-
monious future of American and Asian capital coprosperity. As Wilson
noted, the cold-war legacy of protecting "the American way" from invad-
ing Asian enemies cannot be fully repressed by the demands of global
restructuring for "a utopic discourse of the liberal market, an emerging signifier of transnational aspirations for some higher, supranational
unity."[14] Moreover, the glimmering 1980s record of the "Asian Tigers" was
more than a little vexed as nativist fears of a yellow peril takeover vied for
rhetorical attention: the Pacific Rim nations were still, in the last instance,
capitalist rivals. Any embrace of the Pacific Rim from the vantage point of
contemporary Los Angeles was heavily burdened with the realities of the
past in the present. In response to these troubling specters, the rhetorical
strategy was clear: erase the past and present of U.S. imperialism in Asia,
ignore any hint of class or racial violence in the history or future of Los
Angeles, and evade any question of who stands to lose in this "new global
regionalism." In short, avoid all possible contradictions that might sully
the dream of boundless development.

The second feature troubling a wholesale embrace of this "Asia Pacific"
was the presence in Los Angeles (as elsewhere) of populations that did
not share the enthusiasm for the transnational backroom deals that
would determine their future. For example, in response to the "10 Year
Plan" produced after the Watts riots of 1965, one local resident detected a
curious oversight:

> There were condominiums and townhouses, and there were women
> pushing their babies and there were little grocery and variety stores
> and everything you would need in your community to shop for . . .
> there were no African Americans in those pictures. . . . I asked where
> are the African Americans. I never got an answer to that question.[15]

This would not be the last time that black people were noticeably absent
from official plans dedicated to rebuilding a new Los Angeles in the wake

of mass urban riots. In "Rebuild LA" following the LA riots of 1992, official booster narratives made only the most anemic attempts to engage the
city's black urban poor in the production of the future landscape of Los
Angeles. The erasure of this population from the city's vision of its future
is both a rhetorical sign and a political economic policy that reflects the
processes of urban restructuring aggressively sponsored by the U.S. state.
The writing out of black urban populations from the plans of future prosperity is seen as a necessary condition for economic and social "progress"
in the development of Los Angeles.

The erasure of the black poor from the future of Los Angeles is tied to
larger national scripts in which the black working-class has become a surplus population in the current conditions of globalization. African American scholars like Clarence Lusane voice grave concerns about a global
economy in which black labor is not so much exploited as simply rendered obsolete and irrelevant. In his essay "Persisting Disparities," Lusane
quotes Sidney Wilhelm at length regarding the status of black labor in an
automated economy:

> The Negro moves out of his historical state of oppression into one of
> uselessness . . . he is not needed . . . white America, by a more perfect
> application of mechanization and a vigorous reliance upon automa-
> tion, disposes of the Negro . . . from an exploited labor force into an
> outcast. . . . Wilhelm correctly anticipated . . . the impact of global-
> ized production on the employment and economic life of the Black
> community.[16]

Or again, in his book *When Work Disappears: The World of the Urban
Poor*, William Julius Wilson notes that

> at the same time that changes in technology are producing new jobs,
> however, they are making many others obsolete. The workplace has
> been revolutionized by technological changes that range from the
> development of robotics to the creation of information highways . . .
> less skilled workers, such as those found in many inner-city neigh-
> borhoods, face the growing threat of job displacement.[17]

Thomas Holt states in *The Problem of Race in the Twenty-first Century*, "First of all, it is clear that although race may indeed do conceptual
work in this economy, blacks-as-a-race have no economic role. . . . One of

the clearest consequences of the transformed economy has been the massive exclusion of blacks from the *formal* economy."[18] This discourse of the growing obsolescence of black labor is consistently configured as having a specific gendered dimension, as in Haki Madhubuti's collection of essays, *Black Men: Obsolete, Single, Dangerous?* (1991). And as we will consider in more detail later, some of the earliest depictions of black male surplus came from cultural producers like Ice Cube, Public Enemy, Spike Lee, and the Hughes Brothers.

The concept of surplus labor has, of course, a much longer history. As Karl Marx wrote in the latter half of the nineteenth century, capitalist "development" was predicated on increasing and concentrating wealth for the few while intensifying deprivation for the many. In Marx's analysis, this mode of development turned on the production of a "relative surplus population" or a "reserve army of labor":

> If a surplus population is a necessary product of accumulation or of the development of wealth on a capitalist basis, this surplus population becomes, conversely, the lever of capitalistic accumulation, nay, a condition of existence of the capitalist mode of production. . . . The whole form of the movement of modern industry depends . . . upon the constant transformation of a part of the labouring population into unemployed or half-employed hands.[19]

In the context of U.S. capitalism, this formal economic tendency or law of development has a distinctive racial and gendered cast. In periods of economic contraction, certain racial groups bear the brunt of adjustments in the surplus population. As Ruth Gilmore writes, "Recent changes in labor-market structures have had particularly harsh effects on African-American men while displacing other workers as well."[20] She also notes that "black men are thirty percent more likely than their white counterparts to have lost permanent jobs between 1979 and 1989 with the long-term effect that only 51% of black men have steady employment compared with 73% twenty-five years ago."[21]

Although surplus is most commonly thought of in relation to labor and laboring populations, scholars in the 1980s began to identify other key institutional locations where the signs of surplus were in evidence. Of particular significance in this regard was the site of the prison with its exploding growth starting in the late 1970s. The concept of the "Prison Industrial Complex," a term coined by Mike Davis in the early 1980s, has become a crucial means by which numerous scholars and activists articulate the social and political management of a black urban surplus. With the post-1973 corporate state assault on Keynesian economics, the Prison Industrial Complex has taken the place of the welfare state, as the United States now incarcerates more than two million people, who are disproportionately poor, black, and male.

A 1990 study released the astounding finding that "on an average day in the United States, one in every four African-American men ages 20–29 was either in prison, jail, or on probation/parole."[22] In Los Angeles County, a 1991 study found that "nearly one third of all young black men (ages 20–29) living in Los Angeles County had already been jailed at least once in that same year"[23] and by 1993, black men, who comprised 3 percent of California's population, "accounted for 40% of those entering state prisons."[24] Studies conducted in Baltimore and Washington, D.C., produced similarly stunning statistics showing that these numbers were not local anomalies but a national pattern in the warehousing of black men from urban spaces. In 1991, of all the African American men aged eighteen to thirty-five living in Washington, D.C., more than four out of ten (42 percent) were in jail, in prison, on probation/parole, out on bond, or being sought on arrest warrants. Statistically, 75 percent of all eighteen-year-old black men in Washington could expect to be arrested and jailed at least once before reaching the age of thirty-five.[25] On an average day in Baltimore in 1991, 56 percent of young African American males aged eighteen to thirty-five were in prison, in jail, on probation, on parole, or being sought on arrest warrants, 90 percent of which were for drug-related offenses.[26] The War on Drugs, officially declared in the 1980s by the Reagan administration, has clearly been a significant driving force behind the rapidly expanding prison industry that warehouses young black males and consolidates state resources for the regulation and containment of black urban ghetto space.

The War on Drugs can be regarded as symptomatic of a larger shift in modes of state governance under globalization, in which the elimination of the social wage subsequently redefined the terms by which we understand the entitlements guaranteed by U.S. citizenship. From mass incarceration to postindustrial obsolescence, the black inner-city resident is subject to a wide array of contemporary forms of enclosure marked by a relative immobility, which stands in stark contrast to the imagined hyper-mobilities of the new Pacific Century. Indeed, the fact that U.S. official discourses tend to look to the East for their future development schemes and to erase the presence of blacks from within has become a leitmotif in both utopic and dystopic narratives of our shared global capitalist future. And as we shall see, it is out of this complex ideological matrix that a very particular symbolic economy has emerged to manage the contradictions attending the celebratory discourses of contemporary imperial/capitalist globalization.

Ethics and the Corner Store

KOREAN MERCHANT (Swinging a large push broom while shouting desperately in broken English): "Me no white, me no white, me no white. . . . I'm black . . . I'm black . . . I'm black. . . . You me, same. We same."

ML (indignant to the point of tears): "Same? . . . Me (hitting his own chest) Black. Open your eyes mutherfucker."

This well-known scene in Spike Lee's highly successful and critically acclaimed *Do the Right Thing* (1989) marks a kind of cinematic inauguration for the Korean immigrant merchant, who would become an increasingly significant figure in dominant and black imaginings of postindustrial ghetto space in the 1990s.[27] The film stages potentially explosive antagonisms in New York City between and within multiple racial ethnic groups, including whites, blacks, Asians, Puerto Ricans, and Jews. Lee's *Do the Right Thing* marks a convergence of historical processes by which the Korean immigrant merchant emerged as a highly visible trope in imaginings of the postindustrial urban ghetto: the rapid demographic increase of Korean immigrant businesses in large U.S. cities in the 1980s, mobilizations against Korean merchants in poor black neighborhoods, the unprecedented commercial success of young black filmmakers and other black cultural producers, and the discursive national production of the black urban ghetto as both nightmarish dystopia and object of voyeuristic consumption.[28] In this context, the figure of the Korean immigrant merchant needs to be read as both an empirical fact and a representational image. In other words, representations of the Korean merchant in film, music, or media cannot be seen simply as transparent reflections of "actual" people, dynamics, or events (such as the uprisings and boycotts). Rather, these figures are highly mediated signs engaging multiple ideologies around race, immigration, urban poverty, and citizenship: a narrative mechanism employed by cultural producers in their struggle to tell various stories about the meaning of race, national identity, and urban space in late twentieth-century America.[29] Consequently, these representations, which can be found in various cultural media (film, music, television, literature), are in a mutually constitutive relation with the social conditions they reproduce.

The figure of the Korean immigrant merchant in black neighborhoods is inextricably tied to a discourse of black urban poverty as social crisis and moral lack. In *Do the Right Thing*, we can see the extent to which national imaginings of black ghetto space are saturated by this discourse of ethicality and how Lee attempts to figure and ultimately resolve this burden by staging crucial moments of "choice." From its very title to the story line, *Do the Right Thing* depicts how mounting frustrations on the hottest day of the year in Bed-Stuy compel various characters to make a series of critical decisions that ostensibly shape life conditions in the neighborhood.

Among the multiple ethical choices staged throughout the film, viewers generally interpret Mookie's decision to initiate the destruction of Sal's Pizzeria as the film's key referential moment. As Lee has commented, this dominant reading privileges the destruction of private property as the central locus of concern while subordinating other crucial choices staged throughout the film: Sal's refusal to consider black representation on his "wall of fame"; his enraged decision to smash Raheem's boombox; the Koreans setting up a business in Bed-Stuy; Vino's resistance to completely capitulate to his older brother's antiblack racism; Buggin's declaration to boycott Sal's; and so on. Hence, despite the variety of characters (including business owners, policemen, firemen, the white gentrifier) in Bed-Stuy who make critical decisions throughout the film, audiences invariably fixate on the singular instance of white property destruction—the trash can through the window—as the film's central moral or ethical "moment."

If the urban ghetto constitutes a "social problem," then this pointed projection of ethicality onto ghettoized persons is not so much a nod to black agency as it is a disavowal by a national collective that ostensibly has no ethical matters to deliberate except the choices of the black urban poor. The film underscores irreconcilable subject positions that intersect in Bed-Stuy, complicating the seemingly straightforward imperative to "do the right thing," and thus self-reflexively engages with the burden imposed by a national collective that regards the solution to black poverty as the ethical development of the black poor into normative citizen-subjects. Yet even though Lee's film manages to complicate a reductive binary of right and wrong by generating mutually exclusive voices, the film nonetheless remains wholly within this framework of ethical choice.

As I use the term here, the representational *burden of ethicality* refers to a specific variation of the more general concept of the *burden of representation* facing nonwhite filmmakers and artists. Because racialized communities have been historically denied institutional access to the means of representation and have been subject to representation by dominant (white) imaginings of racial others, minoritized artists confront an "imperative" to produce counterimages and narratives that effectively contest racist ideologies. The most common and readily available representational strategy in response to this obligation is to directly invert dominant depictions, exchanging positive for negative images, good for bad, "real" for stereotypical, and so on. Furthermore, these representational demands extend to the filmmakers themselves insofar as the relative dearth of images burdens each cultural production with the (impossible) injunction to represent an entire community.[30] Kobena Mercer explains that in dominant British cinema and television, "blacks tend to be depicted either as the source and cause of social problems—threatening to disrupt moral equilibrium—or as the passive bearers of social problems—victimized into angst-ridden submission or dependency."[31] For the purposes of this chapter, I extend the notion of the ethical imperative that black artists properly "represent" in order to explain how this burden has been reconfigured in relation to contemporary black American film.

In my analysis, the burden of ethicality is specifically related to the construction of the black urban poor as not just a "social problem" but a problem of black morality. After 1965, when the full rights of citizenship were legally secured for African Americans, discourses of black cultural pathology (operative in various forms since the antebellum period) became a particularly important social force when African Americans gained formal legal equality with white citizens. The Moynihan Report (1965) is so frequently quoted because its discourse on how black social deviance reproduced poverty and black underdevelopment had enormous ideological and policy implications at a crucial moment in the history of black citizenship. The report's identification of single motherhood (emerging from a matriarchal tradition born from slavery) as posing a serious threat to the proper development of black masculinity consolidated social and biological discourses of "reproduction." This so-called deviance of black female sexuality and nonnormative family structures soon became the subtext of neoconservative political ideologies confining the "problem" of black urban poverty to the domain of black morality as part of a larger agenda of dismantling the welfare state.

This relationship between racialized citizenship and heteronormative development is not, by any means, new, having already been clearly visible in nineteenth-century ideologies of black racial uplift that prescribed normative gender and heteropatriarchal conventions as a crucial ideological means to demonstrate black entitlement to citizenship. Contemporary discourses of black social pathology index contradictions of black citizenship in the post–civil rights era, when abstract formal equality and political representation must be reconciled with the deteriorating material conditions of a black urban surplus. Discourses of black social pathology produce a specific narrative that requires black ethical development into a "normative" formation as citizen-subject.

As Roderick Ferguson writes, "The distinction between normative heterosexuality (as the evidence of progress and development) and nonnormative gender and sexual practices and identities (as the woeful signs of social lag and dysfunction) has emerged historically from the field of racialized discourse. Put plainly, racialization has helped to articulate heteropatriarchy as universal."[32] Ferguson's insights clarify the discursive mechanisms by which the black urban poor become signs of stagnation and underdevelopment in relation to contemporary discourses about Asian Americans as model minorities, who, after almost a century of exclusion, immigrated as family units in accordance with specific provisions of the Hart-Celler Act, more commonly known as the 1965 Immigration Act. The ubiquitous discourse about the strength, unity, and discipline of Asian American families is a far cry from the lurid nineteenth-century constructions of unimaginable depravities in Chinatowns crowded with alien male immigrants. As we shift to an analysis of how black film engages with a dominant discourse that demands normative black development as a condition of citizenship, we will see how imaginings of the Korean immigrant variously mediate this demand for ethical normativity.

In response to this dominant discourse, *Do the Right Thing* refuses to construct any of Bed-Stuy's local residents as "underdeveloped," representing the neighborhood alcoholic, the three cornermen, the angry "mob," and Mookie's propensity for taking long breaks as a pizza deliveryman, on their own terms—as already "legitimate" subject formations. However, while Lee rejects the demand for narratives of black development, he nonetheless operates within an overdetermined framework of ethicality. While this burden is elusive insofar as it comes from "outside" the text, Lee attempts to convert the burden of ethicality into a series of existential moments, to make it appear in the representational form of free choice. Hence, as in the case with Sal's Italian American–owned pizzeria, the Korean immigrant merchants in this film appear within this ethical framework, from the debate among the three cornermen about whether to patronize a Korean-owned business in a black neighborhood or in the crowd's deliberation and ultimate decision to not burn down their store: "Leave the Koreans alone. They're all right."

The presence of the Korean immigrant merchant in Bed-Stuy generates a series of competing positions on their place in the neighborhood. Scenes involving Da Mayor and Radio Raheem, who, respectively, purchase beer and batteries in the store, underscore the uneven insider/outsider relationships with the irritated, cursing Korean merchants repeating standard injunctions to "look what we have and buy," while Da Mayor tells them that "this ain't Korea, or China or wherever you come from. You get some Miller High Life in this fuckin joint," and Raheem famously states, "D mutherfucker, learn how to speak English first." But the film resists easy capitulation to these predictable insider/outsider discourses, and when the three cornermen—ML, Sweet Dick Willy, and Coconut Sid—turn to the subject of the merchants, Sweet Dick Willy interrupts ML, who is stating, "Look at those Korean muthafuckas across the street. I bet they haven't been off the boat a year before they open they own place." Intervening in this fairly standard nationalist discourse about black economic autonomy, Sweet Dick interrupts, "Coconut you got a lot of damn nerve, you got off the boat too. Hell leave me alone," punctuating his point by crossing the street to enter the Korean-owned store. While the film clearly exhibits nationalist impulses, from the thumping refrain of Public Enemy's "Fight the Power," to the characters' desires for black representation on Sal's Wall of Fame, the film also rejects purist conceptions of origin, partially due to the transnational formation of Bed-Stuy with its Nuyorican and West Indian black immigrant local residents. For this reason, the construction of the Korean immigrant merchant within the framework of "the foreigner," over and against the black American domestic subject is deliberately destabilized. The place of the Korean immigrant merchants therefore remains ambiguous, and the comic resolution of the scene in the preceding epigraph, "he's black, ain't that a bitch," highlights the absurdity of the Korean's claim while leaving the question open: What role will the merchants play in a low-income, predominantly black neighborhood, and will their racialization as nonwhites make any difference at all?[33]

The Boycotts

Spike Lee's film posed this question at a moment when Korean-owned markets had become the site of increasing conflict in predominantly black neighborhoods in New York City. As a result, merchant boycotts became a privileged means of articulating a range of grievances, from abusive treatment to the high price of goods to the lack of black-owned businesses in the neighborhood to murder.[34] The longest and most publicized of these was the "Red Apple" or Flatbush, Brooklyn, boycott of 1990, although there were at least four major mobilizations as early as 1981 in Jamaica-Queens, Harlem (1982, 1984/85), and Bed-Stuy, Brooklyn (1989). These antagonistic encounters between black residents and Korean green grocers captured national media attention, and the local coverage of the Red Apple boycott was so sustained and intense that it became a critical issue in New York's mayoral election politics.[35] Set in postindustrial black urban ghettos across the country, the dominant interpretive framework for understanding black grievances with Korean immigrant merchants in public discourse was one of "racial conflict" between two minority groups. But in regard to the question of the violent actions undertaken by the "two sides," this conflict was decidedly weighted in favor of the right to property and business. With the conflict prima facie decided on behalf of the owners, the focus more or less shifted to the legitimacy of the black-led boycotts.[36]

African American and Asian American public discourse, ethnic studies scholarship, and the dominant media increasingly questioned whether such black mobilizations represented legitimate political actions or were unseemly expressions of anti-Asian or, more specifically, anti-Korean racialized sentiments in poor black neighborhoods. A range of organizations, politicians, and intellectuals strongly objected to suggestions of anti-Korean racism while the dominant media's generally sympathetic representation of hardworking Korean immigrants either implied that black residents were lazy and resentful or just stated this explicitly while accusing black organizers of being opportunistic racists. Asian American public discourse weighed in ambiguously, fearing that Korean immigrants were functioning as convenient scapegoats, owing to their economic and spatial position as middle-men in a racially stratified society they had only recently entered. Korean immigrant merchants were almost invariably steadfast in regarding themselves as victims of anti-Korean racism, whereas second-generation Korean Americans were more likely to express more complex concerns about the exceptional history of black racialization, inflammatory media coverage, and the antiblack racial attitudes of some Korean merchants.

This discourse on the legitimacy of black critique and political action is carefully delineated in Claire Kim's *Bitter Fruit*, a brilliant sociological analysis of the Red Apple boycott in New York. By providing the context of the 1986 Howard Beach killing of Michael Griffith, and the Bensonhurst mob that killed Yusef Hawkins in 1989, *Bitter Fruit* highlights the deep political stakes (erased by media accounts) of the boycott's demand that two Korean immigrant-owned stores, implicated in assaulting a Haitian immigrant customer, be permanently shut down. Kim's concepts of *racial order* and *racial triangulation* enable a relational analysis of how Asians and other nonwhites are contingently and relatively located between whites and blacks, in which groups are differentially elevated or disciplined, depending on specific and shifting contexts. By constructing a macro paradigm of a U.S. "racial order," *Bitter Fruit* emphasizes that psychologizing and individuating discourses about "misunderstandings" or "intentionality" obfuscate a larger context of power relations in which all racial groups are in continual negotiation.[37] The text demonstrates how the pervasive middle-man, scapegoat, and "wrong place, wrong time" explanations undermine the legitimacy of black political grievances by translating black mobilization into "irrational," "misguided," or "racist" responses to the deplorable conditions of black urban poverty.[38] This dominant argumentative logic either explicitly or implicitly positions Korean immigrant merchants as neutral elements rather than as political/historical agents who are "actively negotiating the distinct opportunities and constraints presented within the American racial order."[39]

Kim's analysis and her concepts of racial ordering and triangulation help bolster my understanding and formulations of black and Asian American discourses of citizenship. *Bitter Fruit* is an urgent intervention in an existing body of scholarship and a dominant national discourse that implicitly or explicitly pathologizes the black urban poor. Consequently, the book must engage the terms by which antiblack racial ideologies are reproduced. These terms hinge on demonstrating the legitimacy of black political organizing against Korean merchants in New York City, as well as showing how Korean immigrant merchants negotiate to secure their position in a racial order. Part of *Bitter Fruit*'s intervention is its final determination that indeed, black political boycotts were both "fair" and decisively not anti-Korean. Kim contextualizes the ubiquitous and predictable racial slurs initially used by some of the boycotting black residents, ("yellow monkey," "fortune cookie," Why don't you go back where you belong," etc.) as the "unsophisticated lay participants [who] sometimes expressed racist sentiments against Koreans, [hence] the activists sought to make them understand that their real enemy was the system, not Koreans themselves . . . boycott leaders sought to discipline participants' behavior, purge racist sentiments from the picket line, and keep the boycott focused on racial oppression."[40] Boycott organizers, who knew that accusations of anti-Korean sentiment had undermined prior mobilizations, worked to eliminate any such traces in boycott flyers, announcements, and in the language of local residents.[41]

This imperative that boycott organizers disassociate black protests from anti-Asian sentiments is an ethical burden that Kim's study also carries, as both must work to "absolve" black political grievances from accusations of anti-Asian prejudice.[42] This burden highlights how the notion of racial fairness or a discourse of ethicality is a constitutive term of the racial order itself, which is reproduced in part through a presumptive evaluation of what constitutes legitimate political action. In various contexts, answering this imperative is a necessary counterresponse to dominant constructions that propagate a disingenuous "color-blind" neoconservative ideology and undermine the articulations of the black urban poor. Refusing to capitulate to the ethical determinations of citizenship, however, can also open up critical space to interrogate the legitimacy of the demand placed on both blacks and Asians for a moral self-accounting that disingenuously implies that racism and the exploitative nature of capitalism are their special burdens. I suggest that we can analytically claim (rather than deny) the "accusations" or "problematics" that are held against vulnerable communities in order to undercut and interrogate the moral authority of this discourse. The following section demonstrates what we can gain from examining how a discourse of black dispossession in relation to Korean immigrant merchants is overdetermined by a genealogy of American Orientalism.[43]

Immobility in the Hood

By the early 1990s, the Asian-owned corner store had become a ubiquitous signifier of an antiblack institution in dystopic cultural representations of black urban ghetto space, particularly in rap music and the related cultural institution known as the *hood film*.[44] The central organizing logic of these films—spatial containment under violent state repression—is not merely a critique of "the police" or even black criminalization but represents the hood as the spatial negation of black citizenship. Manthia Diawara observes that the conventional "escaping the ghetto" narrative is a developmental story in which a young black male protagonist struggles to overcome various obstacles to transcend the space of ghetto particularity and be incorporated into the national body.[45] Most of the films stage a central or subnarrative of failed development in which many main characters are killed as the story concludes, exemplifying the brutal consequences of denied mobility for the black urban male who has become irrelevant surplus to the nation.[46] Scholars of black film and popular culture note that these films consistently represent the black urban ghetto as a hyperregulated space produced by violent forces of state regulation that radically constrain possibilities of mobility.[47] In this manner, hood films explicitly engage and imagine the relationship between a specific black demographic space—the postindustrial black urban ghetto—and its precarious location in the U.S. national body.

John Singleton's seminal debut, *Boyz n the Hood* (1991), was a commercially successful and critically acclaimed film that won two Oscar nominations for best director and screenplay. Set in South Central Los Angeles where Singleton was raised, this particular black ghetto space had already been well inscribed into the national imaginary at the time of the film's release. NWA's phenomenally successful *Straight Outta Compton* (1988) and other "controversial" West Coast gangsta rap productions catapulted highly localized spatial geographies—Inglewood, Compton, Crenshaw, South Central—into international visibility as signifiers of black ghetto dystopias overrun with violence, drugs, and gang warfare. *Boyz n the Hood*, like other films in this loose genre, has a clear intertextual and material relation to rap, which was already generating a rapidly expanding market for music in which the black urban ghetto was a central locus, enabling "cross-promotional strategies" such as hiring high-profile rappers for central roles, soundtrack production, and the like.[48] The growing popularity of rap among white suburban youth remobilized an ever-present moral and social panic regarding black urban crime, primarily gang violence and drug warfare. Accordingly, hood films necessarily engaged with dominant discourses of black deviance and criminality that had become the commonsense lexicon in representations of the black urban poor and the spaces they inhabit.

If discourses of black citizenship demand ethical and moral development into heteronormative patriarchy as a precondition for national inclusion, then *Boyz n the Hood* dutifully responds to the call. The chronological narrative begins in 1984, the year that Tre is sent to live with his father, Furious Styles, after his mother, Reva, becomes alarmed that her intelligent and articulate son is having disciplinary problems at school. The film responds to discourses of black pathology by featuring a strong black father whose authoritative masculinity must displace Tre's strong and competent mother, who ultimately acknowledges that she "cannot teach him to become a man." We learn at the conclusion of the film that Tre, unlike his two closest friends who are shot and killed, has escaped the ghetto and is at Morehouse College, with his high school girlfriend "across the way at Spelman," providing the narrative with heteronormative resolution.

The film's message of racial uplift prescribes education, temperance, normative gender conventions, property ownership, and patriarchy as the means of black progress and survival. Alongside drugs, gang violence, and police repression, which are identified as obstacles to black masculine development, the film also cites Korean capital as a threatening and invasive force of black displacement, and the specter of the "foreign" is continually set in opposition to the domestic space of the hood. *Boyz* refigures the conventional trope of the Korean immigrant merchant into a signifier for much broader and otherwise more abstract processes of economic globalization that have restructured cities like Los Angeles in the post–civil rights period. From Singleton's use of sound to represent the oppressive and relentless hovering of Los Angeles Police Department (LAPD) helicopters to Tre's violent and dehumanizing encounter with the police, South Central ghettos emerge as contained spaces that render physical mobility and escape nearly impossible.

The film also makes frequent and varied references to ostensibly external global processes that shape black urban space. Critics observe that the film's opening shot of a distant plane flying behind a stop sign references a long-standing black leitmotif for the immobility and containment characteristic of the black urban ghetto.[49] Singleton's commitment to local specificity, however, further points to the physical proximity of Inglewood and one of the world's busiest airports, LAX, a literal and symbolic sign of how certain parts of Los Angeles are connected to a daily global flow of im/migrants, business executives, tourists, and commodities.[50] The high-tech warfare technologies that constitute the economic base of "Aerospace Alley" have failed to incorporate Inglewood's black surplus of laborers who are not producers but subjects of warfare technologies that have been adopted by the LAPD, which uses the most advanced technologies of surveillance and communication of any police force in the United States.[51] Inglewood's city borders are just one mile from LAX—the literal gateway to the Pacific Rim—and in contrast to interpretations that the opening shot marks the vast distance and discontinuity between ghettoized subjects and vehicles of mobility, the shot also indexes the film's imagining of how external global forces have already reshaped the black ghetto.

There is yet a more specific way in which external global processes are registered in the representation of ghetto confinement: the presence of Asia. The Korean merchant generally emerges as an index of interracial antagonism generated by the absence of black economic development in urban cities, enabling nonresident racial outsiders (whether Jewish, Arab, or Asian) to profit from the systemic denial of black economic opportunity. Despite the intense black public discourse on Korean-owned liquor stores in South Central when Singleton wrote the screenplay in 1990, the film chooses not to personify this by ever staging a Korean immigrant merchant on-screen. In place of direct characterization, we are offered an oblique form of visual consumption. The camera lingers on liquor storefronts, and parents articulate their fears about their destructive role in the neighborhood, particularly for black men. As she explains the rationale for her painful decision to send her son away to live with his father, Reva positions the liquor store as a privileged symbol in a future trajectory of worst possible nightmares: "I just don't want to see you end up dead, or in jail, or drunk standing in front of one of these liquor stores." The liquor store is clearly identified as an institution that generates a form of black social death akin to the fate of incarceration or actual death. This discourse reemerges when Furious links the ubiquitous presence of liquor stores and gun shops in black urban communities: "Why is it that there's a gun shop on almost every corner in this community? I'll tell you why. For the same reason that there's a liquor store on almost every corner in the black community. Why? They want us to kill ourselves." Although the "they" refers broadly to a historically antiblack dominant society, the immediate ownership of the liquor store is rendered unambiguous, as signs read "Seoul to Seoul Liquor," also written in the foreign script of Korean *hangul.*

In contrast to *Do the Right Thing,* such references are rather subtle, insofar as *Boyz n the Hood* opts to disembody a decade-long discourse about Korean immigrant merchant behavior in order to shift to a more materialist focus on Korean capital. Furious drives Tre and Ricky to an empty corner dirt lot in Compton and gestures toward a large billboard that reads "CASH FOR YOUR HOME: SEOUL TO SEOUL REALTY." As the camera focuses in on Furious with the phrase "SEOUL TO SEOUL" visible behind his face, he tells the boys and a small gathering of Compton locals:

> It's called gentrification. It's what happens when the property values of a certain area is brought down. . . . They bring the property value down, they can buy the land at a lower price, then they move all the people out, raise the property value and sell it at a profit. Now what we need to do is we need to keep everything in our neighborhood, *everything*, Black. Black owned with Black money. Just like the Jews, the Italians, the Mexicans and the Koreans do.

The dialogue itself never spells out what the billboard makes obvious: that Korean capital is identified as one of the driving forces of gentrification and black displacement in Compton, and in fact, this instance in Furious's monologue is the only time that "Koreans" are actually invoked in the film's dialogue. Unlike the South Central liquor stores, the majority of which were owned by South Korean immigrants, there is no similar correspondence to Korean real estate development and speculation in South Central, making the billboard particularly interesting.[52] In other words, the film widely recasts a black public discourse about Korean immigrants as disrespectful, rude, and racist merchants peddling liquor for profit in black neighborhoods and translates that individuated focus into a more critical abstraction of foreign Asian capital.

At one pivotal juncture in the narrative, Furious delivers a lecture on black economic autonomy and temperance, in which his occupation as a mortgage counselor and his general role as a strong, responsible black father consolidate a century-old discourse of black citizenship predicated on securing black patriarchal authority and property. The film generates a spatial map that attempts to reinscribe the hood within the boundaries of the U.S. nation by alluding to foreign interests that undermine possibilities of black citizenship. Korean capital is represented as a clear threat to the development of black masculinity (and consequently black community), in addition to "domestic" forces of repressive state violence, gang warfare, drugs, and irresponsible parenting. The yellow peril is recast here as a form of abstract capital invasion in which black citizenship has no purchase on these global forces of development.

This grievous displacement of black ghettoized communities from the national body due to globalization dramatically concludes the film when Doughboy, a criminalized gangbanger played by Ice Cube, is unable to find any sign that his brother's death has registered for a local or national collective. Still numb from Ricky's murder and from killing the men responsible, Doughboy—by far the film's most compelling character[53]—walks out in the early morning to deliver to Tre what has become an iconic, signature line. There has been little discussion of the larger context of what is considered one of the film's most powerful and moving monologues:

> Turned on the tv this morning. Had this shit on about how we're living . . . living in a violent world. Showed all these foreign places. How foreigners live and all. I started thinking man. Either they don't know, don't show, or don't care about what's going on in the hood. They had *all* this foreign shit. They didn't have shit on my brother man. I ain't got no brother. Got no mother neither.

Doughboy's quietly introspective delivery of this narrative of abandonment is inflected with a deep sense of pathos, and the scene constructs the visibility of "foreign places" and "foreign" people as a force of displacement that obfuscates the violent and brutal conditions that the black urban poor are left to negotiate on their own. The unmarked "they" names both the U.S. media as well as the national collective that forms its audience, and both are implicated in the abandonment of black American men whose nationality is marked by the reiteration of "foreign."

Doughboy's mournful lament of the irrelevance of black citizenship works powerfully as discourses of national and familial abandonment converge at this point in the film. The development of Doughboy's character is largely predicated on his subject position as the unclaimed, devalued, and rejected son in a family to which he nonetheless remains fiercely loyal. This metonymic relationship that the film creates between the national and biological family necessitates scripting the black mother as a key agent of black male abandonment to produce the moving sense of abjection in Doughboy's denied claim to national membership. But as the film attempts to reinscribe the hood within the boundaries of the U.S. nation by referring to foreign interests that undercut black citizenship, black Orientalism reveals the contradictions of this fantasy of the valued black citizen.

While *Boyz n the Hood* produces a narrative of unprecedented crisis in the expendability of black male life under globalization, the film interrupts its own premise as it recalls earlier conditions of black ghetto entrapment and the constrained value of black citizenship. This appears as a fleeting trace in the film when Furious tells Tre that after learning of Reva's pregnancy, he "went to Vietnam" to escape the fate of crime, prison, or death awaiting his friends. Furious's recruitment into the U.S. war in Vietnam is explicitly critiqued while nonetheless figuring as the institutional mechanism that facilitates his "escape" from an earlier formation of the black ghetto.

Such narratives recall the policy recommendations of the Moynihan Report (1965), which suggested that black men could develop into proper citizens, despite deviant black matriarchal communities, by joining the highly disciplined and "utterly masculine world" of the U.S. military.[54] The film's fleeting disclosure underscores the common acknowledgment that the Vietnam War, an unparalleled American signifier for psychotic and traumatized masculinities, offered black soldiers a rather salubrious alternative to living in U.S. ghettos. The recruitment of black males into the U.S. military marks an earlier "ghetto escape" narrative as well as an earlier configuration of the expendability of black life, in which young black men could emerge as U.S. citizens only on the battlefields of Asia, as foot soldiers and fodder of imperialist war.

While this peripheral detail in the film is mobilized to impart the black nationalist principle that "a black man ain't got no place in a white man's army," it simultaneously invokes a U.S. history of imperialist war in Asia, cold-war memories of Asian alien invasion that are now disavowed by contemporary metanational discourses of the "Pacific Century" that celebrate a global future of shared prosperity. Therefore, while the film situates the survival of the black community in opposition to the invasive threat of Asian capital, this discourse of black Orientalism cannot help but disclose the limits of black citizenship as well as how twentieth-century U.S. anticommunist wars in Asia created the conditions of possibility for Asian immigration and Asian foreign capital. In other words, late twentieth-century discourses of black disenfranchisement and black obsolescence under globalization invoke the repressed national history of U.S. imperialist war in Asia, a history that is officially disavowed and now projected as the ideological baggage of the "backward" black urban poor.

Fortified by a self-congratulatory discourse of cosmopolitan multiculturalism, this national displacement of cold-war imperialist memories onto the black poor is affirmed and reproduced in paradigms of interracial relations or black/Asian conflict. The analytic of black Orientalism historicizes the violence of black ghettoization under deindustrialization and globalization, turning to black popular culture to see how these processes are represented and understood and to analyze how Korean immigrant merchants signify in relation to those processes. By not condemning or praising Singleton's film as "hegemonic" or "resistant," this symptomatic analysis reveals that under the violent forces of economic globalization and ghettoization, black Orientalism expresses a yearning for a time and place when black citizenship and black lives were valued by the nation. The discourse itself underscores that such imaginings of black national redemption bear traces of nostalgia for something that never existed, since only earlier conditions of black entrapment can be invoked and recalled. We can recognize these contradictions in the film's fantasies of national redemption and how the discourse of black dispossession invokes the repressed national history of U.S. imperialism in Asia, which is now officially disavowed in the Pacific Century. Reducing this complex discourse to "anti-Asian hostility" capitulates to this national disavowal of violent imperialist militarization in the Asia Pacific, rendering that history as a moral or ethical defect of the black poor.

6

Asian Americans in the
Age of Neoliberalism

Human Capital and Bad Choices in

a.k.a. Don Bonus *(1995) and* Better Luck

Tomorrow *(2002)*

> *I am to be a weapon in the war against black America. . . .*
> *How does it feel to be a solution? Obviously it is easier to*
> *be seen as a solution than as a problem. We don't suffer*
> *genocidal poverty and incarceration rates in the United*
> *States, nor do we walk in fear and a fog of invisibility. To*
> *be both visible (as a threat) and invisible (as a person) is a*
> *strain disproportionately borne by black America.*
>   —Vijay Prashad, *The Karma of Brown Folk*

In most any critical discussion, contemporary discourses of Asian American socioeconomic "success" are regarded as a disciplinary construction deployed by white America against the black poor. Vijay Prashad paraphrases W. E. B. Du Bois's well-known line regarding white America's construction of a "Negro problem," to ask Asian Americans in the new millennium, South Asians in particular, "How does it feel to be a solution"? Prashad's text echoes earlier Asian Americanists in the late 1960s when he exhorts Asian America to refuse to be used by white supremacy as "a weapon against black folk" and to cultivate progressive solidarities with other people of color. Prashad's point that Asian Americans are posited as the "solution" to "the black problem" is an intertextual reference to Du Bois, but his language of "genocidal poverty and incarceration" also invokes the specter of the Holocaust and related questions of complicity in the aftermath of the final solution. The considerable ethical weight placed on Asian Americans "to do the right thing" in response to model minority discourse is one of the foundational elements of Asian American studies. Although this continues to be a necessary intervention, the political imperatives produced by globalization urge ethnic studies to ensure that this conversation remain linked to exploitative processes outside the United States, as it was during anti-imperialist struggles in the late 1960s and 1970s. I suggest that one possible approach is to center a discussion of neoliberalism in relation to Asian American racialization. If our concerns with "genocidal poverty" are broadened to a global scale, we will be prompted to examine discourses of Asian/American industriousness and success in relation to neoliberal ideologies that would link the brutalization of the U.S. black poor to the structural adjustment and austerity programs imposed on the global South in the wake of decolonization. This linkage widens the scope of critical inquiry while calling our attention to broader formations and epistemologies that demand interrogation. This chapter initiates that conversation by looking at how contemporary Asian American film engages with the dominant neoliberal mandates that have become so pervasive under the global restructuring of capitalism. I demonstrate how even a bourgeois, masculinist Asian American film can be read as exposing the dehumanizing instrumentalization of neoliberalism as well as the cynical hypocrisy of mantras of "personal responsibility" on the part of the elite.

Neoliberalism was popularized in the United States in the mid-1960s by a large group of University of Chicago economists whose anti-Keynesian theories served to legitimate the reshaping of national economies and social formations of Latin America and the rest of the global south.[1] More than just an economic program, neoliberalism presents the ideal conditions for global capitalism as the prerequisite for human freedom and liberation, making capitalist economic principles the basis for utopic social abstractions. George Schultz, a key member of the Chicago school and an economic adviser to Presidents Dwight Eisenhower and Richard Nixon before his appointment as secretary of state by President Ronald Reagan in 1982, gave this typical response in an interview, explaining that the Chicago school "stands for the fundamental value of freedom and, of course, in the economics realm its free markets, freedom of enterprise, freedom from undue regulation. So [it stands for] all of those kinds of things."[2] Formed in opposition to Keynesian economic theory, the key tenets of neoliberalism are deregulation, privatization, and the dismantling of social services—or what is now commonly referred to as "getting government out of the way." This often-repeated Americanism points to a particular kind of reorientation to and naturalized resentment of the state that is constituted by a neoliberal social order.[3] We can also see that neoliberalism has transformed dominant notions of citizenship in the United States insofar as the traditional citizen-subject of guarantees and entitlements from the state has been labeled as undeserving and an impediment to economic and social progress. Expectations of basic services and institutions, whether unemployment assistance, social security, health care, or higher education, are increasingly derided by neoliberal ideologies that deplore a national culture of "entitlement" and "handouts."

Since the global recession in the 1970s, neoliberalism has become the dominant political economic logic in opposition to the Keynesian economics that characterized the organization of capitalist expansion after World War II. Broadly understood as part of a "counterrevolt" to global antisystemic movements in the mid-twentieth century, neoliberalism is an ideology that has facilitated "extraordinary concentrations of wealth and power" and unprecedented scales of modern inequality.[4] As a set of theoretical principles legitimating political and economic restructuring in the interests of global capital, neoliberalism "proposes that human well-being can best be advanced by liberating individual entrepreneurial freedoms and skills within an institutional framework characterized by strong private property rights, free markets, and free trade."[5] Of course, the ostensibly noninterventionist state posited by U.S. neoliberalism is a fiction, as the state never ceases to violently facilitate capitalist accumulation, in the form of corporate subsidization, the imposition of structural adjustment programs that entrap the global South into debt dependency, or as a relentlessly aggressive, interventionist geopolitical force that produces and represses surplus populations. In other words, we can understand neoliberalism as a broad set of ideologies that narrate political processes of global class warfare as merely the mechanistic implementation of "free market" economic theory.

Understanding neoliberalism should be critical to the contemporary intellectual and political project of ethnic studies. As a worldview and logic that are to the material detriment of the vast majority who voice its truisms, neoliberalism in the U.S. national context secured ideological hegemony as a racialized gender discourse.[6] As Lisa Duggan concisely argues in *Twilight of Equality*, both white resentment and gendered normative outrage were crucial elements in the ideological project of mobilizing popular consent against not only social welfare programs but also public support of higher education and other publicly funded institutions. The familiar example of the "welfare queen" produced by the Reagan administration effectively mobilized popular support against public assistance (the majority of recipients of which are white) through an image of black female reproduction as a pathological excess sustained by the lifeline of welfare. Embedded in neoliberalism's ostensible rejection of an interventionist state, therefore, is an ethic of "personal responsibility," which in the United States was explicitly defined in negative relation to the black urban poor as subjects of state dependency. This process has been at the center of much of ethnic studies, which has always understood that the dismantling of the welfare state was legitimated by normative racial ideologies. Now, the greatest challenge to the social justice concerns of ethnic studies is no longer a discourse of "white backlash" but a discourse of multiculturalism and the valorization of cultural "difference" that are central to U.S. neoliberalism.[7]

The official discourse of multiculturalism sanctions U.S. military intervention under the auspices of antiracist equality and obfuscates various modes of exploitation under global capitalism. As James Lee argues in *Urban Triage: Race and the Fictions of Multiculturalism*, as both a national and global narrative, multiculturalism has not only done little to "stop the organized killing inherent in racism" but was widely incorporated and implemented as official discourse as poor racialized urban spaces were simultaneously decimated throughout the 1980s.[8] The neoliberal ideologies that attempt to naturalize global capitalism—the most significant existing force of inequality and exploitation—are now inextricably tied to racial inclusion and multicultural representation. In "The Spirit of Neoliberalism," Jodi Melamed writes:

> Multiculturalism portrays neoliberal policy as the key to a post-racist world of freedom and opportunity. Neoliberal policy engenders new racial subjects, as it creates and distinguishes between newly privileged and stigmatized collectivities, yet multiculturalism codes the wealth, mobility, and political power of neoliberalism beneficiaries to be the just deserts of "multicultural world citizens," while representing those neoliberalism dispossesses to be handicapped by their own "monoculturalism" or other historico-cultural deficiencies.[9]

Melamed draws our attention to the ways in which categories of racial difference in the United States have been radically altered in the past half century, shifting from what she terms a racial liberal state to a multicultural neoliberal state. Melamed examines how the inclusion of racial difference (whether into powerful state institutions or the privileged sector of professional labor) under global capitalism has produced a more flexible racialized regime of systemic inclusion and exclusion. Neoliberal multiculturalism

> sutures official antiracism to state policy in a manner that hinders the calling into question of global capitalism, it produces new privileged and stigmatized forms of humanity, and it deploys a normative cultural model of race (which now sometimes displaces conventional racial reference altogether) as a discourse to justify inequality for some as fair or natural.[10]

This incorporation of racial, gender, and cultural difference in multicultural neoliberalism should not be misread as some bad-faith "tokenism," insofar as operations of global capitalism are maximized through forms of inclusion that were denied under earlier regimes of accumulation, such as colonial capitalism or mid-twentieth-century U.S. industrialization. Cultural valuations are now ascribed in what were previously rigid monolithic racial categories: the "patriotic" versus "terrorist" Muslim, the properly developed black professional versus the pathological black poor, the law-abiding Latino distinguished from the *vato*, or the undocumented laborer.

Therefore, multiculturalism displaces white supremacy and racial liberalism in the late twentieth century as a dominant ideology. However, multiculturalism as an inclusive category of cultural difference is governed by a normative logic that is racialized, classed, and gendered. This is why, despite the liberal embrace of multicultural diversity that now extends to the U.S. presidency, the dominant discourses denigrating the black "underclass," the Muslim "radical fundamentalist," and the invasive Mexican "illegal" have remained more or less identical to their earlier incarnations. Such long-standing discourses about the "bad" racial other can remain intact largely because of the capacity of multiculturalism to displace and deflect the relevancy of racialized violence and inequality. In other words, as Melamed observes about the U.S. Patriot Act or about discourses of "cultural respect" at the U.S. prison for "enemy combatants" at Guantánamo, the acknowledgment of "good Arab Americans" or the U.S. state's distribution of Qur'ans to Muslim detainees is what ostensibly makes the detention and torture of a racialized enemy acceptable.

Although racial inclusion and a celebration of "diversity" in the United States are central to the neoliberal obfuscation of intensifying conditions of inequality, discourses of Asian American racial difference have a specific relationship to neoliberalism that demands closer elaboration.[11] Asian American studies has pointed to the emergence of model minority discourse in the mainstream media in the late 1960s (within months of the Watts riots) as an attempt to counter and contain intensifying black demands for redistributive justice.[12] Although historians have recently demonstrated that model minority discourse appeared earlier, in the 1950s,[13] there is ample evidence that since the nineteenth century, capitalists and the petit bourgeoisie have, at various points, favorably compared Asian immigrant workers to both black and white ethnic immigrant labor. I am unconcerned with identifying an originary moment, as it seems clear that relational comparisons arise in response to historically specific crises or configurations. Instead, I focus on post-1965 discourses of Asian American racial difference that emphasize education, family, parenting, and strong cultural values as an ideology that emerges not just in relation to the post–civil rights context of urban rebellion but also in relation to a broader set of neoliberal ideologies and principles that by the 1980s were systematically wreaking economic and political havoc throughout the world.

As Victor Bascara astutely observes, the racial production of Asian Americans as model minority "has uncanny similarities to emergent notions of globalization" and can be "understood as an argument for the changing role of the nation-state . . . bolstering the case for smaller government and privatization."[14] Bascara notes that figuring the Asian American as assimilable by dint of hard work and strong cultural values is part of a larger advocacy for a "noninterventionist" state with respect to racial and socioeconomic equality. We can thus approach the construction of the Asian American model minority not only as a domestic racial discourse but also as an expression of neoliberal principles. This enables us to extend the important point that Asian Americans have been deployed to undermine the legitimacy of black political grievances to a broader set of neoliberal ideologies that work to sanction and naturalize the global restructuring of capitalism. Key neoliberal concepts such as human capital, popularized by the Chicago school in the mid-1960s, are absolutely foundational to the production of the Asian American as an ideally self-enterprising, self-regulating subject. In other words, I contend that the proliferation of model minority discourse, which peaked in the United States in the 1980s, was largely due not only to its ideological function in pathologizing the black urban poor but also because this "model Asian American" embodied the ideal subject of neoliberal ideologies under global capitalism.

When Gary Becker published his seminal study, *Human Capital*, in 1964, he hesitated about the title, concerned about its possibly dehumanizing connotations in defining human beings in terms of market value. Twenty-five years later in 1989, Becker stated in a public lecture, "My, how the world has changed! The name and analysis [of human capital] are now readily accepted by most people not only in all the social sciences, but even in the media."[15] Since the early 1990s, as Becker himself notes, Democratic politicians have routinely used the language of "human investment" when advocating for increased funding in education or health care, in order to dodge the political bullet of Keynesian liberalism. Education, parenting, and job training are all regarded as "investments" in human capital that produce measurable rates of return in both increased productivity and higher wages.

Most simply put, the theory of human capital sidesteps the very notion of the capitalist exploitation of labor by proclaiming every individual a capitalist, the owner of the means of production of himself or herself. In his 1992 Nobel Prize lecture, Becker stated:

> Human capital analysis is so uncontroversial nowadays that it may be difficult to appreciate the hostility in the 1950s and 1960s towards the approach that went with the term. The very concept of human capital was alleged to be demeaning because it treated people like machines. To approach schooling as an investment rather than a cultural experience was considered unfeeling and extremely narrow.[16]

Becker theorizes that individuals (or their parents) rationally seek to increase rates of return through self-development, cultivation, and acquisition of skills and knowledge, and he argues that education is the most important form of human capital, followed by parenting/family and job training.[17] As a Chicago school economist, Becker supports his theories with quantitative methodology to provide empirical and "scientific" explanations for uneven social outcomes. For example:

Therefore, expenditures on children by parents without assets depend not only on endowments of children and public expenditures, as in equation (7), but also on earnings of parents (Yt-1), their generosity toward children (w), and perhaps now also on the uncertainty (e t-1) about the luck of the children and later descendants as in ct-1 = g*(Et', s t-1, Y t-1, e t-1, w), with g*Y >0.[18]

As Becker notes, his economistic approach to education and parenting as rational investments in an individual has become naturalized, as almost all social domains are now routinely understood through cost-benefit analysis. Opposed to recognizing an even potentially exploitative relationship between labor and capital, the theory of human capital evacuates power and politics from its rational choice-based analyses and extends and imposes an economic model on virtually all domains of social life under the authority of scientific empiricism.

The relationship between this concept of human capital and neoliberal economic principles such as privatization and deregulation might not seem immediately apparent, but the theory of human capital marks a radical retheorization of the human subject for a neoliberal global order as the "ultimate step in the elimination of class as a central economic concept."[19] By regarding each individual as an "enterprise" with an almost infinite capacity for "self-development," this kind of hyperprivatizing abstraction, as noted by Michel Foucault, changes the very definition in which "economics is not . . . the analysis of processes; it is the analysis of an activity . . . no longer the analysis of the historical logic of processes; it is the analysis of the internal rationality, the strategic programming of individuals' activity."[20] Drawing on Foucault, Aihwa Ong describes neoliberal governmentality as "resulting from the infiltration of market driven truths and calculations into the domain of politics . . . that inform the government of free individuals who are then induced to self-manage according to market principles of discipline, efficiency, and competitiveness."[21] We can see that the neoliberal theory of human capital and its notion of individual enterprise and self-regulation are not merely evident in Asian American model minority discourse but are also key tenets by which Asian American racial difference came to be defined in the post-1965 period.[22] The centrality of educational achievement and the importance of family in contemporary discourses of Asian American racial difference are no mere coincidence, as neoliberal theories of human capital championed education and parenting as the most critical investments promising the highest rates of return.

Since the late 1960s, Asian Americans have been increasingly represented in terms of socioeconomic mobility, competition, and market-driven instrumentality. These terms resonated quite negatively in the 1970s during U.S. economic recession when the nation was engaged in what was framed as a "trade war" with Japan's expanding export-based economy. Nationalist representations of an invasive enemy in which Asian/American productivity is represented as "robotic" or "machine-like" (thus lacking American ingenuity) were cold-war terms that would be contained and countered by the emergent "metanational" Pacific Rim discourse discussed in the previous chapter. Through the 1980s, Asian/American productivity and self-enterprise were resentfully regarded as racialized threats across class lines, as evidenced by the murder of Vincent Chin in Detroit by white auto workers and the crisis of "too many" Asian American students displacing white candidates at the nation's top universities.[23]

Through the early 1990s, these discourses of Asian/American competitiveness and ascendancy were clearly inflected by yellow peril imaginings, but I argue that characteristics attributed to post-1965 Asian Americans—competitive, self-enterprising, market driven, instrumentalizing, highly productive—are now generally valorized under neoliberalism and globalized capitalism. Although fears of a yellow peril will never disappear completely (history never stays in the past), I contend that an emergent popular discourse of globalization projects a flexible instrumentality (which is readily marked as an Asian/American formation) as universally desirable. For instance, in the celebratory treatise on the wonders of globalization that have "leveled" the world, Thomas Friedman's best-selling *The World Is Flat: A Brief History of the Twenty-first Century* described preparing one's children for the "flat world":

> How does an individual get the best out of it? What do we tell our kids? There is only one message: You have to constantly upgrade your skills. There will be plenty of good jobs out there in the flat world for people with the knowledge and ideas to seize them . . . my advice to them in this flat world is very brief and very blunt: "Girls, when I was growing up, my parents used to say to me, 'Tom, finish your dinner—people in China and India are starving.' My advice to

you is: Girls, finish your homework—people in China and India are starving for your jobs."[24]

Friedman's remarks about China and India are tinged with a U.S. nationalism that pervades his text, but he does not begrudge Asian foreign competition, which he regards as an inevitable force of globalization that produces innovation, growth, and, ultimately, human progress. Asians and Asian Americans appear frequently in his book as paragons of self-enterprise who are successfully riding the wave of globalization—instructive for all Americans who wish to compete in the twenty-first century. That is, Friedman advises jumping on the human capital bandwagon and firmly believes that Americans are situated to maintain global prominence/dominance in the new world economy if they do so.

My focus is not on Friedman's fairly predictable representation of Indians and the Chinese but on how Asian Americans have come to embody an ideal neoliberal subject that is constituted in terms of human capital. In this way, we can understand the rise of a discourse on Asian American "self-enterprise" as a symptom of the proliferation of neoliberal ideologies that not only discipline "bad" racial minorities but also constitute a neoliberal episteme. Asian American cultural production is thus uniquely situated to engage neoliberal "ways of knowing," in which economistic mandates of self-cultivation, self-enterprise, and privatization resonate as an Asian American racial formation.

The contradictions in this relationship between neoliberalism and Asian American racialization are explicit in both Justin Lin's mainstream commercial feature film, *Better Luck Tomorrow* (2002), set in an elite, gated suburban enclave in Orange County, California, and the independent documentary *a.k.a. Don Bonus* (1995), a Cambodian refugee hood narrative set in some of San Francisco's poorest neighborhoods. Both films negotiate neoliberal discipline by recognizing various modes of dislocation as forms of Asian American racial exclusion. My analysis explores the unexpected ways in which these films disclose the violent regulation of neoliberal formations as self-sufficient, multicultural, and market-driven subjects of self-enterprise.

Pairing these two radically disparate films inevitably animates discussion about how to understand Asian American mobility and the significance of Asian American racial difference under global capitalism. In the post–civil rights era, the heterogeneity of any racial group—be it African American, Latino, or Asian American—is indisputable, but class and socioeconomic mobility particularly have emerged as the most visible contradiction of any homogenizing conception of Asian American as a racial identity. For Asian American studies, a field that grew out of an investment in defining Asian Americans as a racial minority in political solidarity with blacks, Native Americans, Latinos, and Vietnamese in anti-imperialist struggle, the class demographics of Asian Americans after 1965 have been largely received as a challenge or a crisis, threatening to undermine a cohesive racially politicized identity. It is important to note that what has been recognized as a crisis in Asian American studies since the 1980s is symptomatic of a larger post–civil rights shift in understanding and theorizing race under neoliberalism. For instance, in the past five years after both Hurricane Katrina and the election of Barack Obama as president, there have been urgent and frequent questions regarding how to understand the violent systemic containment of the black poor in relation to processes of black incorporation.[25]

In Asian American studies, a film like *a.k.a. Don Bonus* gets a tremendous amount of play in courses, colloquia, and cultural events. There is an understandable impulse to screen this documentary about a Cambodian refugee teenager in San Francisco's most impoverished neighborhoods in order to complicate the dominant imaginings of Asian American bourgeois formations that populate U.S. university campuses and corporations. The video-journal form of the documentary easily lends itself to being viewed as self-evident, unmediated "reality," and its representation of Asian refugee/immigrant poverty and displacement is always already the critical intervention, that is, making Asian American poverty visible.

In his reading of *a.k.a. Don Bonus,* Peter Feng warns against having "too much faith" in the "video diary as an organizational conceit."[26] Rather than situating the Cambodian refugee subject as a vague counterpoint to the elite "model minority" formations of *Better Luck Tomorrow,* I examine how both these films bear out various contradictions of neoliberal ideologies. This framework produces a counterintuitive analysis that undercuts the presumption that a refugee working-class narrative is always a "critical" text in opposition to a film that focuses on privileged suburban Asian American youth. Whereas the cynical narrative of *Better Luck Tomorrow* renders the discourse of multicultural neoliberalism as a transparently pathological and instrumentalizing ethos, there is no such leisurely critical distance in the refugee documentary. This juxtaposition clarifies how those who are subjected to the traumatic sociopolitical violences represented in *a.k.a. Don Bonus* are likely to be the most intensely disciplined by the punitive ideologies of neoliberalism.

The Politics of Asian American Suburban Angst

Justin Lin's *Better Luck Tomorrow* (2002) discloses an unexpectedly interesting perspective on the relationship between Asian American racialization and neoliberalism. *Better Luck Tomorrow* has a significant place in Asian American cinematic history as the first independent production to be purchased by a major distributor, MTV Productions, and Paramount Studio. A story about four hyperachieving Asian American male adolescents in their senior year of high school, the film might be easy to dismiss as merely the self-indulgent masculinist angst of privileged Asian American suburban kids. But the film reveals how the market-driven instrumentality of four male teenagers and their high-achieving cohort is a brutally violent mode of dehumanization and alienation, eviscerating all utopic abstractions of neoliberal "freedoms."

The opening shot of *Better Luck Tomorrow* focuses on a slow-moving iron gate that the camera eventually moves past to enter the space of the gated suburban community where the story takes place. Whereas *Boyz n the Hood* (1991) opens with a stop sign that literally signposts the negation of spatial or social mobility in the black urban ghetto, the gates and fences in *Better Luck Tomorrow* signify the privatizing consolidation of abundance for those who have access to these protected resources. We are shown meticulously maintained football fields, basketball courts, parks, schools, homes, and newly paved streets against expansive backdrops of sunny blue skies, and the strategic use of lighting and color heightens the simulacral, artificial quality of this elite suburb. The Asian American protagonist and his three Asian American male friends are located in a space in which the trajectory of socioeconomic mobility is an inevitable part of the film's social landscape. In the film's opening line, "Are you done yet?" the absent referent (early admission Ivy League applications) punctuates the presumption and utter certainty underlying these characters' futures. This ascendant class of Asian American professionals cannot be disentangled from the dominant discourse that pathologizes the black poor, whose absence from this suburban enclave is definitive of racialized economic segregation and the American dream. The film has no visible engagement with the black poor but reacts to model minority discourse with a masculine fantasy of Asian American recalcitrance to neoliberal mandates. Even though the characters appear to be poised for full incorporation into a multiracial global economy, they are nonetheless represented as feeling excluded from a black-white homosociality, which is clearly not the same axis of racial exclusion that we see in *No-No Boy*, operative before 1965.

The film's Filipino American protagonist, Ben Manibag, epitomizes a properly developed subject for the professional labor market under globalization with his wide range of skills and activities that he relentlessly works to cultivate. He catalogs his endless array of college prep activities, from SAT exam prep, training for academic decathlon, varsity sports, and repeated commendations for food court "employee of the month," to more altruistic civic service such as volunteering at the hospital, participating in canned-food drives, and organizing beach litter cleanups, since as he explains, "You just can't count on good grades to get into a decent school anymore." Ben's diversified daily regimen is highly disciplined, precise, and exacting with an emphasis on quantification and measurable returns, down to a hundredth of a point:

> I shoot 215 free throws a day. My goal is beat Calvin Murphy's record of 95.85%. That's 207 baskets. Punctilious: Marked by or concerned about precise and exact accordance with the details of codes and conventions. To get a perfect score on my next SAT, I needed to improve my verbal score by 60 points. I picked a new word everyday and repeated it over and over again. They say if you repeat something enough times it becomes a part of you.

The rigorous self-discipline required to constitute oneself as the ideal candidate for the competitive market is not marked as idiosyncratic but as characteristic of a larger constituency of students, all similarly engaged in a frenzy of self-cultivation: "Lunchtime was clubtime. This was where everyone loaded up on their extracurricular activities for their college app." Such deliberate calculation and empiricist instrumentalization of every social action (what neoliberalism calls "rational choice" or even "freedom") is represented not as heroic self-enterprise but as objectifying and cynical self-interest: "As long as I could put in on my college app, it was worth it."

The shameless drive to compete effectively in the market is shorn of any liberal pretense of principle or anachronistic ideologies of meritocracy. As Ben is shown running down a hospital corridor rushing to his next activity of translating for Spanish-speaking patients, he states, "Unfortunately, all the really worthwhile things in high school were few and far between." We see an organized commercial network by which students are assured of higher grades ("cheating"), and notions of "ethics" necessarily become negligible variables in a calculus of self-interest. As Daric, the most smug and entitled of the group, explains to Ben: "You know this is all bullshit right? It's just a game. People like you and me, we don't have to play by the rules. We can make our own. . . . Cheat sheets? It's easy money. Ben, it's easier than fuck."

The cynicism implicit in neoliberal ideology is represented in the film as utterly pathological, leading to the messy murder and dumping of an Asian American male rival, compelling one of the characters, Virgil, to attempt suicide with a gunshot to the head. Daric's first line when he walks into Virgil's hospital room is a dismissive question of damage assessment, "Is he gonna be retarded or something?" before switching immediately into a mode of self-preservation: "Do you think he's going to talk? Let me think. . . . Let me work this out." This unadorned, transparent logic of "rational" self-interest and cost-benefit analysis is casually captured in peripheral dialogue throughout the film, such as when the students are training for their debates: "All right, the topic is population control. Why retarded children and handicapped people should be executed in order to keep the population down. Ready?"

Even ostensibly "progressive" political activism is repudiated in the film as a meaningful mode of social collectivity. In one of several montages of Ben's dizzying array of extracurricular activities, which include school basketball, choir, volunteer work, and academic decathlon, he is shown carrying a sign, "Vote No on 187," with a look of defiant determination, his mouth open in midchant. The film depicts a process by which all activities are turned into abstract equivalents for the purpose of becoming an ideal, highly competitive candidate for the country's most selective university admission boards. Ben's opposition to draconian state legislation targeting California's undocumented immigrants therefore becomes yet another sign of a neoliberal subject formation that is desirable rather than threatening to the elite Ivy Leagues. All acts of civic participation, whether translating doctor's orders for a Latina mother, collecting cans for the food bank, or organizing an early morning volunteer beach cleanup, are represented as entirely consistent with the neoliberal trumpeting of individual volunteerism that shifts the responsibility of social reproduction away from capital and the state. Although the phrase "compassionate conservatism" might sound like a disingenuous smoke screen, we might understand such notions as less a "ruse" than as critical elements of neoliberalism, in which individual altruism displaces a centralized social safety net.

While the role of parenting is of paramount significance in hood films and black public discourse, it is noteworthy that parents do not appear at all in *Better Luck Tomorrow*. The irrelevance of parental figures to the film's narrative arc underscores how these high-achieving Asian American teens emerge into representation as thoroughly self-regulating subjects. While the absence of black fathers in the hood film genre thematically constitutes the narrative of ghetto entrapment, the nonappearance of parental figures in *Better Luck Tomorrow* implies an Asian American subject formation in which discipline has been thoroughly internalized. Through peripheral detail, we learn that Daric Lu has his own place, since his parents actually live in Vancouver and that Steve's parents are away for months at a time in Europe: traces of the "flexible citizenship" of an Asian diaspora managerial class consisting of "mobile managers, technocrats, and professionals seeking to both circumvent and benefit from different nation-state regimes by selecting different sites for investments, work, and family relocation."[27] The systematic rigor by which these teens strive to increase test scores and performance stats, to compete more effectively in sports, student government, and academic decathlons without parental discipline heightens the sense that each character has become entirely self-regulating in his relentless drive for more human capital.

The strategic instrumentalization of every aspect of social life produces recalcitrant desires, and the four Asian American male protagonists engage in petty crimes, beginning with selling cheat sheets, dealing meth and coke, committing various acts of grand theft, and finally escalating to murder. The line between legality and illegality is almost imperceptible, and the four teenagers continue to build their college applications along with their new exploits: "It just made sense to expand our business into drugs, putting the law of supply and demand into practice. I think our teacher would've been proud." Ben states, however, that they began their stint of petty crime not so much for the money but because "it just felt good to do things that I couldn't put on my college application." Interestingly, because this neoliberal formation is understood in the film as part of the process of being racialized as Asian American, the economization of every domain of social life appears in the film with more critical distance. Recalcitrance for the sake of transgression is racialized for these characters, since their self-cultivation is regarded and experienced (in the film's worldview) as a model minority formation.

Subsequently, the boys struggle against neoliberal mandates in reaction to the passivity and emasculation implied by a racial discourse of

Asian Americans as hardworking, studious, and obedient. Any critical distance in the drive to self-cultivate for the capitalist market emerges as an Asian American masculinist response to being racialized as a model minority. One scene depicts an evening of "study group" (with the rest of the decathlon team) involving an all-nighter of snorting meth and coke, binge drinking, and partying. While the frenetic montage builds to create a sense of transgression, the montage and music wind down, with Daric paying a white stripper at the end of the night, who asks, "So what are you guys? Like a math club or something?" None of the good-looking, chain-smoking cast of Asian American male characters are portrayed as emasculated techno-nerds, yet the film stages scenes of Asian American "exclusion" from an imagined black/white homosociality. At a party, a group of mostly white jocks ridicule the group as they walk in: "Hey, what's up boys . . . uh, I think they have Bible study next door, right? Oh no shit, look at this. It's the Chinese Jordan." The Bible study reference and the absurdity of an Asian male embodying the black masculine prowess of Michael Jordan index the usual elements of the passive and obedient feminized subject of model minority discourse.

As a consequence, the characters recognize the mandate for continual self-cultivation and instrumentalization as part of their gendered racial formation as Asian Americans. Although this is a misrecognition of sorts because neoliberalism is generally a dominant episteme of the U.S. social formation, it is also not inaccurate, insofar as the racialization of Asian Americans as model minority is inextricably bound up with neoliberal precepts of human capital. Subsequently, their masculinist reaction against a racialized "model minority" discourse is the space where an interrogation of neoliberal principles emerges in the absence of a critical vocabulary regarding global capitalism.

Representing Asian American Poverty

In contrast to the "rules don't apply to people like us" ethos that characterizes the hyperelite universe of Better Luck Tomorrow, a.k.a. Don Bonus (1995) emerges from social spaces that neoliberalism has pathologized as impediments to economic progress. Far from the meticulously maintained football fields, basketball courts, parks, schools, and homes in the gated community in Better Luck Tomorrow, this documentary is set in San Francisco's Tenderloin district and one of the city's worst public housing projects. In the early 1990s, filmmaker Spencer Nakasako joined the Vietnamese Youth Development Center in San Francisco to run a media program that lent Southeast Asian teens video cameras to document their lives. Sokly Ny (who renamed himself Don Bonus in a gesture of Americanization) was one of these participants, and Nakasako edited a year's worth of footage to produce the fifty-five-minute documentary, *a.k.a. Don Bonus*, which won an Emmy for cultural programming, in addition to numerous film festival honors.

In Don's documentation of his last year in high school, we see this likable Cambodian teen struggle to negotiate the fragmentation, alienation, and violence of refugee displacement and urban poverty. As the narrative unfolds, we witness Don's isolation, stark living conditions, remote and indifferent teachers, and efforts to graduate from a low-performing working-class high school.[28] Midway through the documentary, Don's younger brother, Touch, is arrested for attempted murder when he fires a gun at a black student at school. The contrast between Don's putative "success" of (barely) graduating and Touch's criminal "failure" provides the narrative with one of its dramatic oppositions. But perhaps the most painful aspect of this documentary is the earnestness with which it reproduces the dominant ethos of neoliberalism that is so casually exposed as an utter fraud in the fictive world of *Better Luck Tomorrow*. In a documentary shot through with violence, we can see neoliberal regulation as the overarching frame through which this working-class refugee teen laments his failure to resolve his life conditions with better choices and more personal responsibility.

The protagonist's sense of being a failed and undeserving subject pervades the film, and he imagines the most trivial instances of undisciplined behavior as signs of the illegitimate deficiency of his subjecthood. Aihwa Ong's ethnographic study of Southeast Asian refugees demonstrates that in daily encounters with state institutions such as the welfare office or hospital, "Cambodian refugees were constituted as particular kinds of unworthy subjects who must be taught to become self-reliant, to be accountable for their situation."[29] Ong argues that from the trauma of being remade under the brutal Khmer Rouge to moving to Thai refugee camps and resettlement agencies, U.S. institutions became an authoritative regime of patronage and pedagogy that refugees negotiated in their struggle for resources. We see the traces of this disciplinary regime that produces a "grateful" self-correcting subject in Don's orientation to his poor educational performance. After failing a proficiency test in composition that is required for graduation, Don returns home and, in confessional mode, faces the camera:

I took the competition [*sic*] test and the result is that I flunk. I fail. . . .
The reason is I cut too much, and didn't pay any attention to teachers. And I don't, I'm also lazy. I don't want to do all the homework.
I feel like, kinda regret it, 'cause actually, I should do this, I should
do that. I should read. I should pay attention. I should ask questions.
I should, you know, ask someone to help me. You know, all of done
with that thing. But I didn't do that, I was so stupid. I had a feeling
I'm not able to be finishing, not finishing high school. Sometime I
feel like, What's the use of going school?[30]

The long monologue has a compulsive quality in its overload of proclama-
tions of individual failure and lack of self-development, a kind of mimetic
recitation of a biopolitical rationality. Despite what his failing grades
might suggest, Don is not simply a "bad" subject who fails to self-regulate.
On the contrary, we see him internalize the mandates of self-cultivation
and discourses of personal deficiency central to the state's processing and
resettlement of Southeast Asian refugees. Fearing that he will not graduate, Don later obtains the test question from other students so he can
write his essay the night before, creating an overstated sense of shame
that emerges privately after passing the exam. Back inside the apartment,
he hangs his head dejectedly as he explains that his family will not attend
his graduation, which falls on the same day as Touch's court hearing: "So
just be me in my graduation. I don't deserve a diploma. I don't deserve
a diploma." Don's intense self-disciplining is symptomatic of not only a
class location subjected to the corrective rationalities of welfare policies
but also of the geopolitical category of racialized refugee, rescued by the
benevolent authority of the U.S. state.

Don's sense of underdevelopment takes on a particular racialized
dimension that is registered in his intense yearning for community in the
form of family. The video-journal form of the documentary highlights the
isolation of the protagonist, who frequently speaks directly to the camera
in his empty apartment that is barely furnished, with clothes and garbage
scattered throughout and a bed sheet tucked behind the barred windows.
Don arrives home and walks us through his apartment, opening up doors
to empty bedrooms to confirm his point:

So now it's 9:31 and guess who's home. My mom, she's not here. My
younger brother Touch, he's not here. Only me at this minute. Well,
it's always been like this. This place, you know, always empty since

my brother Touch ran away. He been gone for like three months 'cause he's scared to live here. . . . My mom, she's not home, 'cause she with her husband Downtown. Actually, this place, she rented for us because me and Touch don't get along with stepfather. I never knew my real father. I never seen his face. I never know what he look like. . . . He sacrifice himself to the Khmer Rouge so he could save us from them. So now, we survive in America. Shit. I don't think nobody think about him no more."

The absence of parental figures in the documentary does not provide the occasion for adolescent freedom but, rather, is the source of Don's greatest trauma as he experiences his family's increasing fragmentation, which had begun in Cambodia. Throughout the film, Don frequently expresses a longing for some form of parental authority: "Some Asian parent . . . they tell the child to be home on a certain day . . . my family's different." He breaks down crying midway through the film about his oldest brother's increasing distance after getting married and having a baby:

And then I started talking. And I start crying some more. I cry and cry. I told him I miss him a lot. And how come he stay away from the family for so long? And he say he gotta take care of his own thing. He's been working hard, do studying. He don't have his time for wife too. Sometime his wife is mad at him, and he say he gotta take care of his wife first, as a family. His family. And that's when I said, *What about me?* To myself, I said to myself, *What about me? I'm your brother. Ain't that family? Ain't that important?*

Don's emotional vulnerability to his eldest brother, Chendara, whom he refers to as "the one who carry me through the jungle" when they fled Cambodia, produces intense sympathy without necessarily indicting Chendara. Instead, his brother's absence is ideologically rationalized by normative gender conventions that shift his patriarchal responsibilities to his wife and child. Although Chendara's increasing distance from Don is explained as regrettable but inevitable, there is no analogous explanation that can sufficiently account for the conspicuous absence of Don's mother.

Consequently, the figure of the mother in the film bears an incredibly heavy burden to somehow compensate for the violences wrought by imperialist war, global capital, and a "noninterventionist" state. Don's mother's absence is frequently highlighted throughout the film, and even though his animus is reserved solely for his stepfather—"I don't give a damn about him. I hate his gut"—the narrative generates an implicit question about the mother's choices and the consequences for the rest of the family. We can see in the following passage that the mother's role as an emotional, nurturing force cannot be disentangled from the reproductive labor necessary to produce the domestic sphere as a site of comfort.

> "Eight days since she been gone and I feel lonely. There's no person that greet me when I go home at end of day, Hi, how you're doing? How's your day today? None of that shit. 'Cause the few times I walk in the house, and I see trash and the dishes not wash. And there's not food and everything. I just get pissed off. I just pick up things and throw it all over the places."

Don's frustration and despair with his sordid, poor living conditions are articulated as a narrative of maternal absence. The discourse of parental responsibility emerges explicitly when after Touch's arrest, Don persuades his reluctant brothers to talk about Asian immigrant teens who end up in the U.S. criminal justice system. An older brother makes the general statement, "Blame the parent. . . . Even this kid, too! Look at him! (points to baby nephew). . . . Blame the parent. If you don't spend more time, the kid will be bad, upset. It go around. Should stay home talk to them a little bit more."[31] While his statement is not directed at their own mother and she is never overtly criticized in the film, this dominant narrative of parental responsibility entails a culturalist explanation that displaces the forces of state violence. This is ideologically reified when toward the end of the film, Don states that "one good thing when Touch got arrested. My mom she's a lot more into the family. Like the family more together now." From the impoverished spaces produced at the nexus of global capitalism, ghettoization, and state violence, we see expressions of the deepest investments in notions of uplift, normative family cohesion, and the importance of good choices.

Don does not link parental absence to Touch's problems, but he produces a narrative of anti-Asian racial antagonism and black criminality to account for Touch's arrest and incarceration. As in many other U.S. urban centers, Southeast Asian refugees have been settled by the state into some of the poorest and, by consequence, predominantly African American residential spaces, and the construction of blackness as a social threat figures prominently in the documentary's narrative. Don is shown frequently lying low in the project apartments, clearly feeling under assault as kids break the apartment windows or when his sister's unit is robbed for the second time. He states:

> We live in Sunnydale for two or three years, and it's the worst. Those people treat us like shit. They call us Chinamen. He tell you from experience, they mugged him, they take his jacket, they take his money. They take his fast pass every day when he go to school. He look around, first look out the window, see any black kids hanging around. 'Cause he scared of black, 'cause what they done to him, they have affected him. Not just black or whatever, it seems like whoever. If you have hard time in life and people push you around too much, black, white, Chinese, Mexican, my own kind, Cambodian, or whatever.

Don's narrative of anti-Asian antagonism and black criminality is seemingly interrupted by a mediating question as the scene has an editing break before his qualifying statement that the problem was "not just black" but anyone who pushes another too far. This modifying qualifier that it could be anyone, however, is not altogether convincing, as the documentary repeatedly shows Don and his sister's family feeling under assault in a black residential space. The housing projects constitute a racialized space of entrapment for Don and his family members, who are afraid to go outside, cautiously peeking out behind blinded windows and turning off lights to avert any possible attention from their neighbors.

After a second robbery, the family moves out of the Sunnydale projects to the skid-row area of San Francisco known as the Tenderloin where this multiracial ghetto space offers both anonymity and familiarity. Although this space allows Don a temporary escape from the projects, this reprieve is qualified by the spatial confines of ten people living in a studio apartment, with their climactic move yet to come. The clearest sign of being freed from black ghetto space arrives in the form of official (state) intervention:

> We're moving out of the TL because of what happened to us back in Sunnydale. When we got harassed and robbed of everything and had to move, we complain to the Housing Authority. Well, the Housing Authority had finally agreed to help us and has given us something called Section 8... [Walking into the new apartment] Wow, mm, Wow. All my life, we never had a house like this, which is big and

nice and in quiet environment. It's right next to Golden Gate Park. We have our own backyard. And I have my own room.

When the family moves into this bright, sunny, large apartment in the Sunset District, the scene constitutes a rare and powerful sign of progress and mobility in a narrative otherwise characterized by fear and isolation. Section 8, in both design and rhetoric, functions to counter the deplorable failure of public housing with superior housing options made possible by the wonders of the private market. The developmental story behind the family's move from the public to private housing sector, however, is much more vexed than it initially appears.

The complaint Don refers to that facilitates the family's move out of Sunnydale was no informal or individual matter but part of a 1993 class-action suit filed by the Asian Law Caucus (ALC) against the San Francisco Housing Authority (SFHA).[32] The ALC filed the suit on behalf of more than one hundred Vietnamese and Cambodian immigrant families in seven separate public housing projects, charging the city with wanton disregard for the safety of Asian American residents. The federal civil rights complaint argued that Asian American residents were essentially being denied fair access to housing when the Housing Authority failed to adequately respond to racially motivated attacks.

The triumphal scene of Don's family walking into an expansive, sunny, second-story apartment functions not only as a narrative trope of progress that hinges on their evacuation from black public housing but is also predicated on a legal conflict that is elided in the film's narrative of Asian uplift. ALC filed two lawsuits, in 1993 and again in 1998, in an effort to pressure the SFHA to respond to the Asian American residents' complaints of being targets of racial violence.[33] Assaults reported by the Asian immigrant residents in public housing ranged from numerous shootings (one of them fatal)[34] to beatings, robbery, vandalism, cars set afire, stone throwing, and children being beaten and spray painted.[35] The ALC argued that the racial epithets "chink," "gook," and "chinaman" were clear evidence that Asian immigrants were being racially targeted, without identifying the race of their antagonists, which was irrelevant to the legal argument as well as politically incendiary in multicultural San Francisco.

The Housing Authority denied liability but reached settlement with the ALC, and officials agreed to a number of procedures to ease racial tensions, including provisions that would "allow Southeast Asian residents to transfer more easily to other housing complexes."[36] The ALC was asked to file a second amended complaint omitting all claims to racial harassment, and the action was dismissed pursuant to the settlement.[37] Neither case produced legal precedent (the ALC's aim was to pressure the Housing Authority to move Asian immigrant families as soon as possible), but both suits provide an instructive index of how racial advocacy groups struggle to work with existing legal parameters of civil rights for disenfranchised minority groups. Signaling a shift in strategy from the previous 1993 case, the discourse of black/Asian racial conflict was minimized by the ALC's lead attorney, Gen Fujioka: "You can't just address the racial tensions without addressing the overall conditions of violence in the projects. . . . I don't see this conflict as being between blacks and Asians. . . . What you have are small groups of people picking on families that are isolated and vulnerable."[38]

In this press statement, Fujioka observes that all residents are entitled to safe and crime-free housing, stressing that the violence endured by Asian immigrant residents would be best eliminated by improving the overall conditions of public housing. Given that there is no legal provision to challenge racialized poverty in this manner, the only strategy available to the ALC is to demonstrate that the racial difference of Asian immigrant residents makes them specifically vulnerable to the crime and violence in the city's worst projects. The racialized warehousing of the black urban poor that produces the conditions of possibility for such violently concentrated spaces of poverty cannot be addressed by the state except through the repressive arm of incarceration. The scope of civil rights as a form of racial protection for impoverished Asian Americans in these instances can address the violence of black criminality but not the larger geopolitical violences of imperialist war, refugee displacement, racialized urban poverty, and racial segregation.

The ideal response that Fujioka astutely suggests—to improve the overall conditions of public housing, racialized poverty, and black ghettoization—reveals an unstated problematic. The limited capacity of the law implied by Fujioka works to highlight that in the absence of racial epithets, black residents cannot challenge their subjection to the violence of public housing as a violation of their civil rights. Nonblack residents in the worst public housing can make such an appeal insofar as the violent crimes they endure are likely to be accompanied by racial epithets—signs of racialized animus. We can see that in this instance, the Fair Housing Act mobilized by the civil rights movement operates as a legal mechanism by which Asian immigrants' access to safe housing effectively means moving away from poor black residents. This equation of better housing conditions with spatial distance from black poverty is not an antiblack attitude or a product of racial prejudice on the part of the ALC or Asian immigrants, but a systemic effect of racial segregation. A century of socioeconomic processes of racial ghettoization has methodically generated real economic value, greater resources, and tremendous wealth for a middle class through the exclusion and spatial containment of poor black communities.[39] The hypersegregation of the black poor through public policy and institutional practices has produced deplorable living conditions that are the most difficult for black residents to leave.

The literal movement away from spaces of black poverty to better living conditions is related yet distinct from the representation of that movement as mobility and progress. For example, the hood films discussed in the previous chapter are characterized by a narrative of black entrapment, in which leaving or escaping the ghetto is the implied resolution. In the case of *a.k.a. Don Bonus*, the family's move from the Sunnydale projects, to the Tenderloin, and finally to the Sunset District entails greater resources and better housing stock owing to the structures of racial segregation. The documentary's narration of that move, however, is always framed by a larger dominant nationalist story of immigrant progress and possibility that adheres to an Asian American story. On multiple levels, the displacement and poverty of this Asian refugee family is sublated by a discourse of Asian uplift, a developmental narrative in which literal and figurative distance from blackness is a critical element of becoming American.

In the context of the late twentieth century, discourses of Asian uplift are overdetermined by neoliberal ideologies that subject Ny and the communities in which he lives to forces of violence across several scales. Such violence is evident not only in the visual documentation of racialized urban poverty but also in the narrative discourse, in which the most structurally vulnerable subjects are compelled to account for their precarious socioeconomic locations and social isolation through neoliberal dicta of private failure. The common critical tendency is to read *a.k.a. Don Bonus* as a text that counters model minority discourse simply by bringing Asian American poverty into representation. Conversely, *Better Luck Tomorrow* can be readily dismissed as a critically bankrupt or self-indulgent text, owing to its focus on privileged model minority subjects. Both misreadings too easily conflate the objective class position of characters with an ideological disposition without providing the necessary analytical framework that would elucidate how particular conditions of inequality are produced and legitimated. Such approaches are symptomatic of an inadequate understanding of the political significance and very nature of cultural production; that is, our critical capacities are constrained by a lingering attachment to a telos of identification with properly politicized subjects. Those of us working in Asian American studies must learn to read—by taking an alternative approach—an emergent language of recalcitrance and dislocation. In so doing, it is not empty expressions of "luck" (or "hope" or "change") that we should turn to as the organizing principles for tomorrow but the contradictions and crises exacerbated by the spread of neoliberalism.

Afterword

Throughout *Race for Citizenship*, I have endeavored to delineate the relational processes by which blacks and Asians in the United States have been differently racialized since the nineteenth century. We have seen how these groups have been racially defined by the ways they have been located across time in relation to the shifting terrains of citizenship, the labor market, and U.S. national culture. I opened this history with the 1992 Los Angeles uprisings as a contemporary flashpoint intended to highlight the complexity of these differential racial formations and how investments in citizenship constrained our capacity to engage that complexity. It seems fitting to close, then, with another, more recent political-economic disaster, Hurricane Katrina, which reveals yet other dimensions of a vexed relational dynamic between discourses of black and Vietnamese displacement.

Since the 1980s, several sizable Vietnamese refugee communities of more than 150,000 persons settled along the Gulf Coast, with a significant proportion joining the commercial fishing industry in Texas, Mississippi, Alabama, and Louisiana. When Katrina hit, at least ten thousand Vietnamese Americans were living in the city of New Orleans, most of them in the working-class districts of Versailles and Avondale. Within four months of the storm, more than three hundred newspaper articles described the displaced Vietnamese with striking thematic consistency: traumatic dislocation and suffering overcome by hard work, independent resilience, strong cultural ties, and survival without complaint. Asian American community activists and academics were quick to point out that such narratives made the work of obtaining resources for evacuees even more difficult. As one team of Asian Americanist scholars put it, "such emphasis on self-sufficiency ignores the voices of some members of the Vietnamese American community who have stated—echoing some African American community members—that federal government assistance is critical to rebuilding. . . . that their community had received inadequate assistance in rebuilding from the state and city."[1]

But while Asian American discourse has convincingly demonstrated that the mainstream coverage of the Vietnamese as model minority was unmistakable and explicit,[2] I would like to expand on other relational aspects that contributed forcefully to the representation of how black and Vietnamese American displacement was figured after Hurricane Katrina. In particular, I want to underscore how images of African American trauma and despair produced an unstable narrative of state shame and crisis owing to a long national history of black racial exclusion, whereas Vietnamese Americans could not signify in the same way. Numerous photos that have become iconic images of Hurricane Katrina all feature the compelling visual detail of an American flag: black Americans on rooftops scrawled with "Help Us"; an elderly woman at the Superdome draped in a flag blanket; a young boy stranded at the edge of a roof in a torn red, white and blue T-shirt. In all these images, the flag visually underscores nationalist elements of place and personhood: black Americans abandoned and betrayed—yet again—by the nation.

Indeed, more than any other recent event, Hurricane Katrina brought the excruciating vulnerability of black poverty into such stark relief that it became difficult, if not impossible, to negate the racial and class dimensions of this ostensibly natural disaster:

> All of us saw on television . . . there is deep, persistent poverty in this region. . . . And that poverty has roots in a history of racial discrimination, which cut off generations from the opportunity of America. We have a duty to confront this poverty with bold action. So let us restore all that we have cherished from yesterday, and let us rise above the legacy of inequality.[3]

What is remarkable about these otherwise mundane declarations of U.S. social inequalities is that they were spoken by President George W. Bush in his live nationally televised special address on September 15, 2005. Notably absent from this speech was the ubiquitous rhetoric of personal responsibility and family values that had been the hallmark of U.S. state policy toward the poor for the past twenty-five years. Ironically forced to take some responsibility for his administration's ineptitude, the president was compelled to acknowledge the depth of a sociopolitical crisis that could not be readily obscured by the usual discourses of black cultural pathology, gender and family deviance, or criminality. And regardless of whether many Americans actually felt any genuine concern about those who were strug-

gling to survive in New Orleans, the complete breakdown in state infrastructure because of a hurricane was a complete shock to the nation's self-
perception as the paragon of an invulnerably modern, first-world nation.

Hurricane Katrina created an anomalous discursive rupture, however
momentary, in a national context in which any invocation of race is quickly
translated into the "race card," as if race were not a decisive factor in the
structuring of everyday life but a worn-out trick or sleight of hand. Within
seventy-two hours after the levees began breaking, shell-shocked mainstream reporters and cameramen were observing that the 40,000-plus
people trapped without food or water in the Superdome, in the Convention
Center, in their homes, and on apartment building rooftops appeared overwhelmingly to be poor and African American. No doubt, familiar discourses
of black criminality quickly gained a foothold as media coverage increasingly
focused on looting and lawlessness. But I would maintain that even these
well-worn discourses were unable to fully dispel the haunting images of black
despair and national abandonment: President George W. Bush's uncharac-
teristic remarks were symptomatic of this momentary ideological rupture.

In a post–civil rights period when the nation is attempting to locate
the relevance of race in the historical past, what kinds of stories could
help reconcile narratives about American opportunity and progress with
the horrifying images that flashed across millions of televisions? It is
here, as Eric Tang suggests, that the Asian American enters. "Local and
national presses," Tang writes, "were thus quick to enlist the Vietnamese
as symbols of survival amid despair, running stories of the peculiar virtues of the Vietnamese."[4] The title of a feature story in the *New York Times*
on October 26, 2005, reads, "Sustained by Close Ties, Vietnamese Toil to
Rebuild." The language of uplift is not particularly subtle:

> The Mary Queen of Vietnam Roman Catholic Church, abandoned
> just a few weeks ago in the deluge, is now bustling with neighbor-
> hood groups planning home repairs and giving out tetanus shots. . . .
> [I]n what could serve as a model for other areas trying to reconstitute
> themselves after Hurricane Katrina, the Vietnamese residents have
> slowly started to reknit their neighborhood. They say the preserva-
> tion of their traditions explains why their ties, stretched thin during
> the upheaval of the hurricane, did not break.

Later in the story the point is repeated: "What they are doing can be a
model for other communities," said Cynthia Willard-Lewis, an African

American city council member. Stephen DeBlasio, chief of the Federal Emergency Management Agency (FEMA)'s direct housing operation in Louisiana, was quoted in several national papers about how impressed he was with the Vietnamese community's ability to care for itself: "They sure want to pick themselves up by their bootstraps. There's no doubt about that."[5] This trope of self-sufficiency appears with remarkable consistency in the majority of hundreds of print articles that mentioned the Vietnamese. Whereas stories involving African Americans also frequently mention desires to rebuild or return to their neighborhoods, the emphasis on the Vietnamese and their independent efforts as a self-organized, model ethnic community is absolutely overwhelming.

The last time this much national media attention focused on the Vietnamese in the Gulf region was in the early 1980s, when a series of violent confrontations were breaking out between white and Vietnamese fishermen. When tens of thousands of refugees began commercial fishing in small coastal towns, competition between white and Vietnamese fishermen escalated into racial violence. In 1979, a Vietnamese man was acquitted after fatally shooting a white fisherman who had frequently threatened him and had cut him with a knife. In Galveston Bay, white fishermen formed an alliance to protect their livelihood from "commie gooks" who could "survive on rice and fish" alone. Some of the fishermen, including the leader of the white alliance, were Vietnam veterans who stated they would die before allowing their livelihoods to be threatened by an enemy that they believed they were fighting a second time. The alliance soon invited the Ku Klux Klan for assistance in handling the matter, quickly organizing a campaign that was intended to intimidate the immigrants into leaving the industry. Public KKK rallies were held, complete with cross burnings, and one evening twenty members in gowns and hoods boarded a boat and cruised past Vietnamese fishing boats and businesses while brandishing firearms and shouting threats. After the fire bombings of three Vietnamese fishing boats in the area, including threats against a white wholesaler and a white dock man, both of whom did business with Vietnamese, an injunction was filed in federal court to protect the Vietnamese right to pursue a livelihood. In 1981, a federal judge approved an injunction that the fishermen and KKK stop their organized campaign of racial intimidation or be charged with contempt but denied the Vietnamese request for federal marshal protection to be present on the opening of shrimp season. James Stanfield, who was the grand titan of the state chapter of Knights of the Ku Klux Klan and who also ran a boat-repair shop, maintained that the "problem between the whites and Vietnamese was never racial . . . but economic."[6] This violent white reaction to the presence of the Vietnamese workers erupted again in 1990 when five commercial fishing boats offshore from New Orleans exchanged gunfire, and at least one boat with a white crew rammed a Vietnamese shrimp boat, resulting in the New Orleans coast guard's confiscating a shotgun and a .22 caliber rifle. White fishermen blamed the confrontation on the "newcomers."

The virtuous Vietnamese "work ethic" that is a model for nonwhite communities is exactly what white fishermen so violently challenged two decades ago, stating that the long working hours of the Vietnamese, who lived "on rice and fish," threatened the livelihood of white American workers.[7]

After Hurricane Katrina, visual images of the Vietnamese returning to sea on their tattered fishing boats were seemingly a welcome relief from the relentless footage of large crowds of black evacuees in massive shelter environments looking shocked and overwhelmed. In a lengthy concluding segment on the NBC Nightly News, anchorman Brian Williams introduced his story on the displaced Vietnamese with the strikingly abstract and ahistorical opening: "There are families who came to this nation's shores from a long distance away to make a living. But now they are going back to the sea in ships. Because it's what they do." The language is peculiar in its near mythical description of a people who came "from a long distance away to make a living," erasing the militarized geopolitical context of their refugee status and migration. The subsequent shots of Vietnamese men fixing their nets, clearing debris, and getting their boats ready contrasted with the preponderance of images of black despair and desperation, large crowds waiting in endless lines, and hands outstretched for supplies of water and food that did not arrive. Such highly visible images of African Americans invoked a sense of historical state failure and inaction as well as black dependency in awaiting state rescue. My point is not that the visual documentation of black suffering at numerous mass shelters was "negative" but that those images created a sense of national indictment that could not be delinked from discourses of black dependency. The story about the Vietnamese concluding the national evening news dramatized just how differently black and Vietnamese trauma can signify in the U.S. imaginary.

For instance, one of the Vietnamese men in this news segment was interviewed while wearing an American flag T-shirt, which resonated in an entirely different way from the disturbing images of black distress in which the visual sign of the American flag could invoke the pathos of abandonment. On the body of the Asian refugee, the U.S. flag generated a radically different script of immigrant possibility and national benevolence. Given the history of violence against Vietnamese fishermen on the Gulf Coast, donning a U.S. flag T-shirt when heading to the docks can be read as analogous to the compulsory display of American flags on South Asian and Middle Eastern bodies and storefronts after the attacks on September 11, 2001, efforts to preempt anticipated racial violence. A reporter does not need to ask Hoang Nguyen to cooperate with the spirit of his story by putting on a U.S.A. T-shirt. For refugees living in a white, working-class coastal town in the Gulf, the violent processes by which the Vietnamese have been incorporated into the United States already compel such necessary acts of adornment.

It is telling that such defensive measures against a history of white racial violence actually help secure the story of hardworking Asian immigrants pursuing the American dream, irrespective of whether it makes sense to do so. The story ends with the image of a boat going out to sea with the voice-over declaring, "Vietnamese shrimpers also know about tough times, and aren't about to quit now." The story about tenacious Vietnamese immigrants asks no questions about their place in a declining industry in which they have dealt with a long history of racial hostility. The substance of the story is rather bleak: the reporter himself states that they might catch $60,000 worth of shrimp but that in doing so, they will pay more than $50,000 for diesel fuel, [and when you] "add in cost of labor, supplies, and loan payments on the boat, there's very little profit." Hoang Nguyen has already told the NBC reporter that he has no other employment options and lacks experience for other kinds of work and asks, "So what can I do?" The fact that these dire conditions nonetheless translate into a feel-good wrap-up to the national evening news is a remarkable testament to how powerfully the Asian immigrant, as signifier, works to restore U.S. nationalist ideologies, irrespective of whether the story actually points to deteriorating opportunity and dead ends.

In a U.S. national imaginary shaped by a century of imperialist benevolence through anticommunist war, occupation, and industrialization, the Asian is readily constituted as the formerly impoverished and incomprehensible peasant in the periphery of MASH episodes, the desperate family airlifted out of Saigon, or the lucky adopted Chinese orphan. Elaine Kim incisively identifies how histories of U.S. imperialism have racialized the Asian American as a perpetually indebted subject to the U.S. nation-state: "Like a guest or a new bride living with her mother-in-law, she needs to be grateful, obedient, and uncomplaining. She needs to be mindful of the rules and of her host's generosity, without which where would she be?"[8] More specifically, Kim notes that it was precisely this state of indebtedness that she violated when she wrote a critique of U.S. racism after the uprisings in Los Angeles, generating piles of virulent hate mail from *Newsweek* readers. "They were furious that I did not express gratitude for being saved from starvation in Asia and given the opportunity to flourish, no doubt beyond my wildest dreams, in America."[9] It goes without saying that after the King verdict and LA uprisings, white Americans did not experience the same kind of shocked outrage when they heard African American critiques of U.S. racism, which they may have readily dismissed but also completely expected from black Americans.

Owing, then, to different histories of racialization, we can see how accounts of African American and Vietnamese displacement after Hurricane Katrina generated radically different narrative possibilities. Images of distraught African Americans carried a power of indictment and were capable of producing national shame based on a long domestic history of black racial exclusion. The U.S. flags that were visible in photos and news footage became signs of the bitter irony of what America promised and denied its black citizens. More a nightmare than a dream, black Americans have long been abandoned by the nation. Representations of the displaced Vietnamese could not possibly resonate in the same way, since a narrative frame of state rescue and immigrant aspiration is always already poised to fix the refugee in a closed structure of debt and gratitude. This is not to say, of course, that the Vietnamese are *actually* entrapped in a state of gratitude: the community's public protests that shut down the nearby toxic landfill, Chef Menteur, is just one clear example of how subjects are always in continual negotiation with processes of racialization.[10] Yet there is no seamless way to "sidestep" narrative frames, and the Vietnamese community's inspiring grassroots mobilization cannot help but emerge in some relation, intended or not, to a subtext of black inaction and/or a galvanizing American story of immigrant development.[11]

To clarify the implications of the strikingly redemptive relationship between citizenship and the Asian American, I turn to one last article, entitled "Displaced New Orleans Family Grows in Omaha," dated December 24, 2005. The article begins:

The photo of a youthful, smiling Thanh Nguyen is not damaged, but a murky water stain creeps across the attached gold-embellished certificate of U.S. citizenship. The brittle, dingy document emits the nauseating stench of a dank cellar, but Nguyen, 30, prizes it nonetheless. He recovered the paper last month from his soggy New Orleans home, along with a passport and birth certificate issued in his native Vietnam, and brought them to his Omaha apartment. . . . The citizenship certificate, which Thanh received in 2001, was salvageable. Thanh hung the soaked paper in the sun to dry, a sign that he was not yet ready to abandon his American dream.[12]

The article imbues the act of preserving these U.S. immigration and citizenship documents with an emotional and symbolic meaning that outweighs the urgency of bureaucratic necessity. The panic and anxious uncertainty associated with losing such critical legal papers, so familiar to many immigrants, are seamlessly rescripted into a celebratory narrative of the American dream. If it seems difficult to imagine a parallel Katrina story about a displaced African American salvaging state records that would signify in such hopeful, rather than bitterly ironic, terms, it is because no such analogy is possible. In these diverging registers, images of black dispossession can evince the specter of state obligation, a historic debt owed and persistently denied to segments of the black community, whereas Asian American displacement is narrated in the discursive frame of their indebtedness to the nation. The point of this contrast is not to suggest that these differential orders of debt afford one aggrieved community greater or lesser latitude than another or to lament that Asian American trauma did not similarly generate national pathos. Rather, it is to underscore how both highly divergent registers are so thoroughly organized and regulated by these bankrupt terms of debt and national belonging that we are obliged to imagine political horizons beyond the citizen and the nation.

Notes

INTRODUCTION

1. Min Hyoung Song, *Strange Future: Pessimism and the 1992 Los Angeles Riots* (Durham, NC: Duke University Press, 2005).

2. For examples of this important work, see such excellent book-length studies as Gary Okihiro's *Margins and Mainstreams* (1994); Vijay Prashad's *Everybody Was Kung-Fu Fighting* (2001); a special issue of *positions* (2003) entitled *the afro-asian century;* Bill Mullen's *Afro-Orientalism* (2004); Laura Pulido's *Black, Brown, Yellow, Left* (2006); Fred Ho and Bill Mullen's *Afro Asia: Revolutionary Political and Cultural Connections between African Americans and Asian Americans* (2008); Scott Kurashige's *The Shifting Grounds of Race: Black and Japanese Americans in the Making of Multiethnic Los Angeles* (2008); and George Lipsitz's work on black identifications with Japan during World War II in "Frantic to Join . . . the Japanese Army."

3. Although W. E. B. Du Bois's theory of double consciousness has been extended to frame many contexts of racialization, it is important to observe how it captures the particularity of a black American formation.

4. Daniel Kim, *Writing Manhood in Black and Yellow: Ralph Ellison, Frank Chin and the Literary Politics of Identity* (Palo Alto, CA: Stanford University Press, 2005).

5. As Daniel Kim writes regarding his analysis of the homosocial articulations of cultural nationalist writers, "The interracialism this study examines, therefore, is not one that is symmetrical. It does not take shape through depictions of black and Asian men standing together in anti-racist homosocial solidarity" (*Writing Manhood in Black and Yellow*, xvii).

6. See Charles J. McClain's excellent study, *In Search of Equality: The Chinese Struggle against Discrimination in Nineteenth-Century America* (Berkeley: University of California Press, 1994). A less conventional but highly instructive archive might include *An English-Chinese Phrase Book* produced by Wong Sam and Assistants (San Francisco: Cubery & Co., 1875), reprinted in *The Big Aiiieeeee! An Anthology of Chinese American and Japanese American Literature*, ed. Jeffrey Paul Chan et al. (New York: Meridian Press, 1991).

PART 1

1. Moon-Ho Jung, *Coolies and Cane: Race, Labor and Sugar in the Age of Emancipation* (Baltimore: Johns Hopkins University, 2008), 7.

2. Ibid.

CHAPTER 1

1. *Chinese Immigration: Its Social, Moral, and Political Effect*. Report to the California Senate of Its Special Committee on Chinese Immigration (Sacramento: State Printing Office, 1878), 247.

2. Brook Thomas, Plessy v. Ferguson: *A Brief History with Documents* (Boston: Bedford Books, 1997), 36–37.

3. The *Yick Wo v. Hopkins* case determined that the Chinese were Mongolian and not white and thus subject to racial segregation. See Charles J. McClain, *In Search of Equality: The Chinese Struggle against Discrimination in Nineteenth-Century America* (Berkeley: University of California Press, 1994), 115–19.

4. The particular racial tandem that I isolate and track here is clearly not "representative" or exhaustive of the meanings generated when blacks and Chinese immigrants were juxtaposed in nineteenth-century America. See Aarim-Heriot's outstanding study of the relationship between the "Negro question" and the "Chinese question," in which she examines the similar degrading traits and characteristics attributed to both groups: Najia Aarim-Heriot, *Chinese Immigrants, African Americans, and Racial Anxiety in the United States, 1848–82* (Champaign: University of Illinois Press, 2003).

5. On the specificity of U.S. Orientalism, see Lisa Lowe, *Immigrant Acts: On Asian American Cultural Politics* (Durham, NC: Duke University Press, 1996), 178, n. 7; and John Tchen, *New York before Chinatown: Orientalism and the Shaping of American Culture, 1776–1882* (Baltimore: Johns Hopkins University Press, 1999).

6. Lowe, *Immigrant Acts*, 19.

7. Tchen, *New York before Chinatown*.

8. Tchen terms this "commercial orientalism"; see *New York before Chinatown*, 63–124.

9. Lowe, *Immigrant Acts*, 5.

10. *Chinese Immigration*, Report to the California Senate, 247.

11. See David Theo Goldberg, *Racist Culture: Philosophy and the Politics of Meaning* (Cambridge: Blackwell, 1993); and Paul Gilroy, *The Black Atlantic: Modernity and Double Consciousness* (Cambridge, MA: Harvard University Press, 1993).

12. For example, we can see this negotiation in Booker T. Washington's statement that

> notwithstanding the cruelty and moral wrong of slavery, the ten million Negroes inhabiting this country who themselves or whose ancestors went through the school of American slavery are in a stronger and more hopeful condition, materially, intellectually, morally, and religiously, than is true of an equal number of black people in any other portion of the globe.

See Booker T. Washington, *Three Negro Classics* (New York: Avon Books, 1965), 37. Washington's striking image of U.S. slavery as a "school" that produced the moral, intellectual, and economic development of blacks in America constructs slavery not as a contradiction to modern ideologies of civilization or democracy but as an institution that enabled black historical progress. Washington's liberal narrative, in which black emancipation is achieved through hard work, humility, and the American ethos of self-help, produces a developmental resolution of this paradox between enslavement and enlightenment.

13. The heterogeneity of black Orientalism can be seen in recent projects such as Bill Mullen's *Afro Orientalism* (Minneapolis: University of Minnesota Press, 2004). Mullen builds on works by Gary Okihiro, *Margins and Mainstreams: Asians in American History and Culture* (Seattle: University of Washington, 1994); Vijay Prashad, *Everyone Was Kung-Fu Fighting: Afro-Asian Connections and the Myth of Cultural Purity* (Boston: Beacon Press, 2001); and Vijay Prashad, *The Karma of Brown Folk* (Minneapolis: University of Minnesota Press, 2000). All these authors delineate a long-standing and global history of black and Asian peoples in "mutual struggle against Western empires" (Mullen, *AfroOrientalism*, xviii). Also see the special issue of *positions: the afro-asian century* (2003).

14. See Mullen, *Afro Orientalism*; and Prashad, *Everyone Was Kung-Fu Fighting* and *The Karma of Brown Folk*. For specific articles focusing on black discourses regarding Japanese imperialism and empire, see George Lipsitz, "Frantic to Join . . . the Japanese Army: The Asia Pacific War in the Lives of African American Soldiers and Civilians," in *The Politics of Culture in the Shadow of Capital*, ed. Lisa Lowe and David Lloyd (Durham, NC: Duke University Press, 1997), 324–53. Also see Ernest Allen, "When Japan Was 'Champion of the Darker Races': Satokata Takahashi and the Flowering of Black Messianic Nationalism," *The Black Scholar* 24, no. 1 (1995): 23–46; and Daniel Widener, "'Perhaps the Japanese Are to Be Thanked?' Asia, Asian Americans, and the Construction of Black California," in the special issue of *positions: the afro-asian century* (2003): 135–81.

15. See Alexander Saxton, *The Indispensable Enemy: Labor and the Anti-Chinese Movement in California* (Berkeley: University of California Press, 1995).

16. In *The Indispensable Enemy*, 59, Saxton is quoting "an address to the working men of Nevada," reprinted in the *Daily Alta*, June 17, 1869.

17. Aarim-Heriot's study does an excellent job of showing how Republicans in the 1870s consistently attempted to disarticulate the Chinese from legislation that enfranchised black Americans (*Chinese Immigrants*, 140–55).

18. Nayan Shah, *Contagious Divides: Epidemics and Race in San Francisco's Chinatown* (Berkeley: University of California Press, 2001), 18.

19. Ibid., 17.

20. In my analysis, the black press refers primarily to newspapers and does not include periodicals or the many newsletters that were circulated by black churches in the nineteenth century. My secondary sources for the black press's representations of Chinese immigrants also examine almost exclusively black newspapers. See David Hellwig, "The Afro-American and the Immigrant, 1880–1930: A Study of Black Social Thought" (PhD diss., Syracuse University, 1974); and Arnold Shankman, "Black on Yellow: Afro-Americans View Chinese-Americans, 1850–1935," *Phylon* 39, no. 1 (spring 1978): 1–17. I regard any press material directed to a black readership and edited and managed by black workers as a "black newspaper."

21. Southern planters expressed considerable interest in importing Chinese labor to replace black sharecroppers during the Reconstruction period. But their efforts resulted in only a "trickle of migrants," and by 1880, the Mississippi census reported only fifty-one Chinese. See James Loewen, *The Mississippi Chinese: Between Black and White* (Prospect Heights, IL: Waveland Press, 1988), 22–26. The few cases in which Chinese immigrants were used in an attempt to displace black workers in the postbellum South ultimately failed owing to a number of factors, including unanticipated

transportation costs, poor productivity, and decreased political necessity (Loewen, *The Mississippi Chinese*, 26).

22. *New Orleans Tribune*, November, 12, 1864, quoted by Hellwig, "The Afro-American and the Immigrant," 112. For an account of the paper's history, see Roland Wolseley, *The Black Press, U.S.A.* (Ames: Iowa State University Press, 1990), 111.

23. "Opium Eating in Chicago," *Topeka Tribune*, October 23, 1880.

24. "The Chinese in New York: Peculiarities of the Orientals Described," *Washington Bee*, November 22, 1884.

25. Shankman, "Black on Yellow," 10.

26. "Chinese Fashions," *Freedom's Journal*, March 16, 1827. I thank Dr. Frances Foster for referring me to this source.

27. "Chinese Fashions."

28. See Benedict Anderson, *Imagined Communities: Reflections on the Origin and Spread of Nationalism* (London: Verso, 1994). During and after the Civil War, hundreds of local black newspapers not only appeared in the larger cities of the North and South but also moved westward, where they were produced and consumed by small black communities in Kansas, California, and throughout the Northwest. See Penelope Bullock, *The Afro-American Periodical Press, 1838–1909* (Baton Rouge: Louisiana State University Press, 1981).

29. This study's focus on the nineteenth-century black press as a site of textual evidence in no way regards these discourses of black citizenship as "representative" of black imaginings of freedom and justice in the nineteenth century. In my attempt to interrogate the limits of citizenship, I look to a cultural institution that has a disproportionately significant role in producing discourses of black national identity.

30. See Jane Rhodes, *Mary Ann Shadd Cary: The Black Press and Protest in the Nineteenth Century* (Bloomington: Indiana University Press, 1998), 100; and Kevin Gaines, *Uplifting the Race: Black Leadership, Politics, and Culture in the Twentieth Century* (Chapel Hill: University of North Carolina Press, 1996).

31. The types of articles that these papers and magazines offered ranged from religious teachings to local community events, sensationalism and gossip, black success stories, politics, and accounts of racial violence, depending more or less on the interests of the press itself. See Bullock, *The Afro-American Periodical Press*, 3.

32. As Gaines notes, it is difficult to categorize the educated black community during this period as "middle class," given that their economic status was not often considerably different from less-privileged blacks. It is precisely this absence of a concrete material distinction between the educated black community and blacks who lacked such "cultural capital," Gaines argues, that made uplift ideology so appealing.

33. The relationship between heteronormative performance and the rehabilitation/development of racialized citizenship has been well theorized by Shah, *Contagious Divides*.

34. For an extensive discussion of black codes and the range of postemancipation practices that produced an "indebted" black subject, see Saidiya Hartman, *Scenes of Subjection: Terror, Slavery, and Self-Making in Nineteenth-Century America* (New York: Oxford University Press, 1997), 125–63. Also, for a discussion of black codes and the convict lease system, see Angela Davis, *Are Prisons Obsolete?* (New York: Seven Stories Press, 2003), 22–39.

35. See W. E. B. Du Bois, *Black Reconstruction in America: 1860–1880* (New York: Simon & Schuster, 1995); and Hartman, *Scenes of Subjection.*

36. Ida B. Wells-Barnett, *On Lynchings: Southern Horrors, A Red Record, Mob Rule in New Orleans* (New York: Arno Press, 1969). Also see Angela Davis, *Women, Race and Class* (New York: Vintage Books, 1983).

37. Hazel V. Carby, *Reconstructing Womanhood: The Emergence of the Afro-American Woman Novelist* (New York: Oxford University Press, 1987), 18.

38. Also see Davis, *Women, Race and Class,* 172–201.

39. Slave narratives of the eighteenth and nineteenth century, as well as the religious discourse of the abolitionist movement, reveal that the enslaved and free black community relied heavily on the discursive terms and narratives of Christianity to repudiate their relegation to property and to critique systematic exploitation. See Saxton, *The Indispensable Enemy,* 227–41; and Frances Smith Foster, *Witnessing Slavery: The Development of Ante-bellum Slave Narratives* (Westport, CT: Greenwood Press, 1979), 42. This strong emphasis on the religious formation of the enslaved was crucial to asserting their humanity as "children of God" and also demonstrated their superior fitness as Christian subjects who survived and escaped the barbarism of slavery through divine intervention and salvation.

40. Pointing to the structural significance of Christianity in developmental narratives of Western modernity is in no way intended to render the importance of religious ideologies to African American history as a sign of "colonized consciousness" or black capitulation to Euro-American hegemony. See Gayraud S. Wilmore, *Black Religion and Black Radicalism: An Interpretation of the Religious History of African Americans* (Maryknoll, NY: Orbis Books, 1998); and Eric Lincoln, *The Black Experience in Religion* (Garden City, NY: Anchor Books, 1974). Also see Karen Baker-Fletcher, *A Singing Something: Womanist Reflections on Anna Julia Cooper* (New York: Crossroad, 1994).

41. For a provocative and thoughtful account of the profound missionary ideologies in the discourses of prominent black nationalist leaders and organizations, see Wilmore, *Black Religion and Black Radicalism,* chap. 3, "Black Religion and Black Nationalism," 125–62.

42. See Alexander Saxton, *The Rise and Fall of the White Republic: Class Politics and Mass Culture in Nineteenth-Century America* (London: Verso, 1990); and George Fredrickson, *The Black Image in the White Mind: The Debate on Afro-American Character and Destiny, 1817–1914* (New York: Harper & Row, 1971). Baker-Fletcher also discusses the use of religious discourse to negotiate scientific racism in the work of Anna Julia Cooper.

43. *Pacific Appeal,* May 17, 1862.

44. Nubia, "Progress of the Colored People of San Francisco," *Frederick Douglass' Paper,* September 22, 1854.

45. Ibid.

46. During this period, anti-Chinese sentiment in California was associated primarily with the white working class, and mainstream publications directed to a middle-class or "not working-class" readership generally condemned anti-Chinese racism and even constructed Chinese immigrants favorably vis-à-vis Irish and other white ethnic immigrants. See Grace Hong's "Race, Empire and the Not Working

Class: Bret Harte's *Overland Monthly* and the Chinatown Photographs of Arnold Genthe," *Journal of the West* 43 (December 2004): 8–14. An educated black community seeking to emulate the values promoted by racial uplift could disavow racist attacks on the Chinese and see themselves as more civilized than the ignorant and vulgar white working class, whose racist class interests also threatened the black community. At the same time, however, Orientalist discourse consolidated a modern black national subject through the logic of cultural dis-identification with Chinese, alien difference.

47. In later issues of *Frederick Douglass' Paper*, the same author reports: "The Chinese have taken the places of the colored people, as victims of oppression. —The poor Chinese are, indeed, a wretched looking set; that they are filthy, immoral, and licentious—according to our notion of things—is unquestionable. But these vices do not justify the whites in oppressing them" (April 16, 1855). Again, the author condemns anti-Chinese racism as she simultaneously recites the "vices" or cultural underdevelopment of the Chinese as "filthy, immoral, and licentious" and implicitly constructs black identification with the culture of Western civilization, which she articulates as "*our* notion of things."

48. Nubia, "Progress of the Colored People."

49. See *The Elevator* (San Francisco), May 24, 1873, December 17, 1869, March 29, 1873, and November 19, 1869. Numerous articles attempted to contrast the "Negro [who] seeks to be an integral part of the nation" with the Chinese who were "unlikely to become converted to the tenets of our religion, incapable to understand the system of our government, to appreciate our civilization, morals and manners, and persistently adhere to the doctrine of the inferiority of the races." Another typical characterization described Chinese immigrants as "people who use no common dictates of reason while among us, who are pagans in religion, inhuman in their traits, most scurrilous when their feelings are irritated, illiterate in intellectual education and of the doctrines of morality, and lastly wholly incompetent to become true citizens" (The *Elevator*, March 29, 1873). While this mode of black dis-identification is clearly linked to the discourse analyzed earlier in "Letters from Nubia," the relationship between black citizenship and oriental alterity is explicitly articulated in response to the growing significance of the anti-Chinese movement in defining the national citizenry.

50. "Democratic Logic," *The Elevator*, August 30, 1867. See Aarim-Heriot's analysis of congressional reconstruction debates, in which proposed legislation was continually engaged in relation to its consequences for the "Chinese question" as Republicans successfully disconnected black enfranchisement from the political costs of Chinese inclusion (Aarim-Heriot, *Chinese Immigrants*, 85–155).

51. Quoted in Hellwig, "The Afro-American and the Immigrant," 105.

52. However, it is clear that anti-Chinese legislation in California was also regarded as an attack on the rights of free and unfree blacks before the Civil War. See, for example, *Frederick Douglass' Paper*, April 13, 1855.

53. *The Elevator*, July 8, 1970.

54. For more than twenty-five citations from a range of black newspapers that spoke out from the 1870s to the 1880s in opposition to Chinese exclusion, see Hellwig, "The Afro-American and the Immigrant," 101–18.

55. *Christian Recorder*, March 30 and April 6, 1882.

56. Other black newspapers on the West Coast, including the *Pacific Appeal* and the *Washington Bee*, also perceived Chinese immigration as a major problem but did not condone race-based legislation as the solution, in part because of their opposition to the white nativist Workingman's Party, which black leaders often described as a group of radical, racist communists, primarily composed of immigrant or first-generation Irish workers. See Francis Lortie's *San Francisco's Black Community, 1870–1890: Dilemmas in the Struggle for Equality* (San Francisco: R and E Research Associates, 1970); and Delilah L. Beasley, *The Negro Trail Blazers of California* (San Francisco: R and E Research Associates, 1919).

57. Because Shankman's analysis interprets the black press's Orientalism as black hostility toward the Chinese (for which his study seeks to account), he states that "curiously enough, there is little evidence of black newspapers being willing to support the various exclusion acts" ("Black on Yellow," 8–9). Conversely, Hellwig's analysis begins with the black press's opposition to Chinese exclusion, arguing that black Americans were largely supportive of Chinese immigrants, despite their admitted "revulsion at the appearance of the alien," which Hellwig tends to naturalize and mitigate in his argument. Thus while Hellwig's and Shankman's analyses emphasize different aspects of the same body of evidence and come to opposite conclusions, their studies together are not contradictory.

58. Hellwig, "The Afro-American and the Immigrant," 99.

59. See ibid., 102.

60. *New Era*, July 14, 1870.

61. *Christian Recorder*, April 6, 1882.

62. Hellwig, "The Afro-American and the Immigrant," 115–16; also see Herbert Hill, *Black Labor and the American Legal System: Race, Work, and the Law* (Madison: University of Wisconsin Press, 1985), 13–21.

63. See Hellwig, "The Afro-American and the Immigrant," 79–98; Noel Ignatiev, *How the Irish Became White* (New York: Routledge, 1995).

64. *The Elevator*, April 26, 1873; *Savannah Tribune*, May 20, 1893.

65. "Have Chinese Any Rights Which Americans Are Bound to Respect," *The Elevator*, May 24, 1873.

66. See "Opium Eating in Chicago," *Topeka Tribune*, October 22, 1880; "The Chinese in New York; Peculiarities of the Orientals Described," *Washington Bee*, November 22, 1884; "The Murderous Mafia," *The Age* (New York); and "One Blessing of the San Francisco Quake," *Alexander's Magazine* (Boston), May 1906. For numerous other articles of similar content, also see Shankman, "Black on Yellow," 10–12.

CHAPTER 2

1. Anna Julia Cooper, *The Voice of Anna Julia Cooper: Including* A Voice from the South *and Other Important Essays, Papers, and Letters*, ed. Charles Lemert and Esme Bhan (Lanham, MD: Rowman & Littlefield, 1998), 53.

2. Ibid., 63.

3. Cooper criticized the white feminist movement for using racialized gender ideologies to legitimate their demands for political participation. As Hazel Carby notes,

the white women's movement's exclusive focus on suffrage rights also resonated as a narrow political objective for black women who had managed to claim an effective political presence as abolitionists and activists in "alternative public spheres," without having waited for the right to vote. See Hazel V. Carby, *Reconstructing Womanhood: The Emergence of the Afro-American Woman Novelist* (New York: Oxford University Press, 1987), 70. Like other black women intellectuals of her period, Cooper did not fixate on political enfranchisement as central to the improvement of black women's conditions. For a thorough discussion of Cooper's critique of the racism of the women's suffragist movement, see Carby, *Reconstructing Womanhood*, 95–120.

4. Ann duCille, *The Coupling Convention: Sex, Text, and Tradition in Black Women's Fiction* (New York: Oxford University Press, 1993), 50.

5. Kevin Gaines, *Uplifting the Race: Black Leadership, Politics, and Culture in the Twentieth Century* (Chapel Hill: University of North Carolina Press, 1996), 5.

6. Ibid., 52.

7. DuCille, *The Coupling Convention*, 30.

8. Cooper, *The Voice of Anna Julia Cooper*, 85.

9. See Min-Jung Kim's discussion of the historical contradiction posed by black women's "specifically situated" location in the ideology of separate spheres in "Renarrating the Private: Gender, Family, and Race in Zora Neale Hurston, Alice Walker, and Toni Morrison" (PhD diss., University of California at San Diego, 1999), on record at Digital publication (AAT 992560).

10. Nancy Fraser, "Rethinking the Public Sphere: A Contribution to the Critique of Actually Existing Democracy," in *Habermas and the Public Sphere*, ed. Craig Calhoun (Cambridge, MA: MIT Press, 1994), 110.

11. See duCille, *The Coupling Convention*; Deborah McDowell, *"The Changing Same": Black Women's Literature, Criticism, and Theory* (Bloomington: Indiana University Press, 1995); and Claudia Tate, *Domestic Allegories of Political Desire: The Black Heroine's Text at the Turn of the Century* (New York: Oxford University Press, 1992).

12. DuCille, *The Coupling Convention*, 34.

13. However, late nineteenth-century black female discourses of domestic civility have been largely dismissed or disparaged by contemporary interpretive paradigms that regard "domesticity as a de-politicized institution" and therefore fail to historicize how Victorian gender ideologies constructed the home as an institution with significant moral, social, and political influence (Tate, *Domestic Allegories*, 131). DuCille also contextualizes the "historically complex and contradictory" significance of marriage in African American culture, stating that

> while modern minds are inclined to view marriage as an oppressive, self-limiting institution, for nineteenth-century African Americans, recently released from slavery and its dramatic disruption of marital and family life, marriage rites were a long-denied basic human right—signs of liberation and entitlement to both democracy and desire. (*The Coupling Convention*, 14)

DuCille's work examines how African American women's fiction has represented and appropriated the "coupling convention" as a means of engaging, revising, and interrogating historically specific ideologies of race and sexuality that shaped the changing and multiple meanings of marriage in the African American community.

14. Cooper, *The Voice of Anna Julia Cooper*, 53.

15. Ibid., 54.

16. According to historian George Fredrickson, white radical conservatives in postbellum America argued that in the absence of the necessary restraints imposed by slavery, the newly emancipated black population would revert to a state of savagery, particularly in the area of sexual excess. Retrogressionism was the social theory that led to this notion of black regression, which was the legitimating ideology for black disenfranchisement, lynching, segregation, and so forth. See George Fredrickson, *The Black Image in the White Mind: The Debate on Afro-American Character and Destiny, 1817–1914* (New York: Harper & Row, 1971).

17. Lisa Lowe, *Critical Terrains: French and British Orientalisms* (Ithaca, NY: Cornell University Press, 1991), 39.

18. Cooper, *The Voice of Anna Julia Cooper*, 53.

19. Ibid., 83.

20. Ibid., 53.

21. Ibid., 55.

22. Carby, *Reconstructing Womanhood*, 30.

23. Gaines, *Uplifting the Race*, 134.

24. Ibid., 135.

25. Cooper, *The Voice of Anna Julia Cooper*, 60–61.

26. Kevin Gaines is correct in noting that Cooper displaces this critique onto the "lower classes of white men," thus absolving the Southern planter class of their participation in institutionalized extramarital sexual arrangements with black women. See Gaines, *Uplifting the Race*, 147. Cooper also addresses the complicity of middle-class black men and women, remarking that "respect for women . . . means to some men in our own day—respect for the elect few whom they expect to consort" (Cooper, *The Voice of Anna Julia Cooper*, 14) and adds that "we need men who can let their interest and gallantry extend outside the circle of their aesthetic appreciation . . . [and] women so sure of their social footing that they need not fear leaning to lend a hand to a fallen or falling sister" (32).

27. Cooper, *The Voice of Anna Julia Cooper*, 64.

28. Ibid., 82.

29. See duCille's discussion of passionlessness as a crucial political ideology for black women writers in the late nineteenth century. She argues that literary passionlessness cannot be reductively understood as black female desire to "assimilate the Victorian values of white society" but rather is a "profoundly political, feminist urge to rewrite those patriarchal structures" (*The Coupling Convention*, 32). DuCille also contends that passionlessness did not necessarily erase black female sexuality, that sexual desire "is not displaced by social purpose but encoded in it" (45). Her insights are highly relevant to understanding Cooper's strategies and negotiations in claiming "the right to both desire and democracy" (46). Cooper's religious fervor in this "disembodied" text culminates in her scathing critiques of the secular rationalism of Enlightenment philosophy, preserving black historical destiny through a religious teleology that can only be described as "passionate."

30. Cooper, *The Voice of Anna Julia Cooper*, 82.

31. Orlando Patterson, *Slavery and Social Death* (Cambridge, MA: Harvard University Press, 1982), vii.

32. Harriet Beecher Stowe's immensely influential text, *Uncle Tom's Cabin*, is considered a classic embodiment of romantic racialism. See Saxton's discussion of the significance of Stowe's analogization of race with gender in providing the Republican Party with a viable racial ideology. Alexander Saxton, *The Rise and Fall of the White Republic: Class Politics and Mass Culture in Nineteenth-Century America* (London: Verso, 1990), 228–41.

33. Fredrickson traces the emergence of a renewed intellectual interest in constructing categorical characteristics of "national stocks" during mid-nineteenth-century America, which amounted to racialist explanations of society and culture. The Romantic movement that had developed in Europe produced a qualified rejection of the universalism of the Enlightenment and was manifested in the United States as a "romantic fascination with differences in the character of nations and peoples" (*The Black Image*, 98). Fredrickson refers to this "comparatively benign view of black peculiarities" as "romantic racialism" and distinguishes this ideology as a distinct racial discourse that emerged in the United States and would prevail in the writings of both blacks and whites throughout the turn of the century (101). Hence, the ideology of progress inherent in the Enlightenment was combined with a racialized civilizationist rhetoric that helped form U.S. nationalism beginning in the 1850s. Scientific racial theories claiming there were inherent differences between Anglo Saxons and nonwhite peoples challenged Enlightenment conceptions of the unity of the human race. Those of Anglo-Saxon stock, these theories determined, possessed an innate "love of liberty, a spirit of individual enterprise and resourcefulness, and a capacity for practical and reasonable behavior, none of which his rivals possessed" (Fredrickson, *The Black Image*, 98). In the antebellum U.S., both proslavery Southerners and many abolitionists embraced theories of "inherent racial differences," but with varying implications.

34. Carby, *Reconstructing Womanhood*, 6.

35. Cooper, *The Voice of Anna Julia Cooper*, 117.

36. In arguing for the necessity of racial heterogeneity in the United States, Cooper sees premodern China as a stagnant civilization whose "arrested development" is the result of the nation's homogeneity and exclusivity (*The Voice of Anna Julia Cooper*, 126–27).

37. Cooper, *The Voice of Anna Julia Cooper*, 74.

38. Ibid., 73.

39. Cooper's disavowal of Orientalist "barbarian brag" also simultaneously identifies her as a civilized subject of Western culture: "How like Longfellow's Iagoo we Westerners are, to be sure! In the few hundred years we have had to strut across our allotted territory and bask in the afternoon sun, we imagine we have exhausted the possibilities of humanity" (*The Voice of Anna Julia Cooper*, 74). While the rhetorical use of "we" clearly is admonishing the presumptuous arrogance of the West, it also situates Cooper in Western civilization, which her reference to the American poet, Longfellow, further consolidates as a demonstration of her cultural knowledge. Cooper's identification as a Western subject is ambiguous, however, as her intervention in Orientalist discourse negotiates the imperative to assimilate into a national culture that circumscribes black subjects as its uncivilized domestic Other.

40. Lisa Lowe, *Immigrant Acts: On Asian American Cultural Politics* (Durham, NC: Duke University Press, 1996), 11–12. See Yen Espiritu, *Asian American Women and Men: Labor, Laws and Love* (Thousand Oaks, CA: Sage, 1997), esp. chap. 1.

41. Cooper, *The Voice of Anna Julia Cooper*, 75.

42. In this sense, I strongly disagree with Gaines's understanding that Cooper has a singular position that can be regarded as nativist or anti-immigrant. At various points, Cooper criticizes the nativism and exclusionist sentiments that are trying to purge America of its perceived Others:

> America for Americans! This is the white man's country! The Chinese must go, shrieks the exclusionist. Exclude the Italians! Colonize the blacks in Mexico or deport them to Africa. Lynch, suppress, drive out, kill out! America for Americans! "Who are Americans?" comes rolling back from ten million throats. . . . Exclusive possession belongs to none. (*The Voice of Anna Julia Cooper*, 127–28)

43. Cooper, *The Voice of Anna Julia Cooper*, 173.

44. Bouglé was a racist post-Durkheimian sociologist whose work claimed that "democratic culture is naturally limited to the more northern, and Euro-American, climactic regions" (Cooper, *The Voice of Anna Julia Cooper*, 270).

45. See Karen Baker-Fletcher, *A Singing Something: Womanist Reflections on Anna Julia Cooper* (New York: Crossroad, 1994).

46. Cooper, *The Voice of Anna Julia Cooper*, 270.

47. There has always been an undercurrent of criticism of Cooper for her "elitism," pointing to both her educational background and her seemingly patronizing words on behalf of poor, less-privileged black women. See Baker-Fletcher, *A Singing Something*. Kevin Gaines extended this point to critique Cooper for her anti-union and anti-immigrant stances (*Uplifting the Race*, 128–51). I do not regard Cooper as having an inadequate or a problematic ideological framework. Even though Cooper (or any other woman, for that matter) is not representative of nineteenth-century postbellum black women, I approach her work as an index of the kinds of ideological negotiations that could be made by a black woman intellectual at the turn of the century. That is, I see Cooper's work in relation to contemporaneous critiques and also scholarship that has examined how Cooper constructs an alternative discourse of black womanhood. See Carby, *Reconstructing Womanhood*; duCille, *The Coupling Convention*; Tate, *Domestic Allegories*; McDowell, *"The Changing Same"*; and Fletcher-Baker, *A Singing Something*.

CHAPTER 3

1. Although it was published during the early civil rights movement, *No-No Boy* could not find an interested or receptive audience for its story of racial alienation and national identity from a Japanese American male perspective. The novel was ignored until its "rediscovery" during the Asian American movement of the 1970s, which emerged in relation to and was inspired by radical black nationalism. While the novel's republication and canonization in Asian American literature therefore owes much to the influence of the Black Power movement, *No-No Boy* anticipates and testifies to the long-standing significance of black masculinity in the Asian American male imaginary.

2. *Nisei* means "second generation," referring to Japanese American citizens who are the U.S.-born children of the *issei*, or "first-generation," Japanese immigrants in the United States, who were ineligible for citizenship.

3. When the U.S. military needed more draftees in 1943, loyalty questionnaires were distributed throughout the internment camps and included the following questions:

> Question 27: Are you willing to serve in the armed forced of the United States on combat duty whenever ordered? Question 28: Will you swear unqualified allegiance to the United States of America and faithfully defend the United States from any or all attack by foreign or domestic forces, and forswear any form of allegiance or obedience to the Japanese emperor, [or] to any other foreign government, power, or organization?

Although most of those questioned replied affirmatively in the hopes that military service would demonstrate their loyalty and the injustice of their internment, those who refused to answer or replied negatively to these two questions were called "no-no boys." They all were placed in federal prison for draft evasion until the war ended.

4. Edward Soja, *Thirdspace: Journeys to Los Angeles and Other Real-and-Imagined Places* (Cambridge: Blackwell, 1996), 74. Building on the work of Henri Lefebvre, geographer Edward Soja uses "third space" to describe the place of culture in the production of social space. While capitalist relations of production and spatial practices such as urban planning determine social space, culture, for Soja, aids in analyzing the production of space as it is "lived, perceived and conceived."

5. See Lisa Lowe, *Immigrant Acts: On Asian American Cultural Politics* (Durham, NC: Duke University Press, 1996); and Bill Ong Hing, *Making and Remaking Asian America through Immigration Policy, 1850–1990* (Palo Alto, CA: Stanford University Press, 1993).

6. See Yen Espiritu, *Asian American Women and Men: Labor, Laws and Love* (Thousand Oaks, CA: Sage, 1997).

7. This exceptional instance in the history of pre-1965 Asian immigration law is a result of at least two key factors. The military power and economic prowess of the Japanese empire seem to have been sufficient in necessitating diplomatic negotiations with the United States. It also is evident that the majority of the picture brides immigrated to Hawaii, a formal colony of the United States since 1898. But in 1907, the migration of Japanese immigrants from Hawaii (and from Canada and Mexico) to the U.S. mainland was prohibited by executive order in response to intensifying anti-Japanese sentiment along the West Coast. The formation of Japanese immigrant family units, reproduction, and permanent settlement may have been regarded as less consequential for Hawaii, which was not a U.S. state and where plantation oligarchies also welcomed a reproducing labor force, since immigration exclusions and mainland migration had depleted their labor population. See Yukiko Kimura, *Issei: Japanese Immigrants in Hawaii* (Honolulu: University of Hawai'i Press, 1988); and Edward D. Beechert, *Working in Hawaii: A Labor History* (Honolulu: University of Hawai'i Press, 1985).

8. Alexander Saxton, *The Indispensable Enemy: Labor and the Anti-Chinese Movement in California* (Berkeley: University of California Press, 1995), 19.

9. See Delilah L. Beasley, *The Negro Trail Blazers of California* (San Francisco: R and E Research Associates, 1919).

10. Saxton, *The Indispensable Enemy*. This is fairly consistent with Saxton's argument, which emphasizes the "ideological baggage" that non-Chinese migrants brought to the Western frontier.

11. Nayan Shah, *Contagious Divides: Epidemics and Race in San Fransisco's Chinatown* (Berkeley: University of California Press, 2001), 120–157.

12. Ibid. Shah's study of San Francisco reveals how these imaginings of Chinatown shaped broader urban policies regarding sanitation, public health, and immigration.

13. Ichiro Murase, *Little Tokyo: One Hundred Years in Pictures* (Los Angeles: Visual Communications, 1983), 11.

14. See Linda N. Espana-Maram, "Brown Hordes and McIntosh Suits: Filipinos, Taxi Dance Halls, and Performing the Immigrant Body in Los Angeles, 1930s and 1940s," in *Generations of Youth: Youth Cultures and History in Twentieth Century America*, ed. Joe Austin and Michel Nevin Willard (New York: New York University Press, 1998), 118–35.

15. See Gary Y. Okihiro, *Whispered Silences: Japanese Americans and World War II* (Seattle: University of Washington Press, 1996).

16. Carole Marks, *Farewell, We're Good and Gone: The Great Black Migration* (Bloomington: Indiana University Press, 1989), 14–17.

17. In the 1890s, the geography of northern cities revealed a trend toward segregation, although most blacks shared larger neighborhoods with white ethnic immigrants and working-class white "natives." Between 1910 and 1930, however, in response to the mass black migration from the South, rigid patterns of residential segregation separated whites and blacks in all northern cities. Black urban ghettos, as one historian notes, are thoroughly "20th century northern creations" in which vast stretches of residential space are occupied solely by blacks and clearly delineated from white areas. See Arnold Hirsch and Raymond Mohl, eds., *Urban Policy in Twentieth-Century America* (New Brunswick, NJ: Rutgers University Press, 1993).

18. Black urbanization in the first half of the twentieth century followed the moral panic and progressive reformism that attempted to discipline and regulate millions of white ethnic immigrants living in urban slums. This underdeveloped multitude of foreigners created a "crisis" regarding national culture and identity. Progressive reformers had already coded the city as a degenerative and corrupting environment for "underdeveloped" working-class white ethnic immigrants.

19. See Dorothy Roberts, *Killing the Black Body: Race, Reproduction, and the Meaning of Liberty* (New York: Vintage Books, 1997); and George Frederickson's *The Black Image in the White Mind: The Debate on Afro-American Character and Destiny, 1817–1914* (New York: Harper & Row, 1971).

20. Quoted in Kevin Gaines, *Uplifting the Race: Black Leadership, Politics, and Culture in the Twentieth Century* (Chapel Hill: University of North Carolina Press, 1996), 92–93.

21. Kevin Mumford, *Interzones: Black/White Sex Districts in Chicago and New York in the Early Twentieth Century* (New York: Columbia University Press, 1997), 143.

22. Ibid.

23. Ibid.

24. Quoted in Hazel V. Carby, *Reconstructing Womanhood: The Emergence of the Afro-American Woman Novelist* (New York: Oxford University Press, 1987), 745.

25. Black middle-class discourses of urban pathology that sought to regulate and discipline the black working class were already evident in W. E. B. Du Bois's sociological study *The Philadelphia Negro*. While Du Bois clearly challenged the prevailing scholarship attributing to blacks a biologistic propensity for criminal behavior and vice, he also voices concerns about working-class black sexuality and criminality as impediments to uplifting the race.

26. I have chosen to use the term *Asian uplift* to contest the ideological presumptions of contemporary racial discourses that position Asian Americans as "model minorities" in order to discipline blacks and Latinos. Since the notion of "racial uplift" is predominantly recognized as a form of black cultural politics, the term *Asian uplift* emphasizes that Asian American racialization and discourses of Asian American citizenship are always predicated on black racial formation, rather than being a discrete and distinct process. For this reason, I distinguish Asian uplift from the processes by which nineteenth-century ethnic immigrants became "white."

27. The ideology of assimilation that was intellectually institutionalized by the Chicago school of sociology in the 1920s asserts that U.S. society inevitably incorporates all its ethnic immigrants as they acculturate to the nation's dominant norms and institutions. The naturalization of the selective incorporation of white ethnic immigrants implies that racial groups eventually are absorbed into the "universal" citizenry as white immigrants had, notwithstanding group "deficiencies" or "shortcomings." However, the hegemonic ideology of assimilation, which disavows systemic racialization, derives from the state's racialized institution of citizenship that regulates Asian American subject formation. For a concise review of the notion of assimilation as posited by the Chicago school, see Michael Omi and Howard Winant, *Racial Formation in the United States: From the 1960s to the Present*, 2d ed. (New York: Routledge, 1994), 9–23.

28. Lowe, *Immigrant Acts*, 9. Lowe argues that this incorporation into national culture is crucial to resolving the inequalities that cannot be resolved through the political sphere of representative democracy.

29. Both quotations, Lowe, *Immigrant Acts*, 6.

30. Ibid., 214, n. 18.

31. Ibid., 56.

32. Quintard Taylor, *The Forging of a Black Community: Seattle's Central District from 1870 through the Civil Rights Era* (Seattle: University of Washington Press, 1994), 86–87.

33. See Espiritu, *Asian American Men and Women*; and Lowe, *Immigrant Acts*.

34. Taylor, *The Forging of a Black Community*, 112.

35. Ibid., 115. The second Chinatown and its residents, primarily middle-aged men who had migrated from other areas, also consisted of a bachelor society. The prostitution, dancing halls, and gambling enterprises in the area were contained

through zoning laws that made Jackson Street a vice district that served all of Seattle's residents throughout the twentieth century.

36. Taylor, *The Forging of a Black Community*, 115–16.

37. Ibid., 116. Japanese immigrants in Seattle were actively recruited to work in railroad construction and other jobs similar to those held by the Chinese, but they also began small-scale farming and fishing.

38. The Japanese American population grew large enough to support numerous community institutions, such as churches, presses, and social clubs. Since the 1900s, the Japanese have easily been the largest racial minority in Seattle, growing from 2,900 in 1900 to 8,448 in 1930 (Taylor, *The Forging of a Black Community*, 108). The community was composed largely of family units, and despite the alien land laws of 1908, 1912, and 1922 that were specifically directed at Japanese immigrants, some managed to secure property through their U.S.-born children or other pseudolegal arrangements, operating restaurants, hotels, and markets that served a multiracial clientele who could not find service in white establishments (Taylor, *The Forging of a Black Community*, 118).

39. As in other West Coast urban centers before the economic boom following World War II, Seattle had a small black population in all respects, particularly compared with the Asian American community. Quintard Taylor's study shows that in 1900, only 406 black persons lived in Seattle, which still represented a 42 percent increase from the previous decade (52). By 1910, the black population had jumped to 2,296, a 466 percent increase, although the community was still much smaller and less visible than the 6,127 Japanese who resided in Seattle at that time (108). Between 1910 and 1940, the black population grew slowly to only an average of 510 new residents per decade (86). Before the mid-1940s, the majority of this small black community worked in domestic service, often competing directly with the larger (and primarily male) Asian community for jobs, which included waiters, busboys, maids, launderers, and menial laborers.

40. Neil Wynn, *The Afro-American and the Second World War* (New York: Holmes & Meier, 1993), 86. In Seattle, shipbuilding and aircraft industries boomed with federal contracts, making Boeing the city's largest employer, with 50,000 workers in 1944. Boeing gradually began integrating its workforce in 1942, with two black women workers, and by July 1943, black women represented 86 percent of the 329 black workers. Boeing and its union, however, were largely resistant to hiring more than a nominal black workforce, in accordance with Executive Order 8802. Seattle had twenty-seven shipyards, however, which hired thousands of black workers who were incorporated into racially integrated unions such as the ILWU and the Marine Cooks and Stewards and Ship Scalers (166). Black workers were earning exponentially higher wages than they ever had, due to the wartime labor shortage and black political mobilization that forced the desegregation of defense industrial labor.

41. Wynn, *The Afro-American and the Second World War*, 172–73. Prewar black residents resented the influx of largely black southern migrants, regarding them as vulgar, backward, uneducated "sharecroppers" and holding them responsible for the intensification of racial restrictions against all black residents in the city.

42. Wynn, *The Afro-American and the Second World War*, 86. Before 1942, only 65 percent of Seattle's black residents lived in the Southside ghetto, but the proliferation of restrictive covenants moved virtually all the black World War II migrants into this four-square-mile area.

43. Wynn, *The Afro-American and the Second World War*, 169. By 1945, Seattle's black population had grown to approximately 10,000 persons, who were now "living in the same buildings that had housed 3,700 five years earlier."

44. See Robin Kelley, "The Riddle of the Zoot: Malcolm Little and Black Cultural Politics during World War II," chap. 7 of his *Race Rebels: Culture, Politics, and the Black Working Class* (New York: Free Press, 1994).

45. What is most problematic is how this fantasy obscures the fact that it was black men who had been the relentless targets of white hostility and antagonism in the industrial workplace since World War I, attacks that were also driven by imaginings of the hypermasculinity of the black male body.

46. Their home is clearly distinguished from the middle-class aspiring, normative home of the Kumasakas. The "freshly painted frame house that was situated behind a neatly kept lawn" is filled with the appropriate commodities that define normative domesticity, and the Kumasakas perform gender roles appropriate to the home and nation. Having lost their *nisei* son who died fighting in Germany, the positioning of the Kumasakas as having a place in the nation is manifested in the home where they reside. As in virtually all the spaces he occupies throughout the novel, Ichiro feels mislocated in this house, which he values for being "undifferentiated" from all other homes, a space of universality that he knows he cannot inhabit.

47. Patricia Chu, *Assimilating Asians: Gendered Strategies of Authorship in Asian America* (Durham, NC: Duke University Press, 2000), 58.

48. The passage is hardly subtle in identifying the Japanese immigrant mother as the contaminating and dominating agent of foreign difference that is ultimately to blame for Ichiro's predicament:

> It was to please her, he said to himself with teeth clamped together to imprison the wild, meaningless, despairing cry which he was forever straining inside of him. Pa's okay but he's a nobody. He's a goddamned, fat, grinning, spineless nobody. Ma is the rock that's always hammering, pounding, pounding, pounding in her unobtrusive, determined, fanatical way until nothing left to call one's self. She's cursed me with her meanness and the hatred that you cannot see but which is always hating. It was she who opened my mouth and made my lips move to sound the words which got me two years in prison and an emptiness that is more empty and frightening than the caverns of hell. (*No-No Boy*, 12)

49. Chu, *Assimilating Asians*, 59.

50. Many of these numerous passages not only acknowledge that Ichiro's hatred of his mother is an act of displacement but even reframe the mother's "insane" Japanese fanaticism as a "rational" response to U.S. racialization, which legally defined her as a perpetual alien of the nation:

> Through his anger crept up a sudden feeling of remorse and pity. It was an uneasy, guilty sort of sensation. . . . Was it she who was wrong and crazy not to have found in herself the capacity to accept a country which repeatedly refused

to accept her or her sons unquestioningly, or was it the others who were being deluded, the ones, like Kenji, who believed and fought and even gave their lives to protect this country where they could still not rate as first-class citizens because of the unseen walls? (*No-No Boy*, 104)

In addition, while these recurrent instances always accompany equally recurrent pathologizations of the mother, the U.S. nationalist demand to disavow the feminized racial family is ultimately denied when Ichiro is forced to partially acknowledge that he cannot escape the contradictions of racialized citizenship by simply moving away:

A man does not start totally anew . . . having lived and laughed and cried for twenty or thirty or fifty years and there is no way to destroy them without destroying life itself . . . the past had been shared with a mother and father and whatever they were, he too was a part of them and they a part of him. (*No-No Boy*, 154)

While the passage still "alien"-ates the immigrant parents, "whatever they were," and does not explicitly acknowledge that he cannot become a universal subject irrespective of where his family is, history and memory are invoked in contradiction to the liberal democratic promise of universality.

CHAPTER 4

1. Michael Rogin, *Blackface, White Noise: Jewish Immigrants in the Hollywood Melting Pot* (Berkeley: University of California Press, 1996), 5. Also see pp. 27–44.

2. Haesu makes her "delightful discovery" during the first year of her immigration in 1920. Her last child, Faye, is named after a Hollywood actress, and up through the novel's conclusion in 1945, Faye's narrative is filled with countless references to Hollywood stars.

3. Rogin, *Blackface, White Noise*, 78.

4. Ibid.

5. Quoted in Rogin, *Blackface, White Noise*, 25.

6. Rogin, *Blackface, White Noise*, 25.

7. Ibid., 39.

8. Ibid., 52.

9. The minstrel show faded at the turn of century with the rise of vaudeville and film. However, as Rogin demonstrates in *Blackface, White Noise*, the cultural logic of blackface was variously incorporated into these new institutions of American popular culture. Rogin's study demonstrates that blackface minstrelsy was not just a nineteenth-century form of U.S. popular culture but also provided the formal and ideological foundation for twentieth-century motion pictures (12). The four most historically definitive films in the United States before World War II—*Uncle Tom's Cabin* (1903), *Birth of a Nation* (1915), *The Jazz Singer* (1927), and *Gone with the Wind* (1939)—all were "blackface" narratives produced through what Rogin calls "the surplus symbolic value of blacks." Rogin's analyses of these films show that blackface is not merely a descriptive term for white actors in burnt cork but a complex discursive nexus that variously enables the reconciliation or subsumption of ethnic or regional particularities into the universality of the nation. Rogin's project is much more complex than what this partial characterization implies. He looks backward to

examine the historical relationship between Jews and African Americans, identifying blackface as a legacy that transformed Jews into Americans in the first half of the twentieth century and continued to burden Jewish cultural productions and collaborations with African Americans during the civil rights movement. Rogin not only reveals that a meticulous and seemingly exhaustive analysis of mass culture delineates the formation of U.S. nationalism, which is predicated on black exclusion, but also pushes at troubling yet necessary questions of the historical relations between Jews and African Americans in culture and politics.

10. This is different from how Asian uplift is framed by Okada, who constructs this process of Americanization as an "ethical" and politicized choice that can be refused or rejected. For instance, *No-No Boy* stages this process of Americanization through black displacement in various passages, including the white immigrant woman on the bus and Ichiro's refusal to return to the church that excludes the old black man. In *Clay Walls*, black exclusion and repudiation are implicitly part of U.S. national culture and processes of assimilation. Okada makes virtually no reference to popular culture in his novel, whose subjects are racialization and contradiction, whereas in *Clay Walls*, the centrality of Hollywood and U.S. popular culture only implicitly figures a relationship between black exclusion and blackface to national assimilation.

11. Rogin, *Blackface, White Noise*, 167.

12. Ibid., 163.

13. Ibid., 175.

14. Ibid.

15. Ibid., 162.

16. Ibid., 167.

17. Ibid.

18. Ibid., 177–91.

19. Nick Browne, "Race: The Political Unconscious in American Film," *East-West Film Journal* 6, no. 1 (January 1992): 11–12.

20. Japan's efforts to remake Koreans into loyal subjects of the Japanese empire included the brutal military suppression of numerous revolts and uprisings. These massacres were relentlessly retold and remembered to produce Korean nationalist dis-identification from the national identity and culture coercively imposed by the colonial state. Along with militarized repressive measures by the state, the colonial educational system performed a cultural and historiographical intervention that renarrated Koreans into a subordinating official history of Japan and eradicated all cultural practices coded as "Korean," including a formal prohibition against speaking the Korean language.

21. Angela Davis's "Rape, Racism and the Myth of Black Rapist," in her *Women, Race and Class* (New York: Vintage Books, 1983), provides an intersectional analysis of nineteenth- and twentieth-century discourses of the black male rapist and its erasure of the institutionalized sexual violence waged against black women, revealing how rape has been historically constructed to maintain the property rights of white men of privilege. Davis asserts that sexual violence against women cannot be adequately addressed through this historically produced concept of rape but must be situated in an intersectional analytical paradigm that seeks to understand how racism and sexism work together to reproduce capitalist relations of production.

22. George Lipsitz, "From Chester Himes to Nursery Rhymes: Local Television and the Politics of Cultural Space in Post-War Los Angeles," unpublished manuscript, 1990.

23. In 1940, only 2.2 percent of the black population lived west of the Mississippi, but as historian Lawrence De Graaf pointed out, one-fourth of this percentage resided in the city of Los Angeles, which "already ranked fourteenth among the nation's cities in Negro population." See Lawrence De Graaf, "Negro Migration to Los Angeles, 1930–1950" (PhD diss., University of California, Los Angeles, 1974), 323.

24. Ibid., 330.

25. Ibid.

26. From 1940 to 1944, black migrants accounted for almost one-third of the city's population growth, but there was no significant expansion in available housing, which doubled the number of black residents occupying the same housing structures in the oldest parts of the city (De Graaf, "Negro Migration," 201). As in all other urban areas in the West, the internment of Japanese Americans opened up some housing in Little Tokyo, which was already "conveniently" located along black districts at the northern tip of Central Avenue. Renamed Bronzeville, black residents swiftly faced severe overcrowding and deterioration as several families and occupants were forced into a single housing structure with makeshift additions and inadequate plumbing (De Graaf, "Negro Migration," 199). Federal Housing Administration policies continued to subsidize white suburbanization and sponsor residential segregation in postwar Los Angeles, at the expense of property devaluation and other impediments to asset accumulation suffered by black residents and black property and business owners confined to the inner city. See George Lipsitz, *The Possessive Investment in Whiteness: How White People Benefit from Identity Politics* (Philadelphia: Temple University Press, 1998).

27. Quoted in Clora Bryant, Buddy Collette, William Green, Steve Isoardi, and Marl Young, eds., *Central Avenue Sounds: Jazz in Los Angeles* (Berkeley: University of California Press, 1998), 87.

28. Ibid., 217.

29. See Robin Kelley, "The Riddle of the Zoot: Malcolm Little and Black Cultural Politics during World War II," chap. 7 of his *Race Rebels: Culture, Politics, and the Black Working Class* (New York: Free Press, 1994).

30. Bryant et al., *Central Avenue Sounds*, 216–17.

31. Horace Tapscott, *Songs of the Unsung: The Musical and Social Journey of Horace Tapscott* (Durham, NC: Duke University Press, 2001), 14.

32. Tapscott's organization of the Pan Afrikan Peoples Arkestra and the Underground Musicians Association (UGMA) in the early 1960s is remarkable in this regard. Although segregation was no longer formally sanctioned, these cultural institutions grew out of what had become a predominantly working-class black community as a result of the out-migration of black middle-class residents as South Central deteriorated. UGMA was a band of musicians and artists as well as a grassroots political organization that contested police brutality, ran breakfast programs for schoolchildren, provided music lessons that were also black history courses, played for senior citizens, and basically responded to whatever arose as a community need. By providing consistent public cultural venues, the UGMA helped

revitalize areas of South Central by facilitating a sense of community and collective struggle for social justice. Tapscott's rejection of commercial success in favor of local, community-focused cultural praxis produced a formation that made it impossible to separate political and economic conditions from cultural production. See Tapscott's *Songs of the Unsung.*

33. George Lipsitz, "From Chester Himes to Nursery Rhymes."

34. See Peter Stallybrass and Allon White, *The Politics and Poetics of Transgression* (Ithaca, NY: Cornell University Press, 1986).

35. Repeated references to the lindy hop, a popular version of the jitterbug, in the *Autobiography of Malcolm X*, are central to Malcolm's memories of the awe and joy of being introduced to a vibrant black urban youth culture.

36. The distinction is noteworthy, since Benny Goodman, or the King of Swing, adopted Basie's "One O'Clock Jump," which had been recorded seven months before Goodman's recording of the same song. Goodman's version of "One O'Clock Jump" was his first record to make more than $1 million, whereas Basie obviously had much lower sales and distribution. Goodman's version of swing differed from black ensembles in that he stressed "precision and accurate pitch essential to European harmony, and worked unceasingly toward that goal." However, as jazz historian Marshall Stevens put it, if Benny Goodman was the King of Swing by 1935, the real man behind the throne was Count Basie, who "gave depth and momentum to the whole swing era while planting seeds that later gave birth to bop and the 'cool' school of jazz." See Marshall Stevens, "The Swing Era and the Revivalists," chap. 17 of his *The Story of Jazz* (New York: Oxford University Press, 1970), 211.

37. The restructuring of global capital moved industrial production overseas in search of cheaper labor sources, and as a result, unemployed workers faced downward mobility in a growing service-sector economy that offered lower wages, job instability, and few or no benefits. This deindustrialization of the U.S. economy in the early 1970s was devastating to racialized minorities, who occupied low-wage, unskilled positions in the industrial labor market. As industries closed down and service-sector jobs were moved to suburban areas, those who were confined to the inner city faced severe unemployment. The frustration of unemployed and laid-off industrial white workers, however, was directed not at the mobility of transnational capital but at immigrants and racial minorities, who were increasingly constructed as unworthy "beneficiaries" of affirmative action programs and state resources.

CHAPTER 5

1. As Giovanni Arrighi argued, "When the history of the second half of the twentieth century will be written . . . the chances are that no single theme will prove to be of greater significance than the economic renaissance of East Asia." See Giovanni Arrighi, *Adam Smith in Beijing: Lineages of the Twenty-first Century* (London: Verso Books, 2007), 1.

2. As in the nineteenth-century context, U.S. blacks are always already racialized as unincorporable; however, the distinct discourse about the black urban poor after 1965 is particularly striking in its emphasis on underdevelopment and stagnation.

3. Karl Marx, *The 18th Brumaire of Louis Bonaparte* (New York: International Publishers, 1998), 15.

4. For his contextualization of these relationships, see Robert Lee, *Orientals: Asian Americans in Popular Culture* (Philadelphia: Temple University Press, 1999), esp. chap 7, "After L.A.," and the section "Orientalizing Capital."

5. Paul Ong et al., *The Widening Divide: Income Inequality and Poverty in Los Angeles* (Los Angeles: Graduate School of Architecture and Urban Planning, University of California, Los Angeles, 1989), 4.

6. David Harvey, *The Condition of Postmodernity: An Inquiry into the Origins of Cultural Change* (Cambridge: Blackwell, 1993), 166.

7. Chris Connery, "Pacific Rim Discourse: The U.S. Global Imaginary in the Late Cold War Years," in *Asia/Pacific as Space of Cultural Production*, ed. Rob Wilson and Arif Dirlik (Durham, NC: Duke University Press, 1995), 36.

8. Ong et al., *The Widening Divide*, 10.

9. "Of the 78 foreign agents of international banks in California, 57 are based in Los Angeles, the largest number being Asian, especially Japanese." See Edward Soja, *Postmodern Geographies: The Reassertion of Space in Critical Social Theory* (New York: Verso, 1989), 222–24.

10. See Rob Wilson, "Tracking the 'China Peril' along the U.S. Pacific Rim: Carpet Baggers, Yacht People, 1.2 Billion Cyborg Consumers, and the Bamboo Gang. Coming Soon to a Neighborhood Near You!" in *Imagining Our Americas: Toward a Transnational Frame*, ed. Sandhya Shukla and Heidi Tinsman (Durham, NC: Duke University Press, 2007), 169–73. By critically reading recent "social science" narratives and American films and novels, Wilson demonstrates that yellow peril discourses have reemerged in the current context of "techno-Orientalism" and the alarming specter of transnational dispersion and infiltration. Wilson points to journalistic studies such as *Lords of the Rim* (1996), which describes the ascendance of a mobile group of overseas Chinese ("Rim Lords") acting as the brainy new masters of the latest technologies. He also looks at films and the popular cyberpunk novel *RIM* (1994), in which the Pacific Rim has merged into one border-fusing culture of cybernetic capitalism over which Japan and the United States both compete and protect from lesser-developed Asian nations.

11. Wilson, "Tracking the China Peril," 178–80.

12. Bruce Cumings, *Parallax Visions: Making Sense of American–East Asian Relations at the End of the Century* (Durham, NC: Duke University Press, 2002), 178–79.

13. Los Angeles 2000 Committee, *LA 2000: A City for the Future* (Los Angeles, 1988), 59.

14. Rob Wilson, *Reimagining the American Pacific: From South Pacific to Bamboo Ridge and Beyond* (Durham, NC: Duke University Press, 2000), 31–32.

15. Randy Holland's documentary on South Central Los Angeles, *The Fire This Time* (1994), skillfully negotiates this discourse through references to local policies and economic transnationalism, subtly linking the mobility of Asian capital to the forced removal of displaced inner-city residents, who are likely to be relocated to state prisons.

16. Clarence Lusane, "Persisting Disparities: Globalization and the Economic Status of African Americans," *Howard Law Journal* 42 (1999): 435.

178 ǀ Notes to Chapter 5

17. William Julius Wilson, *When Work Disappears: The World of the New Urban Poor* (New York: Vintage Press, 1997), 152.

18. Thomas Holt, *The Problem of Race in the Twenty-first Century* (Cambridge, MA: Harvard University Press, 2002), 102.

19. Karl Marx, *Capital*, vol. 1, *A Critique of Political Economy* (New York: Penguin, 1990), 641–42.

20. Ruth Wilson Gilmore, *Golden Gulag: Prisons, Surplus, Crisis, and Opposition in Globalizing California* (Berkeley: University of California Press, 2007), 75.

21. Gilmore, *Golden Gulag*, 75. African Americans, and particularly African American men, have not been the only ones adversely affected by the most recent economic downturns. "Between 1970 and 1980, the earnings of Chicanos aged 25–34 in the Los Angeles region declined from those of the previous decade, and the state registers its indifference in the growing dropout rate—as high as 63–79 percent in some black and Latino high schools" (76).

22. Jerome Miller, *Search and Destroy: African American Males in the Criminal Justice System* (Cambridge: Cambridge University Press, 1997), 7.

23. Ibid., 5.

24. Ibid., 8.

25. Miller, *Search and Destroy*; Steven Donzinger, *The Real War on Crime: The Report of the National Criminal Justice Commission* (New York: Harper Perennial, 1996).

26. Donzinger, *The Real War*; Marc Mauer and the Sentencing Project, *Race to Incarcerate*, rev. and updated ed. (New York: New Press, 2006).

27. Lee's film is radically distinctive from the "postindustrial ghetto films" that soon followed, insofar as *Do the Right Thing* rejects a realist mode of representation and Bed-Stuy is not constructed as a space of utter entrapment: black characters do not struggle to escape the neighborhood but attempt to claim it.

28. The most widely circulated and visible representations of Korean immigrants in the United States appeared between 1989 and 1993 in black film (particularly ghettocentric film), rap music, and media coverage of the LA uprisings. Hood films of the 1990s (alternately referred to in critical discourse as ghettocentric, postindustrial ghetto, black gangsta, or ghetto action films) are a cinematic form that many critics have linked to a larger body of hip-hop cultural production. See Manthia Diawara, *Black American Cinema* (New York: Routledge, 1993), 272; Craig Watkins, *Representing: Hip Hop Culture and the Production of Black Cinema* (Chicago: University of Chicago Press, 1999), 169–243; Todd Boyd, *Am I Black Enough for You: Popular Culture from the 'Hood and Beyond* (Bloomington: Indiana University Press, 1997); and Ed Guerrero, *Framing Blackness* (Philadelphia: Temple University Press, 1993), 159, 184. The character of the Korean immigrant merchant is most familiar in black LA-based cultural production, and although it does not appear in every black postindustrial ghetto film, its presence in some of the most commercially successful and critically discussed black films during this period—*Do the Right Thing* (1989), *Boyz n the Hood* (1991), and *Menace II Society* (1993)—is highly significant.

29. Lee stated that at the numerous lectures and talks he is invited to give throughout the country, nonblack viewers frequently ask whether he or his film "condones" Mookie's choice or, in another form, ask him to "rationalize" or explain Mookie's motivation (reissue DVD, interview).

30. Kobena Mercer tracks how black British filmmakers negotiated their particular burden of representation through a range of aesthetic forms, from documentary-like realism to a formal code that "demonstrates a conception of representation not as mimetic correspondence with the 'real,' but as a process of selection, combination, and articulation of signifying elements . . . to reveal the nature of the problems of representation." See Kobena Mercer, *Welcome to the Jungle: New Positions in Black Cultural Studies* (New York: Routledge, 1994), 88–89.

31. Mercer, *Welcome to the Jungle*, 82.

32. Roderick Ferguson, *Aberrations in Black: Toward a Queer of Color Critique* (Minneapolis: University of Minnesota Press, 2004), 6.

33. Min Hyoung Song, *Strange Future: Pessimism and the 1992 Los Angeles Riots* (Durham, NC: Duke University Press), 2005.

34. Black-organized merchant boycotts were not exclusive to the New York City area, but they were most visible there.

35. Claire Kim, *Bitter Fruit: The Politics of Black/Korean Conflict in New York City* (New Haven, CT: Yale University Press, 2003).

36. The ethics of Koreans profiting from liquor stores in poor black neighborhoods was, however, more prominent in Los Angeles.

37. Kim rejects structuralist arguments, which she regards as psychologically deterministic, even though a Marxist analysis would readily support her central argument that black boycotters are legitimate political actors rather than "irrational" and "angry" subjects. She states that "the idea here is that certain structural conditions lead to mass psychological disruption, which leads inexorably to chaotic collective outbursts. . . . Denied political agency, black collective actors appear as little more than water molecules that predictably come to a boil under specified conditions" (5). While I see why Kim must be dismissive of historically overdetermined terms such as black "anger," "outrage," and "resentment," it is important not to capitulate entirely to the dominant ideologies that depoliticize these sensibilities, which are often at the heart of many powerful social movements.

38. Kim, *Bitter Fruit*, 4–5.

39. Ibid., 5.

40. Ibid., 132.

41. Kim points to the lack of explicitly anti-Korean or anti-Asian rhetoric in the flyers and official literature of the 1989 boycott, a political lesson learned, Kim states, from earlier boycotts that were less aware of the strategic importance of not exploiting anti-Asian racism. To explore this issue further, Kim interviewed the black nationalist leaders who organized the boycott and who tended to characterize the racial slurs as unfortunate manifestations of the community's lack of political sophistication: "The issues around the boycott, I mean, they get distorted. . . . They get distorted by some of the more backward elements in the community because that's the level of their consciousness. . . . That's why there's a responsibility [on the part of the activists]. . . . [People who] have some politics [must help others]" (132).

42. I do not question the political necessity of the organization's efforts to downplay and "purge" the movement of anti-Korean sentiments, since accusations of black racism were continually deployed by mainstream media, producing a national "outrage" directed against the boycott. See Kim, *Bitter Fruit*, "Manufacturing Outrage," 188–220.

43. This question of anti-Asian racism has created factions in black political organizations and generated ambivalence in leftist Asian American organizations and in antiracist critical discourse in general.

44. Hood films are shot to play up the surveillance and spatial containment, and the narratives are organized as "ghetto escape" stories in which the successful resolution into adult black masculinity can be achieved only by moving out of the ghetto. Narratives of denied spatial mobility characterize a wide range of black hood films, beginning with Singleton's *Boyz n the Hood (1991)*, the Hughes Brothers' *Menace II Society*, Matty Rich's *Straight Out of Brooklyn* (1991), and F. Gary Grey's *Set It Off* (1996), in which young black characters struggle and generally fail to escape the violent conditions that entrap them.

45. Diawara, *Black American Cinema*.

46. As Houston Baker observes, "It is not incidental that we call to mind at this point the energy that John Singleton's film *Boyz n the Hood* acquires at the very moment that its athletic hero is gratuitously murdered. The moment of Ricky's death represents an epic erasure of black youth energy." See Houston Baker, *Black Studies, Rap, and the Academy* (Chicago: University of Chicago Press, 1993), 59.

47. See Baker, *Black Studies*; Diawara, *Black American Cinema*; Boyd, *Am I Black Enough for You*; Watkins, *Representing*; and Guerrero, *Framing Blackness*. Also see Paula Massood, *Black City Cinema: African American Urban Experience in Film* (Philadelphia: Temple University Press, 2003).

48. Watkins, *Representing*, 11; Boyd, *Am I Black Enough for You*, 92; Massood, *Black City Cinema*, 152–53.

49. Several critics have commented that this scene is analogous to the literary representation of Bigger Thomas's recognition of an airplane as a humiliating and demoralizing symbol of denied opportunities and entrapment in the slums of Chicago's Southside. See Guerrero, *Framing Blackness*, 184; Diawara, *Black American Cinema*, 22.

50. Edward Soja identifies LAX as being in the center of a third outer-region area, as the airport is surrounded by "the agglomeration of office buildings, hotels, and high-technology research and manufacturing establishments that surround it . . . contains what is probably the country's largest concentration of the American military industrial complex." See Allan J. Scott and Edward Soja, ed., *The City: Los Angeles and Urban Theory at the End of the Twentieth Century* (Berkeley: University of California Press), 1996.

51. Mike Davis observes that the

> Astro program LAPD helicopters maintain an average nineteen-hour-per day vigil over "high crime areas," tactically coordinated to patrol car forces and exceeding even the British Army's aerial surveillance of Belfast . . . thousands of residential rooftops have been painted with identifying numbers, transforming the aerial view of the city into a huge police grid.

See Mike Davis, *City of Quartz: Excavating the Future in Los Angeles* (New York: Vintage Books, 1992), 250–53.

52. However, the highly publicized influx of Japanese capital into downtown Los Angeles in the early 1980s and the less visible movement of Korean and Taiwanese capital investment in Koreatown, Monterey Park, and Santa Monica may have led to Singleton's view of Korean land speculation (Davis, *City of Quartz*, 101–49). In 2007, fifteen years after the film's release, Korean capital was still being directed to the

development of Koreatown as well as large commercial buildings in the mid-Wilshire area. Even though multiracial gentrification has had some impact in Inglewood, what has radically changed the geography of South Central is the increasing number of Latinos who have reached majority numbers in what have been considered historically black areas: Watts, Compton, Inglewood, Crenshaw, and so on.

53. See bell hooks, "Ice Cube Culture," in her *Outlaw Culture: Resisting Representations* (New York: Routledge, 2006).

54. Lee Rainwater and William Yancey, eds., *The Moynihan Report and the Politics of Controversy* (Cambridge, MA: MIT Press, 1967), 88.

CHAPTER 6

1. This large group at the University of Chicago was formed primarily by members of the economics department and the business school. They included Milton Friedman, George Schultz, George Stigler, Robert Lucas, Richard Posner, Ronald Coase, Robert Fogel, and a score of other Nobel Prize recipients, many of whom were enlisted as economic advisers to the U.S. state. Neoliberal frameworks eventually extended to both sociology and history. Fogel, for instance (another Nobel laureate), wrote the notorious study in which he argued that the lives of American slaves were quantitatively superior to those of industrial workers in the North. See Robert Fogel, *Time on the Cross: The Economics of American Negro Slavery* (New York: Norton, 1995). The Chicago school's neoliberal agenda throughout the global south was implemented largely by the International Monetary Fund and the World Bank. These key institutional mechanisms were established after World War II to extend U.S. global hegemony under Keynesian capitalism.

2. George Schultz, interview, *Commanding Heights*, PBS, October 2, 2000.

3. Michel Foucault, *The Birth of Biopolitics: Lectures at the Collège de France, 1978–1979* (New York: Palgrave Macmillan, 2008), 247.

4. David Harvey, *A Brief History of Neoliberalism* (New York: Oxford University Press, 2005); Midnight Notes Collective, *Midnight Oil: Work, Energy, War* (Brooklyn, NY: Autonomedia, 1992), 273–333.

5. Harvey, *A Brief History of Neoliberalism*, 2.

6. It is important to distinguish between the reception of neoliberalism in the U.S. national context and in the developing nations brutalized by the International Monetary Fund's neoliberal mandates that wiped out emergent systems of national production and ordered state disinvestment in social reproduction, such as health care, education, housing, and infrastructure. Throughout Latin America, the Caribbean, Asia, and Africa, there is a pervasive, popular recognition of neoliberalism as a transparent neocolonial ideology.

7. This differs from Omi and Winant's definition of racial neoliberalism (written during the Clinton administration), in which they regard racial neoliberalism as rejecting the neoconservative insistence on a "color-blind" formation while avoiding the explicit language of race in fear of being politically divisive. See Michael Omi and Howard Winant, *Racial Formation in the United States: From the 1960s to the Present*, 2nd ed. (New York: Routledge, 1994), 148.

8. James Lee, *Urban Triage: Race and the Fictions of Multiculturalism* (Minneapolis: University of Minnesota Press, 2004).

9. Jodi Melamed, "The Spirit of Neoliberalism: From Racial Liberalism to Neoliberal Multiculturalism," *Social Text* 89, no. 4 (2006): 1.

10. Ibid., 14.

11. Well over a decade ago, Elaine Kim asked that we explore the particular place that Asian Americans occupied in relation to the massive inequalities produced by neoliberalism:

> It seems clear that these days we are hurtling toward the bifurcation of U.S. society into two major economic classes—the very rich and the poor. . . . We are all facing the enormous challenge of the direct and indirect impact of a shameful assault on the poor, immigrants, and people of color in this country. How will Asian Americans face this challenge?

See Elaine Kim, "'At Least You're Not Black': Asian Americans in U.S. Race Relations," *Social Justice* 25, no. 3 (fall 1998): 5.

12. See "Success Story of One Minority Group in U.S.," *U.S. News & World Report*, December 1966, reprinted in *Asian American Studies, A Reader*, ed. Jean Yu-Wen Shen Wu and Min Song (New Brunswick, NJ: Rutgers University Press, 2000); William Peterson, "Success Story, Japanese American Style," *New York Magazine*, January 6, 1966; "Success Story: Outwhiting the Whites," *Newsweek*, June 21, 1971, 24–25; "Japanese in U.S. Outdo Horatio Alger," *Los Angeles Times*, October 17, 1977, l-1; "Korean Americans: Pursuing Economic Success," *Washington Post*, July 13, 1978, 1.7. For a summary of social science studies, see Ki-Taek Chun, "The Myth of Asian American Success and its Educational Ramifications," in *The Asian American Educational Experience: A Sourcebook for Teachers and Students*, ed. Don Nakanishi and Tina Yamano Nishida (London: Routledge, 1995), 95–112. For an extensive list of more than forty of these sociological articles, as well as critiques and counterarguments from Asian American studies, see Frank Wu, *Yellow: Race in America beyond Black and White* (New York: Basic Books, 2003), 350–51.

13. Robert G. Lee, *Orientals: Asian Americans in Popular Culture* (Philadelphia: Temple University Press, 1999), 145–79.

14. Victor Bascara, *Model Minority Imperialism* (Minneapolis: University of Minnesota Press, 2006), 4–5.

15. Gary Becker, *Human Capital: A Theoretical and Empirical Analysis with Special Emphasis on Education*, 3rd ed. (Chicago: University of Chicago Press, 2002), 16.

16. Gary Becker, "Nobel Lecture: The Economic Way of Looking at Human Behavior," *Journal of Political Economy* 101, no. 31 (1995): 392.

17. Becker, *Human Capital*.

18. Ibid.

19. Herbert Gintis, "The Problem with Human Capital Theory—A Marxian Critique," *American Economic Review* 65, no. 2 (1975): 74–82.

20. Foucault, *The Birth of Biopolitics*, 223.

21. Aihwa Ong, *Neoliberalism as Exception: Mutations in Citizenship and Sovereignty* (Durham, NC: Duke University Press, 2006), 4.

22. See Sumi Cho, "Korean Americans vs. African Americans: Conflict and Construction," in *Reading Rodney King / Reading Urban Uprising*, ed. Robert Gooding-Williams (New York: Routledge, 1993), 196–211. Cho explains that

the human-capital model is a variant of neoclassical economic theory applied to labor-market economics. The model attempts to explain a dependent variable such as income inequality as derivative of independent variables such as educational attainment, work experience, total number of hours worked per year, marital status, and English proficiency, among others. It explains Asian Americans' advancement by foregrounding their investments in human capital such as educational attainment. It would also explain the lack of mobility of certain groups such as Southeast Asians or African Americans who had not yet invested appropriately in human capital. (p. 210, n. 1)

23. On the Chin case, see Helen Zia, *Asian American Dreams: The Emergence of an American People* (New York: Farrar, Straus & Giroux, 2001); and for a discussion of a "crisis" produced by rising Asian American college admissions, see Dana Takagi, *The Retreat from Race: Asian-American Admissions and Racial Politics* (New Brunswick, NJ: Rutgers University Press, 1993).

24. Thomas Friedman, *The World Is Flat: A Brief History of the Twenty-first Century* (New York: Farrar, Straus & Giroux, 2007), 278–79.

25. For a book-length study, see Houston Baker, *Betrayal: How Black Intellectuals Have Abandoned the Ideals of the Civil Rights Era* (New York: Columbia University Press, 2008).

26. Peter Feng, *Identities in Motion: Asian American Film and Video* (Durham, NC: Duke University Press, 2002), 11.

27. Aihwa Ong, *Flexible Citizenship: The Cultural Logics of Transnationality* (Durham, NC: Duke University Press, 1999), 112.

28. In 1991, Galileo High School, with 65 percent Asian American students and 17 percent African Americans, was largely working class, with less than 8 percent of graduating seniors considered to be eligible for California universities. The school was restructured in 1995 and has shed its reputation as a poor high school with relatively high rates of crime and violence.

29. Aihwa Ong's ethnographic study of Southeast Asian refugees in the late 1980s examines "the policies, programs, codes, and practices (unbounded by the concept of culture) that attempt to instill in citizen-subjects particular values (self-reliance, freedom, individualism, calculation, or flexibility) in a variety of domains." See Aihwa Ong, *Buddha Is Hiding: Refugees, Citizenship, the New America* (Berkeley: University of California Press, 2003), 6. Ong uses the Foucauldian notion of biopolitics while still maintaining a notion of agency, arguing that refugees are never simply compliant subjects of regulatory institutions with which they negotiate.

30. Ong, *Buddha Is Hiding*, 124.

31. Transcript of *a.k.a. Don Bonus* by Lindsay Gervacio. I corrected Gervacio's transcription here.

32. *Hai Nguyen et al. v. San Francisco Housing Authority* (C93 1127-JPV).

33. *Truong v. Housing Authority* (C98-0956 CW). The seven housing projects named were Alice Griffith, Potrero Terrace, Potrero Annex, Hunter's Point, Hunter's View, Westbrook, and Sunnydale.

34. Xuyen Nguyen was eighteen years old when he was shot and killed at Potrero Terrace. His mother, Ut Doen, was part of the 1993 lawsuit.

35. *Truong v. Housing Authority of San Francisco* (April 3, 1998), no. C980956; and *Memorandum of Points and Authorities In Support of Mtn for Prelim Inj*, no. C98-0956 CW.

36. *San Francisco Chronicle*, July 21, 1993, A18.

37. This official cleanup seems to indicate how the state struggles to contain various contradictions of federal mandates to racially integrate public housing without unsettling a national housing industry and economy founded on the urban warehousing of the black poor.

38. *San Francisco Gate*, November 27, 1996.

39. Douglas Massey and Nancy Denton, *American Apartheid: Segregation and the Making of the Underclass* (Cambridge, MA: Harvard University Press, 1998).

AFTERWORD

1. Karen Leong et al., "Resilient History and the Rebuilding of a Community," *Journal of American History* 94 (2007): 772.

2. Eric Tang, "Boat People," *Colorlines Magazine* 32 (spring 2006): 25.

3. The transcript of Bush's address is available at http://www.cnn.com/2005/POLITICS/09/15/bush.transcript/.

4. Tang, "Boat People," 23.

5. *Times-Picayune*, "'Home' Has New Meaning; Vietnamese Vow to Rebuild N.O. Enclave," October 22, 2005, 1.

6. *New York Times*, "Klan Inflames Gulf Fishing Fight between Whites and Vietnamese," April 25, 1981, sec. 1, p. 1.

7. *United Press International*, June 4, 1982, sec. Domestic News.

8. Elaine Kim, "'At Least You're Not Black': Asian Americans in U.S. Race Relations," *Social Justice* 25, no. 3 (fall 1998): 7.

9. Elaine Kim, "Home Is Where the Han Is: A Korean American Perspective on the Los Angeles Upheavals," in *Reading Rodney King / Reading Urban Uprising*, ed. Robert Gooding-Williams (New York: Routledge, 1993), 224.

10. See the powerful documentary *A Village Called Versailles* (2009), directed by Leo Chiang.

11. Examples of this inevitably relational dynamic abound, whether in the *New York Times*, CNN, or more progressive media outlets. For a particularly egregious example, see Adam Lashinky, "New Orleans: An Immigrant Community Thrives," *Fortune*, August 10, 2007, available at http://money.cnn.com/2007/08/10/magazines/fortune/no vietnamese.fortune/index.htm. Also see the following study, which includes discussion of media and community perceptions of the protest and their general efforts to rebuild: Leong et al., "Resilient History and the Rebuilding of a Community," 770–79. Note the inevitable tension between the imperative to negate model minority discourse while accounting for the community's impressive achievements.

12. *Omaha World-Herald*, "Displaced New Orleans Family Grows in Omaha," December 24, 2004, sec. News, 1A.

Selected Bibliography

Aarim-Heriot, Najia. *Chinese Immigrants, African Americans, and Racial Anxiety in the United States, 1848–82.* Champaign: University of Illinois Press, 2003.

Allen, Ernest. "When Japan Was 'Champion of the Darker Races': Satokata Takahashi and the Flowering of Black Messianic Nationalism." *The Black Scholar* 24, no.1 (1995): 23–46.

Almaguer, Tomás. *Racial Fault Lines: The Historical Origins of White Supremacy in California.* Berkeley: University of California Press, 1994.

Anderson, Benedict. *Imagined Communities: Reflections on the Origin and Spread of Nationalism.* London: Verso, 1994.

Andrews, William L. *To Tell a Free Story: The First Century of Afro-American Autobiography, 1760–1865.* Champaign: University of Illinois Press, 1986.

Arrighi, Giovanni. *The Long Twentieth Century: Money, Power and the Origins of Our Times.* New York: Verso, 1999.

Baker, Houston. *Betrayal: How Black Intellectuals Have Abandoned the Ideals of the Civil Rights Era.* New York: Columbia University Press, 2008.

———. *Black Studies, Rap, and the Academy.* Chicago: University of Chicago Press, 1993.

Baker-Fletcher, Karen. *A Singing Something: Womanist Reflections on Anna Julia Cooper.* New York: Crossroad, 1994.

Bascara, Victor. *Model Minority Imperialism.* Minneapolis: University of Minnesota Press, 2006.

Beasley, Delilah L. *The Negro Trail Blazers of California.* San Francisco: R and E Research Associates, 1919.

Becker, Gary. *Human Capital: A Theoretical and Empirical Analysis with Special Emphasis on Education.* 3rd ed. Chicago: University of Chicago Press, 2002.

Beechert, Edward D. *Working in Hawaii: A Labor History.* Honolulu: University of Hawai'i Press, 1985.

Bond, Max J. *The Negro in Los Angeles.* San Francisco: R and E Research Associates, 1972.

Bowles, Samuel, and Herbert Gintis. "The Problem with Human Capital Theory—A Marxian Critique." *American Economic Review* 65, no. 2 (1975): 74–82.

Boyd, Todd. *Am I Black Enough for You: Popular Culture from the 'Hood and Beyond.* Bloomington: Indiana University Press, 1997.

Browne, Nick. "Race: The Political Unconscious in American Film." *East-West Film Journal* 6, no. 1 (January 1992): 5–16.

Bryant, Clora, et al. *Central Avenue Sounds: Jazz in Los Angeles.* Berkeley: University of California Press, 1998.

Bullock, Penelope. *The Afro-American Periodical Press, 1838–1909.* Baton Rouge: Louisiana State University Press, 1981.

Cacho, Lisa. "The Rights of Respectability: Ambivalent Allies, Reluctant Rivals, and Disavowed Deviants." In *Immigrant Rights in the Shadows of Citizenship*, ed. Rachel Buff, 190–206. New York: New York University Press, 2008.

Carby, Hazel V. *Reconstructing Womanhood: The Emergence of the Afro-American Woman Novelist.* New York: Oxford University Press, 1987.

Chiang, S. Leo. *A Village Called Versailles.* Walking Iris Film, 2009.

Chinese Immigration: Its Social, Moral, and Political Effect. Report to the California Senate of its Special Committee on Chinese Immigration. Sacramento: State Printing Office, 1878.

Cho, Sumi. "Korean Americans vs. African Americans: Conflict and Construction." In *Reading Rodney King / Reading Urban Uprising*, ed. Robert Gooding-Williams, 196–214. New York: Routledge, 1993.

Chu, Patricia. *Assimilating Asians: Gendered Strategies of Authorship in Asian America.* Durham, NC: Duke University Press, 2000.

Chun, Ki-Taek. "The Myth of Asian American Success and its Educational Ramifications." In *The Asian American Educational Experience*, ed. Don Nakanishi and Tina Yaman Nishida, 95–112. New York: Routledge, 1995.

Collins, Keith. *Black Los Angeles: The Maturing of the Black Ghetto, 1940–1950.* Saratoga, NY: Century Twenty-One Publishing, 1980.

Connery, Chris. "Pacific Rim Discourse: The U.S. Global Imaginary in the Late Cold War Years." In *Asia/Pacific as Space of Cultural Production*, ed. Rob Wilson and Arif Dirlik, 30–56. Durham, NC: Duke University Press, 1995.

Cooper, Anna Julia. *The Voice of Anna Julia Cooper: Including A Voice from the South and Other Important Essays, Papers, and Letters*, ed. Charles Lemert and Esme Bhan. Lanham, MD: Rowman & Littlefield, 1998.

Cumings, Bruce. *Parallax Visions: Making Sense of American—East Asian Relations at the End of the Century.* Durham, NC: Duke University Press, 2002.

Davis, Angela. *Women, Race & Class.* New York: Vintage Books, 1983.

———. *Are Prisons Obsolete?* New York: Seven Stories Press, 2003.

Davis, Mike. *City of Quartz: Excavating the Future in Los Angeles.* New York: Vintage Books, 1992.

De Graaf, Lawrence. "Negro Migration to Los Angeles, 1930–1950." PhD diss., University of California at Los Angeles, 1974.

Diawara, Manthia. *Black American Cinema.* New York: Routledge, 1993.

Donzinger, Steven. *The Real War on Crime: The Report of the National Criminal Justice Commission.* New York: Harper Perennial, 1996.

Doreski, C. K. *Writing America Black: Race Rhetoric in the Public Sphere.* Cambridge: Cambridge University Press, 1998.

Du Bois, W. E. B. *Black Reconstruction in America: 1860–1880.* New York: Simon & Schuster, 1995.

———. *The Souls of Black Folk, Three Negro Classics.* New York: Avon Books, 1965.

DuCille, Ann. *The Coupling Convention: Sex, Text, and Tradition in Black Women's Fiction*. New York: Oxford University Press, 1993.

Duggan, Lisa. *The Twilight of Equality: Neoliberalism, Cultural Politics, and the Attack on Democracy*. Boston: Beacon Press, 2003.

Espana-Maram, Linda N. "Brown Hordes and McIntosh Suits: Filipinos, Taxi Dance Halls, and Performing the Immigrant Body in Los Angeles, 1930s and 1940s." In *Generations of Youth: Youth Cultures and History in Twentieth Century America*, ed. Joe Austin and Michel Nevin Willard, 118–35. New York: New York University Press, 1998.

Espiritu, Yen. *Asian American Women and Men: Labor, Laws and Love*. Thousand Oaks, CA: Sage, 1997.

Feng, Peter. *Identities in Motion: Asian American Film and Video*. Durham, NC: Duke University Press, 2002.

Ferguson, Roderick. *Aberrations in Black: Toward a Queer of Color Critique*. Minneapolis: University of Minnesota Press, 2004.

Foster, Frances Smith. *Witnessing Slavery: The Development of Ante-bellum Slave Narratives*. Westport, CT: Greenwood Press, 1979.

Foucault, Michel. *The Birth of Biopolitics: Lectures at the College de France, 1978–1979*. New York: Palgrave Macmillan, 2008.

Franklin, John Hope. *From Slavery to Freedom: A History of Negro Americans*. 6th ed. New York: Random House, 1988.

Fraser, Nancy. "Rethinking the Public Sphere: A Contribution to the Critique of Actually Existing Democracy." In *Habermas and the Public Sphere*, ed. Craig Calhoun, 109–42. Cambridge, MA: MIT Press, 1994.

Fredrickson, George. *The Black Image in the White Mind: The Debate on Afro-American Character and Destiny, 1817–1914*. New York: Harper & Row, 1971.

Friedman, Thomas. *The World Is Flat: A Brief History of the Twenty-first Century*. New York: Farrar, Straus & Giroux, 2007.

Gaines, Kevin. *Uplifting the Race: Black Leadership, Politics, and Culture in the Twentieth Century*. Chapel Hill: University of North Carolina Press, 1996.

Gilmore, Ruth Wilson. *Golden Gulag: Prisons, Surplus, Crisis, and Opposition in Globalizing California*. Berkeley: University of California Press, 2007.

Gilroy, Paul. *The Black Atlantic: Modernity and Double Consciousness*. Cambridge, MA: Harvard University Press, 1993.

Goings, Kenneth. *The New African American Urban History*. Thousand Oaks, CA: Sage, 1996.

Goldberg, David Theo. *Racist Culture: Philosophy and the Politics of Meaning*. Cambridge: Blackwell, 1993.

Grey, F. Gary, director. *Set It Off*. 1996.

Guerrero, Ed. *Framing Blackness*. Philadelphia: Temple University Press, 1993.

Gutman, Herbert. *Work, Culture, and Society in Industrializing America: Essays in American Working Class and Social History*. New York: Knopf, 1976.

Hartman, Saidiya V. *Scenes of Subjection: Terror, Slavery, and Self-Making in Nineteenth-Century America*. New York: Oxford University Press, 1997.

Harvey, David. *A Brief History of Neoliberalism*. New York: Oxford University Press, 2005.

————. *The Condition of Postmodernity: An Inquiry into the Origins of Cultural Change.* Cambridge: Blackwell, 1993.

Hellwig, David. "The Afro-American and the Immigrant, 1880–1930: A Study of Black Social Thought." PhD diss., Syracuse University, 1974.

Hill, Herbert. *Black Labor and the American Legal System: Race, Work, and the Law.* Madison: University of Wisconsin Press, 1985.

Hing, Bill Ong. *Making and Remaking Asian America through Immigration Policy, 1850–1990.* Palo Alto, CA: Stanford University Press, 1993.

Ho, Fred, and Bill Mullen, eds. *Afro Asia: Revolutionary Political and Cultural Connections between African Americans and Asian Americans.* Durham, NC: Duke University Press, 2008.

Holland, Randy, dir. *The Fire This Time.* 1994.

Holland, Sharon. *Raising the Dead: Readings of Death and (Black) Subjectivity.* Durham, NC: Duke University Press, 2000.

Holt, Thomas. *The Problem of Race in the Twenty-first Century.* Cambridge, MA: Harvard University Press, 2002.

Hong, Grace. *The Ruptures of American Capital: Women of Color Feminism and the Culture of Immigrant Labor.* Minneapolis: University of Minnesota Press, 2006.

————. "Race, Empire and the Not Working Class: Brete Harte's *Overland Monthly* and the Chinatown Photographs of Arnold Genthe." *Journal of the West* 43 (December 2004): 8–14.

hooks, bell. "Ice Cube Culture" in *Outlaw Culture: Resisting Representations.* New York: Routledge, 2006.

Hughes, Allen, and Albert Hughes, dir. *Menace II Society.* 1993.

James, C. L. R., et al. *Fighting Racism in World War II.* New York: Monad Press, 1980.

Jung, Moon-Ho. *Coolies and Cane: Race, Labor and Sugar in the Age of Emancipation.* Baltimore: Johns Hopkins University Press, 2008.

Kelley, Robin. *Race Rebels: Culture, Politics, and the Black Working Class.* New York: Free Press, 1994.

Kim, Claire. *Bitter Fruit: The Politics of Black/Korean Conflict in New York City.* New Haven, CT: Yale University Press, 2003.

Kim, Daniel. *Writing Manhood in Black and Yellow: Ralph Ellison, Frank Chin, and the Literary Politics of Identity.* Palo Alto, CA: Stanford University Press, 2005.

Kim, Elaine. "'At Least You're Not Black': Asian Americans in U.S. Race Relations." *Social Justice* 25, no. 3 (fall 1998): 3–10.

————. "Home Is Where the Han Is: A Korean American Perspective on the Los Angeles Upheavals." In *Reading Rodney King / Reading Urban Uprising*, ed. Robert Gooding-Williams, 215–35. New York: Routledge, 1993.

Kim, Min-Jung. "Renarrating the Private: Gender, Family, and Race in Zora Neale Hurston, Alice Walker, and Toni Morrison." PhD diss., University of California at San Diego, 1999.

Kim, Ronyoung. *Clay Walls.* New York: Permanent Press, 1986.

Kurashige, Scott. *The Shifting Grounds of Race: Black and Japanese Americans in the Making of Los Angeles.* Princeton, NJ: Princeton University Press, 2008.

Lee, James. *Urban Triage: Race and the Fictions of Multiculturalism.* Minneapolis: University of Minnesota Press, 2004.

Lee, Robert. *Orientals: Asian Americans in Popular Culture*. Philadelphia: Temple University Press, 1999.

Lee, Spike, dir. *Do the Right Thing*. 1989.

Leong, Karen, Christopher Airriess, Wei Li, Chia-Chen Chen, and Verna Keith. "Resilient History and the Rebuilding of a Community." *Journal of American History* 94 (2007): 770–79.

Lin, Justin, dir. *Better Luck Tomorrow*. 2002.

Lincoln, C. Eric, ed. *The Black Experience in Religion*. Garden City, NY: Anchor Books, 1974.

Lipsitz, George. "Frantic to Join . . . the Japanese Army: The Asia Pacific War in the Lives of African American Soldiers and Civilians," in *The Politics of Culture in the Shadow of Capital*, ed. Lisa Lowe and David Lloyd, 324–53. Durham, NC: Duke University Press, 1997.

———."From Chester Himes to Nursery Rhymes: Local Television and the Politics of Cultural Space in Post-War Los Angeles." Unpublished manuscript, 1990.

———. *The Possessive Investment in Whiteness: How White People Benefit from Identity Politics*. Philadelphia: Temple University Press, 1998.

Liu, David Palumbo. *Asian/American: Historical Crossings of a Racial Frontier*. Palo Alto, CA: Stanford University Press, 1999.

Loewen, James. *The Mississippi Chinese: Between Black and White*. Prospect Heights, IL: Waveland Press, 1988.

Logan, John, and Harvey Moltoch. *Urban Fortunes: The Political Economy of Place*. Berkeley: University of California Press, 1987.

Lortie, Francis. *San Francisco's Black Community, 1870–1890: Dilemmas in the Struggle for Equality*. San Francisco: R and E Research Associates, 1970.

Los Angeles 2000 Committee. *LA 2000: A City for the Future*. Los Angeles: 1988.

Los Angeles Community Analysis Bureau. Population and Housing Trend 1940–1970. The State of the City, 1975.

Lou, Raymond. "The Chinese American Community of Los Angeles, 1870–1900: A Case of Resistance, Organization, and Participation." PhD diss., University of California at Irvine, 1982.

Lowe, Lisa. *Critical Terrains: French and British Orientalisms*. Ithaca, NY: Cornell University Press, 1991.

———. *Immigrant Acts: On Asian American Cultural Politics*. Durham, NC: Duke University Press, 1996.

Lusane, Clarence. "Persisting Disparities: Globalization and the Economic Status of African Americans." *Howard Law Journal* 42 (1999): 431–50.

———. *Race in the Global Era: African Americans in the New Millennium*. Brooklyn, NY: South End Press, 1999.

Madhubuti, Haki. *Black Men: Obsolete, Single, Dangerous?* Chicago: Third World Press, 1990.

Marks, Carole. *Farewell, We're Good and Gone: The Great Black Migration*. Bloomington: Indiana University Press, 1989.

Marx, Karl. *Capital*. Vol. 1, *A Critique of Political Economy*. New York: Penguin, 1990.

———. *The 18th Brumaire of Louis Bonaparte*. New York: International Publishers, 1998.

Massey, Douglas, and Nancy Denton. *American Apartheid: Segregation and the Making of the Underclass.* Cambridge, MA: Harvard University Press, 1998.

Massood, Paula. *Black City Cinema: African American Urban Experience in Film.* Philadelphia: Temple University Press, 2003.

Mauer, Mark, and the Sentencing Project. *Race to Incarcerate.* Rev. and updated ed. New York: New Press, 2006.

McClain, Charles J. *In Search of Equality: The Chinese Struggle against Discrimination in Nineteenth-Century America.* Berkeley: University of California Press, 1994.

McDowell, Deborah. *"The Changing Same": Black Women's Literature, Criticism, and Theory.* Bloomington: Indiana University Press, 1995.

Melamed, Jodi. "The Spirit of Neoliberalism: From Racial Liberalism to Neoliberal Multiculturalism." *Social Text* 28, no. 4 (2006): 1–24.

Mercer, Kobena. *Welcome to the Jungle: New Positions in Black Cultural Studies.* New York: Routledge, 1994.

Midnight Notes Collective. *Midnight Oil: Work, Energy, War.* Brooklyn, NY: Autonomedia, 1992.

Miller, Jerome. *Search and Destroy: African American Males in the Criminal Justice System.* Cambridge: Cambridge University Press, 1997.

Mullen, Bill V. *Afro Orientalism.* Minneapolis: University of Minnesota Press, 2004.

Mumford, Kevin. *Interzones: Black/White Sex Districts in Chicago and New York in the Early Twentieth Century.* New York: Columbia University Press, 1997.

Murase, Ichiro. *Little Tokyo: One Hundred Years in Pictures.* Los Angeles: Visual Communications, 1983.

Nakasako, Spencer, and Sokly Ny, dir. *a.k.a. Don Bonus.* 1995.

O'Brien, Kenneth. *The Home-Front War: World War II and American Society.* Westport, CT: Greenwood Press, 1995.

Okada, John. *No-No Boy.* Seattle: University of Washington Press, 1957.

Okihiro, Gary Y. *Margins and Mainstreams: Asians in American History and Culture.* Seattle: University of Washington Press, 1994.

———. *Whispered Silences: Japanese Americans and World War II.* Seattle: University of Washington Press, 1996.

Omi, Michael, and Howard Winant. *Racial Formation in the United States: From the 1960s to the Present.* 2nd ed. New York: Routledge, 1994.

Ong, Aihwa. *Buddha Is Hiding: Refugees, Citizenship, the New America.* Berkeley: University of California Press, 2003.

———. *Flexible Citizenship: The Cultural Logics of Transnationality.* Durham, NC: Duke University Press, 1999.

———. *Neoliberalism as Exception: Mutations in Citizenship and Sovereignty.* Durham, NC: Duke University Press, 2006.

Ong, Paul, Eulalia Castellanos, and Luz Echavarria. *The Widening Divide: Income Inequality and Poverty in Los Angeles.* Los Angeles: Graduate School of Architecture and Urban Planning, University of California at Los Angeles, 1989.

Patterson, Orlando. *Slavery and Social Death.* Cambridge, MA: Harvard University Press, 1982.

Prashad, Vijay. *Everybody Was Kung-Fu Fighting: Afro-Asian Connections and the Myth of Cultural Purity.* Boston: Beacon Press, 2001.

———. *The Karma of Brown Folk*. Minneapolis: University of Minnesota Press, 2000.

Pulido, Laura. *Black, Brown, Yellow, Left: Radical Activism in Los Angeles*. Berkeley: University of California Press, 2006.

Rhodes, Jane. *Mary Ann Shadd Cary: The Black Press and Protest in the Nineteenth Century*. Bloomington: Indiana University Press, 1998.

Rich, Matty, et al. *Straight Out of Brooklyn*. New York: HBO Entertainment, 1991.

Roberts, Dorothy. *Killing the Black Body: Race, Reproduction, and the Meaning of Liberty*. New York: Vintage Books, 1997.

Rogin, Michael. *Blackface, White Noise: Jewish Immigrants in the Hollywood Melting Pot*. Berkeley: University of California Press, 1996.

Said, Edward. *Orientalism*. New York: Random House, 1994.

Saxton, Alexander. *The Indispensable Enemy: Labor and the Anti-Chinese Movement in California*. Berkeley: University of California Press, 1995.

———. *The Rise and Fall of the White Republic: Class Politics and Mass Culture in Nineteenth-Century America*. London: Verso, 1990.

Scott, Allan J., and Edward Soja, eds. *The City: Los Angeles and Urban Theory at the End of the Twentieth Century*. Berkeley: University of California Press, 1996.

Shah, Nayan. *Contagious Divides: Epidemics and Race in San Francisco's Chinatown*. Berkeley: University of California Press, 2001.

Shankman, Arnold. "Black on Yellow: Afro-Americans View Chinese-Americans, 1850–1935." *Phylon* 39, no.1 (Spring 1978):1–17.

Singleton, John, dir. *Boyz n the Hood*. 1991.

Soja, Edward. *Postmodern Geographies: The Reassertion of Space in Critical Social Theory*. New York: Verso, 1989.

Song, Min Hyoung. *Strange Future: Pessimism and the 1992 Los Angeles Riots*. Durham, NC: Duke University Press, 2005.

Stallybrass, Peter, and Allon White. *The Politics and Poetics of Transgression*. Ithaca, NY: Cornell University Press, 1986.

Stevens, Marshall. *The Story of Jazz*. New York: Oxford University Press, 1970.

Takagi, Dana. *The Retreat from Race: Asian-American Admissions and Racial Politics*. New Brunswick, NJ: Rutgers University Press, 1993.

Tang, Eric. "Boat People." *Colorlines Magazine* 32 (spring 2006): 22–25.

Tapscott, Horace. *Songs of the Unsung: The Musical and Social Journey of Horace Tapscott*. Durham, NC: Duke University Press, 2001.

Tate, Claudia. *Domestic Allegories of Political Desire: The Black Heroine's Text at the Turn of the Century*. New York: Oxford University Press, 1992.

Taylor, Quintard. *The Forging of a Black Community: Seattle's Central District from 1870 through the Civil Rights Era*. Seattle: University of Washington Press, 1994.

Tchen, John. *New York before Chinatown: Orientalism and the Shaping of American Culture, 1776–1882*. Baltimore: Johns Hopkins University Press, 1999.

Thomas, Brook. *Plessy v. Ferguson: A Brief History with Documents*. Boston: Bedford Books, 1997.

Watkins, Craig. *Representing: Hip Hop Culture and the Production of Black Cinema*. Chicago: University of Chicago Press, 1999.

Wells-Barnett, Ida B. *On Lynchings: Southern Horrors, A Red Record, Mob Rule in New Orleans*. New York: Arno Press, 1969.

Widener, Daniel. "'Perhaps the Japanese Are to Be Thanked?' Asia, Asian Americans, and the Construction of Black California," in the special issue of *positions: the afro-asian century* (2003): 135–81.

Williams, Randall. *The Divided World: Human Rights and Its Violence*. Minneapolis: University of Minnesota Press, 2010.

Wilmore, Gayraud S. *Black Religion and Black Radicalism: An Interpretation of the Religious History of African Americans*. Maryknoll, NY: Orbis Books, 1998.

Wilson, Rob. "Imagining 'Asia-Pacific': Forgetting Politics and Colonialism in the Magical Waters of the Pacific. An Americanist Critique." *Cultural Studies* 14, nos. 3–4 (2000): 562–92.

———. *Reimagining the American Pacific: From South Pacific to Bamboo Ridge and Beyond*. Durham, NC: Duke University Press, 2000.

———. "Tracking the 'China Peril' along the U.S. Pacific Rim: Carpet Baggers, Yacht People, 1.2 Billion Cyborg Consumers, and the Bamboo Gang. Coming Soon to a Neighborhood Near You!" In *Imagining Our Americas: Toward a Transnational Frame*, ed. Sandhya Shukla and Heidi Tinsman, 168–89. Durham, NC: Duke University Press, 2007.

Wilson, William Julius. *When Work Disappears: The World of the New Urban Poor*. New York: Vintage Press, 1997.

Wolseley, Roland. *The Black Press, U.S.A.* Ames: Iowa State University Press, 1990.

Wu, Frank. *Yellow: Race in America Beyond Black and White*. New York: Basic Books, 2003.

Wu, Jean Yu-Wen Shen, and Min Song, eds. *Asian American Studies: A Reader*. New Brunswick, NJ: Rutgers University Press, 2000.

Wynn, Neil. *The Afro-American and the Second World War*. New York: Holmes & Meier, 1993.

Zia, Helen. *Asian American Dreams: The Emergence of an American People*. New York: Farrar, Straus and Giroux, 2001.

Index

About the Author

HELEN HERAN JUN is an associate professor of English and African American studies at the University of Illinois at Chicago.